HISPANICS
IN THE
UNITED STATES

Joan Moore
UNIVERSITY OF WISCONSIN, MILWAUKEE

Harry Pachon
BARUCH COLLEGE, CUNY

HISPANICS IN THE UNITED STATES

PRENTICE-HALL, INC., ENGLEWOOD CLIFFS, NEW JERSEY 07632

Library of Congress Cataloging in Publication Data

MOORE, JOAN W.
　　Hispanics in the United States.

　　Bibliography: p.
　　Includes index.
　　1. Hispanic Americans.　　I. Pachon, Harry.　　II. Title.
EL84.S75M66　　1985　　　　305.8'68'073　　　　84-26290
ISBN 0-13-388984-X

Editorial/Production supervision: *Edith Riker*
Manufacturing buyer: *John Hall*
Cover design: *Diane Saxe*
Cover photos: *Marc Anderson; Laimute E. Druskis; Marc Anderson*

Printed in the United States of America

10　9　8

ISBN　0-13-388984-X　　01

Prentice-Hall International, Inc., *London*
Prentice-Hall of Australia Pty. Limited, *Sydney*
Editora Prentice-Hall do Brasil, Ltda., *Rio de Janeiro*
Prentice-Hall Canada Inc., *Toronto*
Prentice-Hall Hispanoamericana, S.A., *Mexico*
Prentice-Hall of India Private Limited, *New Delhi*
Prentice-Hall of Japan, Inc., *Tokyo*
Prentice-Hall of Southeast Asia Pte. Ltd., *Singapore*
Whitehall Books Limited, *Wellington, New Zealand*

CONTENTS

PREFACE

It is the purpose of this book to offer a meaningful description and analysis of a large and growing segment of American society—the Hispanics. Both the high rates of immigration and a high birth rate mean that it is only a matter of time before Hispanics assume a dominant position among American minorities. Meanwhile, a traditional concentration in the Southwest and New York City is dispersing—a process that is abruptly bringing the Hispanics into new areas of the nation and into national consciousness.

Because it is impossible to give more than the barest sketch of this highly diverse group of people, we concentrate on three important factors. The first of these is the history of these populations. Not only is this history unfamiliar to most Americans, but it is critical in understanding the life conditions of Hispanics. The range of the environments is almost inconceivable, ranging as it does from the poorest slums of Manhattan to the ancient cultures of northern New Mexico which antedate the Anglo settlement of North America.

Second, we include comprehensive surveys of the best and latest socioeconomic information. Included are sketches of immigration and settlement patterns, employment and income, educational status, family and community patterns, and language and culture. There is special attention to recent developments and research in Hispanic education.

Third, we examine with care the impact of modern American institutions on Hispanics. Certain of these are critical, including the American systems of education, health and mental health care, welfare services, criminal justice, and immigration control. Even the church, an institution normally thought of as belonging to the community, has operated with the Hispanics as an institution of the larger society. In addition, a full chapter surveys for the first time the history, main trends, and current status of Mexican-American, Puerto Rican, and Cuban political life—an area that is assuming great new importance.

The book builds on the work of many Hispanic researchers, particularly Mexican-American. Several generations of agitation for equality have produced a growing number of young scholars able to research their own people: much of this material is included. Because of their work it is possible to view the Mexican-Americans in this country with a depth and certainty not possible in earlier years. We hope that in the near future the more recently arrived Hispanics will develop a similar volume of literature.

Finally, our best insights and most fruitful approaches came through many years of interaction with Mexican, Puerto Rican, and other Hispanic scholars, students, and community people from all over the nation. Mutual interaction and mutual research is an important road to increased understanding. We owe particular gratitude to Leo Grebler for his extraordinary qualities as director of the UCLA Mexican-American Study Project, one of the first large-scale studies of Chicano Life in this country. Further thanks are due to Robert S. Garcia, for his years of dedication to the principle of community-based research on Hispanics, and to Congressman Edward Roybal, an individual who has championed and who embodies Hispanic unity.

CHAPTER ONE
HISPANICS
IN AMERICAN LIFE

This book is about more than 15 million persons of Hispanic ancestry who live in the United States. These are the people who describe themselves in the U.S. Census as "Mexican American, Chicano, Mexican, Mexicano, Puerto Rican, Cuban, Central or South American, or other Spanish origin."

Slightly more than half of this very diverse group is of Mexican descent and is concentrated in the American Southwest. About a sixth of the Hispanics are Puerto Rican in origin and now tend to live in or near New York City. The third largest group of Hispanics is Cuban. Although Cubans make up only about a twelfth of the total, they are heavily concentrated in the one city of Miami, Florida. Small as it is, the Cuban population greatly outnumbers Hispanics from any other single nation except Mexico. But added up together, these "others" are quite a large group—a fifth of all Hispanics.

Some of the differences between these subpopulations are very great. The Hispanics of northern New Mexico and Cuban refugees in Miami both speak varieties of Spanish, yet they seem to share little else. Moreover, each group became part of the larger American population in a different manner. Each faced different experiences in the larger American society. Each lived through different economic, political, and environmental situations. Each group has a different sense of its own identity. And even within some of the larger groups, there are sharp divisions. The *Hispanos* of New Mexico are descendants of sixteenth-century Spanish Conquistadors and often see themselves as quite different from other "Mexican origin" immigrants. The *Mariel* wave of Cuban refugees in 1980 is quite different from the anti-Castro professionals and middle-class people who left Cuba in the 1950s.

Why then should these groups be treated in one book as one group? There are several reasons, all of them centered on the growth and acceptance of the idea that Hispanics have become a *national* minority.

First, regardless of distinctive histories and separate identities, the life situations of all Hispanic minorities in the United States are converging. In fact, they are converging with other racial minorities as well. All segments of the Hispanic community are predominantly urban; many are locked into poverty and face prejudice and discrimination.

Second, the Hispanic populations are increasingly being treated by the larger society as a group with common characteristics and common problems. In some respects, they are beginning to think of themselves as sharing many problems. This is happening mostly in political life, as when separate Hispanic populations find themselves negotiating together for a special program that will benefit all kinds of Hispanics. The shared interest in bilingual education is a good example. Congressman Robert Garcia is a New York–born Puerto Rican who said recently, "When I first came to Washington I saw myself as a Puerto Rican. I quickly realized that the majority society saw me as a member of a larger group called Hispanic."[1]

Third, the subpopulations are beginning to disperse outside of their traditional areas. People of Mexican origin are found increasingly in such northern industrial cities as Chicago and Detroit as well as in the Southwest. Puerto Ricans live in industrial cities in the Northeast and Middle West outside of New York. Cubans are now found in large colonies in New York, New Jersey, and Los Angeles as well as in Florida.

Fourth, accompanying the dispersal of the Hispanics is a very large increase in their total number. In fact, Hispanics are one of the fastest-growing segments of the American population. There is every reason to believe that this growth from immigration and from natural increase will continue to be high.

So it is reasonable to think of all segments of the American Spanish-speaking population as "Hispanics." The facts of their life in modern America are rapidly creating such a polyglot minority.

Each of these topics of diversity and commonality will be discussed at length in the following chapters. In general, we will focus on the three dominant Hispanic groups—Mexican Americans, Puerto Ricans, and Cubans. Smaller groups tend to be quite recent immigrants, and most of them are appearing in milieus in which the meaning of their ethnicity is established by other Hispanics who are already in place. Thus, most of several hundred thousand Dominican and Colombian arrivals go to New York City where to most Anglos they are indistinguishable from Puerto Ricans.[2] In Los Angeles the Cubans, Guatemalans, and Salvadorans live in their own distinctive communities but all of them take part in programs designed for and by the overwhelmingly large Mexican-American population of Los Angeles.

---

[1] Personal communication.

[2] Many Dominicans are in the United States as undocumented aliens, and estimates run as high as 300,000. See Antonio Ugalde et al., "International Migration from the Dominican Republic: Findings from a National Survey," *International Migration Review,* Vol. 13 (1979), pp. 235–254. G. Hendricks, *The Dominican Diaspora* (New York: Teachers College Press, 1974), presents an excellent portrait of village Dominicans at home and in their New York "diaspora."

HISPANICS: THE CONFUSION OF RACE AND ETHNICITY

In this chapter we will focus on the ways in which Hispanics are viewed by other Americans and on the ways in which they see themselves and each other. These are stereotypes and issues related to ethnic identity.

Stereotypes are assumptions that allow a society to classify individuals into groups. These "beliefs" then "support, justify, and determine the character of inter-racial relationships."[3] So once they are established, stereotypes then can lead to or justify discriminatory treatment of a minority. (Sociologists agree that discrimination can also take place even in the absence of stereotypes. In some cases, discriminatory behavior is built into an institution. As an example, height requirements for police officers have the unintended consequence of discriminating against short people: historically, many Hispanics have not been tall. More subtly, discrimination results from de facto exclusion, as when Hispanics do not serve on a Grand Jury because none of the people who nominate members for the Grand Jury happen to know any Hispanics.)

Stereotypes about Hispanics developed within Anglo-American culture from the very earliest contacts. Yet there has also been persistent confusion about whether Hispanics should be considered a racial minority or simply another predominantly Catholic ethnic group like the Italians, for example. For most Americans, "race" means black and white, as does the word "minority." This idea is helped along by the persistent use of the word "minority" to refer only to blacks. An important illustration of this narrow biracial assumption is enshrined in the U.S. Census.[4]

Because it used "White" and "Nonwhite" for categories, the census has had great difficulty in its task of classifying Hispanics. (Blacks were the largest nonwhite group.) Mexicans so baffled these categories that they were moved back and forth from a racial ("other nonwhite") category in 1930 to a kind of ethnic group ("persons of Spanish mother tongue") in 1940. An even more ambiguous classification ("white persons of Spanish surname") was used in 1950 and 1960, but only in five states of the "Mexican" Southwest. In 1970, the classification was changed to "persons of both Spanish surname and Spanish mother tongue." Then, in 1980, Mexican Americans, Puerto Ricans, and other Hispanics became a kind of "super" ethnic group: they are listed along with other national descent groups, and they are *also* in a separate category, sometimes as a "race," along with white, black, and other nonwhite. This confusion is a consequence of the biracialist assumption and a grudging and inconsistent acknowledgment that Chicanos, Puerto Ricans, and other Hispanics are something other than a simple ethnic group.

Hispanics share some of the features of American blacks. Both groups are racially distinctive. And even though color differences do not appear to hurt Hispanics as much as they do blacks, darker Chicanos, Puerto Ricans, and other Hispanics experience serious discrimination.[5] Hispanics also share many of the features

[3] Alfred R. Lindesmith and Anselm L. Strauss, *Social Psychology* (Hinsdale, IL: The Dryden Press, 1950), p. 396.

[4] Clara Rodríguez, *The Ethnic Queue in the U.S.: The Case of the Puerto Ricans* (San Francisco: R&E Research Associates, 1974).

[5] Joe Hakken, *Discrimination Against Chicanos in the Dallas Rental Housing Market: An Experimental Extension of the Housing Market Practices Survey* (Washington, D.C.: U.S. Department of Housing and Urban Development, Office of Policy Development and Research, August 1979).

of white ethnic groups because, like them, most Hispanics speak a language other than English and trace their origins to another modern nation with its own culture and traditions. But even here there is an exception. The Hispanos of New Mexico are all Americans with no tradition outside the United States—an exception that emphasizes the need to be careful about generalizations. Hispanics are thus a category unto themselves. Hispanics are an important minority that needs understanding quite apart from old ideas about other immigrant groups.

HISPANICS AS ANGLOS SEE THEM

The three major Hispanic groups have had very different kinds of contact with Anglo-American society, in different regions of this nation, and at different eras of American history. Accordingly, the images of each group vary. Yet there are many common themes. These themes show that Hispanics *are* seen as having some common features.

The historical images. American views of Hispanics are influenced by roots that go as far back as England's conflict with Spain in the sixteenth century. As one scholar noted, English colonists "believed the Roman Church to be corrupt and ostentatious. . . . As for the Spaniards, they were the perfect adherents of the Papacy—cruel, treacherous, avaricious and tyrannical." Perceptions were also molded by the widespread distribution of Bartolomé de las Casas's attack on Spanish rule in Latin America, *The Spanish Colonie.*[6] The first encounters between Mexicans and Americans occurred when the Southwest was still firmly occupied by Mexicans. Because of this long contact from the early years of the nineteenth century, the images that Anglos hold of Mexican Americans are far more complex and varied than they are for other Hispanics. Yet these first encounters with Mexicans tended to fix some basic outlines and to become the prototypes of later Anglo-Saxon images of all Hispanics.

In the first half of the nineteenth century, Americans came to Texas as colonists with Stephen Austin. Traders made the long journey to New Mexico on the Santa Fe Trail. They came to California with the clipper ships from New England and to wilderness areas as explorers. As soldiers and irregular militia, Anglo Americans reached many parts of the northern provinces of Mexico. Whatever their role, Anglo visitors did not hesitate to record their scorn for what they felt to be a backward people in a backward land. "To the early writers, the Mexican was just plain lazy and deserved to lose out, as he surely would, to the energetic, productive Northerner."[7] It was during these years of the 1840s that the observed contrast between Anglo-Saxon vigor and Mexican sloth seemed to justify the violent over-

[6] Ray Paredes, "The Origins of Anti-Mexican Sentiment in the United States," in R. Romo and R. Paredes, eds., *New Directions in Chicano Scholarship* (La Jolla: University of California at San Diego, 1978).

[7] Cecil Robinson, *With the Ears of Strangers: The Mexican in American Literature* (Tucson: University of Arizona Press, 1963), p. 33. This book is an exhaustive analysis of the portrayal of Mexican Americans in literature from the earliest contacts. Arnoldo De León, *They Called Them Greasers* (Austin: University of Texas Press, 1983), deals with Anglos' attitudes toward Mexicans in Texas from 1821 to 1900.

throw of the Mexican government in Texas. The famous Sam Houston, leader of the Texas Americans, "consistently thought of the struggle in his region as one between a glorious Anglo Saxon race and an inferior Mexican rabble."[8] It was easy enough to extend the same racist image far enough to justify the idea that it was the "manifest destiny" of the United States "to overspread and to possess the whole of the continent allotted by Providence for the free development of our yearly multiplying millions."[9] One of the first consequences of this "Providential" plan was the war with Mexico from 1846 to 1848 (Chapter 2).

During this war, simple hatred crept into the American image of Mexicans. Americans began to call the Mexicans "yellow-bellied greasers" and to develop the notion that Mexicans by race were naturally cowards. The belief in the cowardice of Mexicans is commemorated most strikingly in the simplified popular Anglo mythology about the defense of the Alamo. Legend built a story about how a small, brave band of Anglo Texas rebels defied overwhelming numbers of cowardly Mexican troops. A spate of popular novels followed the Mexican-American war and with them a set of clear stereotypes. In the fiction, we read about the three types of male Mexicans: the "pureblood" but effete Spanish aristocrats who "melted and crumbled 'like sugar'" before the virile Anglo-Saxons. Then there were the cowardly "half-breed greasers" who flee before any sign of danger. Third, from the guerilla warfare of this period and later years, the dangerous and cruel "'mestizo bandido,' ... whose combination of Spanish intelligence and 'Indian' savagery makes tougher and more courageous than the decadent hidalgos.... [They] have no moral scruples ... [or] sense of fair play."[10]

Another set of stereotypes is developed about Mexican women, but these are not so negative. Some of the early explorers expressed the usual contempt for upper-class Mexican men but found the Mexican women to be "'joyous, sociable, kind-hearted creatures." The stereotype of exotic, receptive Mexican women and lazy, inept Mexican men was to sink deep into American racial mythology."[11] In later years the popular novels distinguished between the "proud pureblood Castilian" beauties of the upper class and the available, even sexually aggressive, "half-breed temptresses," who are attractive but of "loose morals." Later, a parallel stereotype was to emerge about Puerto Rican women.

Thus, important negative and positive stereotypes of Hispanics were established very early. On the positive side, Anglo Americans met an intact society offering a full range of social classes from aristocrat to peon. This exposure to upper-class and lower-class life-styles meant that the image could acquire some social depth. But in the process, the Anglo-American racism of the period was strongly reinforced by Mexican upper-class ideas of race. As in most of Latin America, the upper classes in Mexico believed themselves to be of "pure blood," untainted by any mixture of Indian intermarriage or *sangre india.*" It was easy for the new

---

[8] Reginald Horsman, *Race and Manifest Destiny* (Cambridge, Mass.: Harvard University Press, 1981), p. 213.

[9] Horsman, *Race and Manifest Destiny,* p. 219.

[10] A. Pettit, *Images of the Mexican American in Fiction and Film* (College Station: Texas A&M Press, 1980), pp. 28, 96. See also Diego Vigil, *Early Chicano Guerrilla Fighters* (La Mirada, Calif.: Advanced Graphics, 1974).

[11] Horsman, *Race and Manifest Destiny,* p. 234.

Anglos in the Southwest to assume that the aristocratic people and the elaborate fiestas of rancho life were "Spanish" whereas the lower classes and rural people were "Mexican." On the negative side, American settlers fought Mexicans not only in open warfare between sovereign states, but also later in guerilla-style encounters so similar to that waged against Southwestern Indians. These latter encounters brought with them the same deep legacy of hatred as they had toward the Indians.

But in time the memories of warfare and border killings faded, and the benevolent stereotypes grew more elaborate. A highly romanticized popular literature appeared, which repeated early themes about aristocratic life. Perhaps the best example is Helen Hunt Jackson's *Ramona.* In her novel of 1884, rancho owners were painted as cultivated, gentle, exploited people. Throughout the twentieth century, American writers continued to build the benevolent stereotypes when they wrote about the Mexican Americans of Texas (as did Tom Lea and J. Frank Dobie) and the *Hispanos* of New Mexico (as did Paul Horgan and John Nichols). Something of the same romanticism continued with the poor wage earners of Monterey, California, as seen by John Steinbeck. The strongly folkloric themes of these writers appealed to thousands of readers. Implicit in these works of fact and fiction is a very real admiration for the Mexicans of Tortilla Flat in Monterey or the loyal Kineños of the King Ranch. The appeal is romantic and nostalgic: it follows a theme also found in writings about the American Indians of a life that is unspoiled, close to nature, strong and unchanging, and lived simply by peasants without neurotic complications.[12] But inevitably and tragically, the peasant must fall prey to a more sophisticated and exploiting society.

Cultural stereotypes have certain important social functions. Historically, they tended to permit Anglo Americans to stifle any guilt feelings about the rapid conquest of Mexican and other Hispanic territories. Anglo Americans were bombarded with a political rhetoric of racial inferiority and by a century of fiction with images identical to the political message: Anglo Americans are superior beings. Hispanics (even the upper classes, but especially the lower classes) are inferior.

It was a myth of racial inferiority that very conveniently justified the low status of Mexicans in the developing Southwest. The new Anglo settlers established ranches and towns and brought in a network of services to an area seen by the newcomers as a wilderness. Most of the Mexicans already living there did not participate in this work and did not share its rewards. For Anglo Americans, the moral equation was easily completed—Mexicans were poor *because* they were unwilling to suffer hard work and boredom. Moreover (so runs the argument), they are quite content with their status; they even prefer the life of the casual laborer and do not really mind poverty. Indeed, a general movement out of poverty might spoil them and make them unhappy. Thus the comfortable Anglo-Protestant moral equation of

---

[12] Leslie Fiedler is fascinated by the ambivalence in American literature about portrayals of Indians and blacks. Alternately, these people represent a lost Eden of strength and innocence and yet a hell of uncontrolled lustfulness and cruelty. Much the same is true of literary images of Mexicans and other Hispanics. Fiedler follows general theories of prejudice in suggesting that such ambivalence, deeply embedded in American culture, permits Anglo Americans to project their own unwanted impulses on the members of minorities. This is a cultural-psychological function of racial stereotypes, and it helps to explain why it is the *mestizo* (mixed-blood Hispanics) about whom the literary stereotyping was most glaring. The "pureblood Castilians," men and women alike, were seen in a relatively favorable light. See *Waiting for the End* (New York: Stein and Day, 1964).

vice and punishment, hard work, and material reward can remain intact. Poverty becomes a just return for laziness or a necessary condition for maintaining virtue rather than a reminder to Anglos of social injustice.

These new images were available and easily extended when another war forced close contact between Americans and a new group of Hispanics. The war against Spain began as a lightly considered effort to "free Cuba." A quick naval victory in 1898 brought the United States control of Cuba, Puerto Rico, and the Philippines. Although many American notables felt that it was part of America's manifest destiny to annex all the Caribbean Islands, it soon became evident that most American policymakers did not feel that Puerto Rico and the other islands could be self-governing states in the ordinary process of statehood. Not only were their inhabitants tropical people and, therefore, decadent, but they were culturally alien and racially "mongrelized." As one author of the time commented, "A country in which the mass of the population has been kept in either slavery or in a condition of social and economic inferiority is certain to retain the sexual relations of a primitive period for a long time after the causes giving rise to these relations have disappeared."[13] White Americans should be encouraged to settle in these new colonial possessions, but "there was absolute hostility to the possibility that the new subjects might emigrate to the United States."[14] Even political liberals like Carl Schurz called the Cubans "'a sorry lot' of Spanish creoles and Negroes," while the powerful speaker of the House of Representatives, Joseph Cannon of Illinois, "felt that Puerto Ricans did not 'understand, as we understand it, government of the people, and by the people . . . because . . . 75 or 80 percent of these people are mixed blood in part and are not equal to the full-blooded Spaniard and not equal, in my judgment, to the unmixed African.' "[15]

These themes surfaced again in 1928 when (for the first time in U.S. history) a congressional committee on immigration began to consider limits on immigration from the Western hemisphere, notably Mexico. Congressman John Box argued for the restriction of immigration from Mexico because "the Mexican peon is a mixture of Mediterranean-blooded Spanish peasants with low-grade Indians who did not fight to extinction but submitted and multiplied as serfs. Into this was fused much negro slave blood. . . . The prevention of such mongrelization and the degradation it causes is one of the purposes of our laws."[16] It was argued that race mixture and the Indian-Spanish mixture were bars to participation in American democracy. In the case of Puerto Ricans, the mixture of blackness and Spanishness was feared. These racial themes were repeated in the 1940s when large numbers of Puerto Ricans began to appear in New York City. One journalist commented about this wave of immigration: "they are mostly crude farmers, subject to congenital tropical diseases . . . almost impossible to assimilate and condition . . . they turn to guile

[13] Leo Stanton Rowe, *The United States and Puerto Rico* (New York: Longman, Green, 1904), p. 98.

[14] Cited in David Healy, *U.S. Expansionism* (Madison: University of Wisconsin Press, 1970), p. 244.

[15] Rubin F. Weston, *Racism in U.S. Imperialism* (Columbia: University of South Carolina Press, 1965).

[16] *Congressional Record,* 2817–18, cited in Gilberto Cárdenas, "United States Immigration Policy Toward Mexico: An Historical Perspective," *Chicano Law Review,* Vol. 2 (1975), pp. 66–99.

and wile and the steel blade, the traditional weapon of the sugar cane cutter, mark of their blood and heritage."[17] Not surprisingly, the first Cuban exodus of the early 1960s did not evoke racist sentiments because the refugees were "fleeing communism" and were largely white. The most recent wave of Cuban emigrés, by contrast, were, to Anglo-American eyes, largely black and evoked racist concerns.

RECENT IMAGES

For more than 50 years, a series of American public opinion surveys have reflected distasteful images of persons of Mexican descent (and, more recently, Puerto Ricans and Cubans). In 1926, 1946, 1956, and 1966, Emory Bogardus measured the "social distance" that American college students felt about 30 different ethnic groups. In every one of the surveys, Mexicans and Puerto Ricans ranked in the bottom third, along with other non-European stock such as Koreans, Indians, Turks, Japanese, and Negroes.[18] In 1978, 500 men and women with annual incomes above $25,000 were interviewed about their perceptions of various ethnic groups. Only 23 percent had positive feelings about Mexican Americans (compared with 44 percent with positive feelings about blacks and 66 percent about Chinese Americans). When asked for the first three words that they would associate with Mexican Americans, 21 percent offered positive stereotypes (such as "they're hard working," "good-humored"), 15 percent negative stereotypes ("they're lazy," "dirty," "ignorant"), while 43 percent responded with some descriptive phrase ("they're poor," "migrant workers," "discriminated against"). Puerto Ricans elicit more negative associations. Only 10 percent of the persons interviewed responded with positive images ("they're hard-working," "friendly"), while 25 percent offered negative images ("always want welfare handouts," "lazy," "dirty," "criminal") and 47 percent agreed on more neutral descriptive statements ("poverty," "slums," "under educated"). Well over half the respondents (59 percent) felt that Puerto Ricans living on the mainland are a drain on the economy, compared with 42 percent who felt that way about the Mexican Americans, 47 percent about blacks, and 15 percent about Chinese Americans. (By contrast, almost half the respondents felt that Chinese Americans were an asset, 18 percent for blacks, 17 percent for Chicanos, and 9 percent for Puerto Ricans.)[19] As recently as 1982, a Roper public opinion poll found that only 25 percent of a national sample felt that Mexicans were "good for the country" while 17 percent felt that Puerto Ricans were good and 9 percent that Cubans were good for the country. Stated negatively, 34 percent felt that Mexicans were bad for the country, 43 percent that Puerto Ricans were bad, and 59 percent that Cubans were bad.[20]

[17] Jack Lait and Lee Mortimer, *New York Confidential* (Chicago: Ziff Davis, 1948), pp. 126-132, cited in C. Wright Mills, Clarence Senior, and Rose Kohn Goldsen, *The Puerto Rican Journey* (New York: Harper, 1950), p. 80.

[18] Emory S. Bogardus, "Comparing Racial Distance in Ethiopia, South Africa, and the United States," *Sociology and Social Research,* Vol. 52 (1968), pp. 149-156. Bogardus's surveys were among college students, a group of reasonably well-educated Americans.

[19] Cambridge Research Associates, "The Island's Tarnished Image: The Mainland Survey on Puerto Rico and Its People," *The San Juan Star,* July 30, 1978.

[20] Dialogo: Quarterly Newsletter of the National Puerto Rican Policy Network, Vol. 1 (1982), p. 3.

A particularly persistent factor in the image of Hispanics is the idea of innate stupidity (euphemistically called "lower intelligence"). In 1982, to cite a damaging example, the U.S. Department of Defense released a study in which the authors argue that the lower test scores for Hispanics and blacks (as compared with whites) showed genetic differences in addition to cultural differences.[21] In the same year, the National Educational Testing Service (which administers the Scholastic Aptitude Tests to high school students) was apparently so surprised by the high scores of 18 Mexican-American students in Los Angeles that they required the students to re-take the examination. (The students maintained their high scores the second time around.)[22]

Harmful stereotypes persist and are used against Hispanics. One of the most glaring occurred in 1969 when a juvenile court judge in California drew on stereo-types of Hispanic sexual looseness to say to a youthful offender, "Mexican people, after 13 years of age, think it's perfectly all right to go out and act like an animal. . . . Your parents won't teach you what is right or wrong and won't watch out. . . . We ought to send you out of the country—send you back to Mexico."[23]

Pervasive stereotypes of Mexican Americans and other Hispanics are still disseminated through advertising. In the late 1960s, to cite only one example, Arrid underarm deodorant was advertised by showing a Mexican *bandido*. The bandit sprays himself with deodorant, and we are told that "if it works for him, it will work for you." Particularly irritating for many years was the "Frito Bandido"—a fat, supposedly funny caricature of the *bandido* character.[24] During the early 1970s, Chicano activists mounted national and local campaigns to sensitize advertisers to harmful advertising, and some of the more damaging caricatures disappeared. Advertising people are much more sensitive to Hispanics now, primarily because of the rapid growth of the Hispanic market for goods and services. But in time advertising agencies specializing in the perceived foibles and whims of a generalized Hispanic audience may create yet more stereotypes. Late in 1983, between 20 and 25 New York agencies were specialists in Hispanic marketing, and all of the 5 largest agencies were equipped with bilingual specialty divisions.[25]

Early portrayals of Hispanics in American literature were as stereotypically negative as the images in American politics. The Mexicans were the chief targets, caught up as they were in the environment of the dime novels and, later, the "Western" novels. Yet during the last few years, particularly since World War II,

[21] D. Bock and E. Moore, *Profile of American Youth: Demographic Influences on ASVAB Test Performance,* cited in National Council of La Raza news release, February 25, 1982. Bock and Moore state that these "differences in the average vocational test performance reflect the present social separation of these groups both reproductively and culturally" and that this isolation "raises the possibility that the differences in test performance arise from differences in the respective gene pools." Stephen Jay Gould's history of mental measurement shows the strong racial biases built into this kind of endeavor from its origins; see his *The Mismeasure of Man* (New York: W. W. Norton, 1982).

[22] *LaRed: The Net,* Newsletter of the National Chicano Council on Higher Education, no. 63 (January 1983), p. 1.

[23] Judge Gerald Chargin, on September 2, 1969, reprinted in Carrol A. Hernandez et al., *Chicanos: Social and Psychological Perspectives* (St. Louis: C. V. Mosby, 1976), pp. 61–62.

[24] Tomás M. Martinez, "Advertising and Racism: The Case of the Mexican American," Octavio L. Romano-V., ed., *Voices* (Berkeley, Calif.: Quinto Sol, 1971), pp. 48–58.

[25] *The New York Times,* December 13, 1983.

American literature has grown up enough to see frontier and urban Mexican Americans as a varied and interesting group of people—not always good and not always bad. Arthur Pettit remarks that the Mexican most often appears nowadays as "struggling to survive as a human being in a degraded and prejudiced America." These "persecuted pawns" of American novels come in four distinct fictional forms. They are harassed victims, Americanized Mexicans who "make it" in Anglo worlds, and avengers of injustice. But then there are still the "jolly loafers" who are just helpless clowns.[26] Pettit's careful book is too interesting to abbreviate here, except to note his remark that the idea of American Hispanics as persecuted pawns is yet another fictional stereotype.

In American movies images of Mexicans have improved from those of the 1920s and 1930s. Vicious and funny *bandidos* have been replaced by more complex characters, including the memorable role in *High Noon* of Katy Jurado. More recently a spate of movies about Chicano youth violence (*Boulevard Nights,* as an example) revived Chicano protests. *West Side Story,* an earlier movie about Puerto Rican gangs in New York City (with a notable cast and music by Leonard Bernstein), created an image of Puerto Rican life that still hurts all Hispanics. *Fort Apache: The Bronx* is a recent example of movies emphasizing the stereotypes of criminality and social deviance in the Puerto Rican community, and other Hispanic groups are also now being included in the stereotype, as the sensationalist movie *Scarface* (the story of the rise of a Cuban cocaine dealer) clearly shows.

From the earliest days, Hispanics have suffered from their image in the daily news media. A 1980 study reports "The English language news media, in their choice of presentation of stories about Latinos, still tend to report only the problem or sensational aspects: illegal immigration, poverty, gang activity, and violence. Even when such stories are accurate, they add up to a persistent impression of a problem people, an impression that leaves out the contributions and advances made by Latinos in the United States and so makes harder their full acceptance and participation as fellow citizens."[27]

A careful recent study shows that media perceptions may change very rapidly. Coverage of Mexican-American affairs by *The New York Times* was generally neglected from 1951 to 1958, except for a single concern about undocumented Mexican workers. From 1959 to 1964, the *Times* stressed an increased interest with Mexican poverty, but viewed it largely through statements by Anglo liberals. Then, rather abruptly in 1964, the *Times* began to see Mexican organizations as active agents, most particularly the actions of such Mexican leaders as César Chávez, Rodolfo (Corky) Gonzáles, and Reies Tijerina.[28]

Social scientists themselves have had serious problems with stereotypes. Many studies of Hispanics used the not very apt model of the European immigrant without any real understanding of its defects. These studies argue that Hispanics are well on their way to acculturation and assimilation, ignoring the history of conflict and conquest and the retention of the Spanish language after a century and a half of

---

[26] Pettit, *Images of the Mexican American.*

[27] Quoted in "From Bylines to Bottomlines," *Perspectives,* Vol. 13 (1983), pp. 18–21.

[28] James S. Olson, "The New York Times Index and Mexican Americans, 1951–1972," *Journal of Mexican American History,* Vol. 5 (1975), pp. 91–102.

life under the United States flag.[29] These stereotypes from the social sciences also creep into policy perspectives on the Hispanics. Thus Patricia Harris, President Carter's secretary of Housing and Urban Development, commented rather blandly that the problems of Hispanics would largely disappear within 20 years. More recently, Chicano and Puerto Rican social scientists have criticized Anglo scholars for their distorted or inadequate understanding of Hispanics[30] (see Chapter 7).

HISPANICS AS THEY SEE THEMSELVES

But what do Hispanics themselves think of this long history of stereotypes? In fact, Mexican and Puerto Rican identity has been explored for a very long time by Hispanic intellectuals.[31] It is a constant theme in most of the Hispanic literature that is based on Mexican experience in the United States. It is echoed endlessly on the popular level and surfaces in politics and many other areas of action. One particular point now at issue: How much do Hispanics think of themselves as a distinctive group, as "a people?" It is often hard for non-Hispanics to identify Hispanics or to tell the difference between one or another type of Hispanic.[32] (Puerto Ricans and Dominicans are often confused.)

We can get some idea how Hispanics think of *themselves* by asking what they want to be called. For Mexican Americans, we have clear evidence: most people interviewed in various areas of the Southwest want to be called "Mexican," "Mexican American," "Spanish American," "Latin American," or "Chicano."[33] In short, they see themselves as a distinctive people rather than as fully merged into an all-

[29] See Joan W. Moore, "Minorities in the American Class System," *Daedalus,* Vol. 110 (1981), pp. 275–298, for a critical view of the social science models that have been applied to Hispanics. Velez, in "Puerto Rico: Submerged or Emerging Nation?" discusses controversies in conceptualizing Puerto Ricans.

[30] For example, Octavio Romano-V., "The Anthropology and Sociology of the Mexican-Americans: The Distortion of Mexican American History (A Review Essay)," *El Grito* (1968), pp. 13–26; José Hernández, "Social Science and the Puerto Rican Community," in Clara Rodriguez et al., eds., *The Puerto Rican Struggle* (New York: Puerto Rican Migration Research Consortium, 1980).

[31] For example, see Octavio Paz, *The Labyrinth of Solitude* (New York: Grove Press, 1961), for the view of a Mexican philosopher looking at Chicanos.

[32] Anglos and black children cannot distinguish between Anglos and Chicanos. Chicanos can. A. S. Rice et al., "Person Perception, Self-identity, and Ethnic Group Preference in Anglo, Black and Chicano Preschool and Third-Grade Children," *Journal of Cross-Cultural Psychology,* Vol. 5 (1974), pp. 100–108.

[33] Survey data for Los Angeles and San Antonio (1965–1966) are reported in Leo Grebler, Joan Moore, and Ralph Guzmán, *The Mexican American People* (New York: The Free Press, 1970), and from Albuquerque from samples drawn by Operation SER in an unpublished study. Recent data and interesting changes are reported by Biliana Ambrecht and Harry Pachon, "Ethnic Political Mobilization in a Mexican American Community," *Western Political Quarterly,* Vol. 27 (1974), pp. 500–519. Analysis of a national sample drawn in 1976 (*Survey of Income and Education*) showed that for Mexican origin people 50.7 percent wanted to be called "Mexican American" and "Mexican" was chosen by 20.1 percent. Some variant of "Spanish" was chosen by 20.7 percent; 4.4 percent chose "Mexicano," and 4.0 percent chose "Chicano." John A. Garcia, "Yo Soy Mexicano: Self-identity and Sociodemographic Correlates," *Social Science Quarterly,* Vol. 62 (1981), pp. 88–98.

encompassing American identity. Adult Hispanics usually do not want to be identified as just "American."

Among Mexican Americans, the name may vary greatly from area to area. Traditionally, the residents of New Mexico have wanted to be known as "Spanish Americans" or "Hispanos," reflecting the fact that their earliest ancestors settled this area when it was "New Spain" rather than Mexico. Persons of Mexican origin who live in Texas were more inclined to accept Anglo euphemisms—or terms that avoid the reference to Mexico entirely. (This included "Latin American.") The terms "Mexican" and "Chicano" may be more common in cities like Los Angeles. Puerto Ricans and Cubans show fewer variations in terms.

It is clear that these preferences change over time as the Hispanics themselves shift. For people of Mexican origin, each variant has a special historical root and special historical meanings. "Chicano" appeared as a term of choice for many Mexican Americans in the context of youthful political militancy. Older and more middle-class Mexican Americans may still find the term insulting because the word was once almost entirely an in-group word and implied new immigrant arrivals with lack of sophistication. This very quality, once depreciated in the nation's Chicano communities, became exalted as "soul." Much the same phenomenon occurred in Puerto Rican communities. Thus, in the 1950s, many Puerto Ricans preferred "Latino" to the term Puerto Rican.

Very few Hispanics would choose a collective term of self-designation (either "Hispanic" or "Latino") even though this may be the term by which the rest of the nation generally knows them. A collective term is most likely to be used in certain areas such as the Midwest where people of Mexican origin live as neighbors with Puerto Ricans and other Hispanics and are treated by their larger communities as exactly the same kind of people. But no collective designation can evoke the power of symbols of national origin.[34] Furthermore, many Hispanics are somewhat suspicious of the word "Hispanic," believing that such bureaucratic labels were often used as a mask for political manipulation.[35]

Some of this attitude is changing. In Chicago, for example, the collective designation "Latino" has allowed political mobilization in Puerto Rican and Chicano coalitions to resolve problems that neither group could resolve separately. Job discrimination in specific companies is an example.[36] Felix Padilla gives a clue to the political utility of collective designations when he observes that Chicago leaders talk about local community problems in terms of "Puerto Ricans" or "Mexicans"

---

[34] It is through this power that Chicano activists have been able to play increasingly important roles in local politics because they find roots in the "political, economic and cultural nationalism of post-revolutionary Mexico [which] supplies a source of ideological inspiration." See Larry Trujillo, "Parlier, The Hub of Raisin America, A Local History of Capitalist Development" (Berkeley, Calif.: Institute for the Study of Social Change, 1978), Ch. 3, p. 9.

[35] It is true that often low-status Hispanic laborers found themselves supervised and exploited by Anglo-designated upper-status Cubans, Peruvians, and other Latin Americans, with resentment as a consequence. On the other hand, small and outnumbered components of the total Hispanic population often see the collective designation as a way of establishing their commonality with Hispanics who have more clout.

[36] Felix Padilla, "The Theoretical and Practical Sides of Latino Ethnicity in Chicago," manuscript, 1982, p. 63.

but citywide problems are discussed in terms of "Latinos." This need for coalition is even more obvious on the national level. Some decades back, the American Indians struggled with exactly the same problem and in the process began to develop a generalized "Indian" identity. This new identity appeared in addition to their primary tribal identity as Navajos, Oneidas, or Seminoles. It may well be that Hispanics will also develop this kind of "secondary identity."

Pointing to this possible development is the peculiar nature of American "ethnicity." Padilla thinks that to a very large extent it is a creation of the American experience, especially in the mix and merger and contrast of ethnicity in large American cities. Until very recently, Hispanics have not had this kind of experience. Mexicans have been isolated in the Southwest and were not in contact with other ethnic groups. Earlier Mexican Americans tended to live in rural settings where they were the *only* people who were not Anglos. There were not very many Puerto Ricans or Cubans to be found anywhere in this country before World War II. In recent years, Mexicans, Puerto Ricans, Cubans, and other groups of Latin Americans have begun to mix and merge, both in local areas such as Chicago and in the national political arena. The results of this contact may produce a new kind of identity, especially since the national media often treat Hispanics as a single group.

A comparatively new and interesting accompaniment to this self-definition and self-awareness is the appearance of a new literature.[37] These novels, essays, and poems by Hispanics are highly autobiographical. Some were first written under the impetus of the Chicano movement in the Southwest and other movements elsewhere. All the new writers are preoccupied by their need to "find themselves" and to "define their heritage and their people." In one of the earlier Chicano novels, for example, José Antonio Villareal describes the evolution of a *"pocho"*—a person who is neither American nor Mexican. The theme is repeated in a more positive way by Richard Vasquez in describing the slow and painful adaptation of a farm worker family to life in Los Angeles—the process, in short, of becoming a Chicano.[38] The novel by Texas-born Tomás Rivera[39] *". . . y no se lo trago la tierra"* (". . . and the earth did not swallow him") is a poetic view of the social reality of farm workers. It was written in Spanish and translated by the author and a colleague. In a series of 12 archetypal anecdotes (one for each month of "the lost year"), Rivera tells of both the suffering and the rich personal cultural resources of the Chicano farm worker. But for Chicanos, it is Oscar Acosta who tells of the Mexican American as an urban person, doomed to live in Anglo cities and to confront Anglo discrimination. Acosta's two books picture the Chicanos as a people who can achieve nothing except in full battle against a destructive Anglo society. *The Autobiography of a*

[37]This literature is produced primarily by Mexican Americans and Puerto Ricans. Cubans have been in the United States a shorter time, and their literature is still emerging.

[38]José Antonio Villareal, *Pocho* (Garden City, N.Y.: Doubleday, 1959), and Richard Vasquez, *Chicano* (Garden City, N.Y.: Doubleday, 1970). "Pocho" is the name used in Mexico to refer to the non-Mexican and negative qualities of Mexican Americans, while "Chicano," the title of the second novel, refers to the pride in that identity which is scorned in Mexico. See also essays in Joseph Sommer and Tomás Ybarra-Fausto, eds., *Modern Chicano Writers* (Englewood Cliffs, N.J.: Prentice-Hall, 1979), and Arnulfo Trejo, ed., *The Chicanos: As We See Ourselves* (Tucson: University of Arizona Press, 1979).

[39]Tomás Rivera, ". . . *y no se lo trago la tierra*" (Berkeley, Calif.: Quinto Sol, 1971).

Brown Buffalo is a perceptive look at a Chicano childhood and coming of age, of an outsider forced to fight for acceptance and then realizing the hypocrisy of that acceptance.[40] *The Revolt of the Cockroach People* continues the story in fiction form.[41] It deals primarily with the intense political activity from 1968 to 1970 in East Los Angeles where Acosta, as an activist lawyer, played a major role. Acosta continues in this book to sharpen his definition of himself—a "brown buffalo" because he and his people are unwanted survivors of the Western past, doomed to be hunted to death like cockroaches. For Acosta there is no alternative but apartness, an active condition of being a minority, and fighting back with the sophisticated institutional weapons of the Anglo himself.[42]

The creative literature of Puerto Ricans shares much with that of the Chicanos, especially the concern with identity. Thus, one of the classic pieces of Chicano literature is the lyric and moving epic poem, *Yo Soy Joaquin*.[43] It is a long evocation of Mexican history as a tribute to the endurance of the Mexican people and "defines" (if such a lackluster word is appropriate) the Chicano as a many and various person with an unconquerable appetite for freedom. The counterpart for Puerto Ricans might be Pedro Pietri's *Puerto Rican Obituary*, a short epic poem about the various dreams and disappointments of life in New York.[44] The *Obituary* is gloomier than *Yo Soy Joaquin*, reflecting the destructive experiences of Puerto Ricans in the city, the nervous stress, the high rates of heroin addiction, the desire for a quick score through lotteries, numbers, or sweepstakes; the hopeless entrapment in poor drab jobs. Much better known outside the Puerto Rican community is a book by Piri Thomas, *Down These Mean Streets*.[45] This is an important novel to emerge from Spanish Harlem, and the first. Thomas deals eloquently with experiences on the streets of the Puerto Rican and black districts of New York City—and the dark side of those streets, the narcotics, robbery, and prison.

Thomas's book reflects not only the greater degradation of the Puerto Rican experience but also a greater emotionalism about race. Although "Indianness" is an issue to many Mexican Americans, it is relatively muted as compared with the importance of "blackness" to Puerto Ricans. Color is defined differently in Puerto

[40] Oscar Z. Acosta, *The Autobiography of a Brown Buffalo* (San Francisco: Straight Arrow Books, 1972).

[41] Oscar Z. Acosta, *The Revolt of the Cockroach People* (San Francisco: Straight Arrow Books, 1973).

[42] One Chicano literary critic contrasts Acosta's "brown buffalo" to earlier folk heroes in the Mexican-American tradition, especially Gregório Cortéz, a Texas farmer whose flight from Texas law enforcement takes on epic proportions. "The hero of an incipient pre-capitalist mode of production is projected within the folk epic context, promoting romantic identification with the protagonist, Gregório Cortéz. In the case of the Acosta/Buffalo persona, individual urbanity and modern capitalist conditions produced an anti-hero to grotesquely and caricaturistically personify the struggle of the 'cockroadh people.'" Alurista, "From Tragedy to Caricature . . . and Beyond," *Aztlán*, Vol. 11 (1980), pp. 89–98.

[43] Rodolfo González, *Yo Soy Joaquin (I Am Joaquin)* (New York: Bantam Books, 1972). This poem is very popular, often reprinted, and has been made into a film. It is an important document of *Chicanismo*.

[44] *Puerto Rican Obituary* (New York: Monthly Review Press, 1973).

[45] Piri Thomas, *Down These Mean Streets* (New York: Alfred A. Knopf, 1967).

Rico itself. Puerto Rico is a racially mixed society, with African, Spanish, and other Europeans mixed with the tiny remnant of Indians. This racial mixture is glorified ideologically, much as the Indian and Spanish mixture is in Mexico.[46] Immigrant Puerto Ricans and their children adjust with difficulty to the sharp racial distinctions of American culture. Black Puerto Ricans face the usual discrimination confronting all black Americans. This is true even if, as for Piri Thomas, many of the families and friends are blond and blue-eyed. As Clara Rodríguez comments, the consequences can be devastating:

> There are only two options open in biracial New York—to be white or black. These options negate the cultural existence of Puerto Ricans and ignore their insistence on being treated, irrespective of race, as a culturally intact group. Thus, U.S. racial attitudes necessarily make Puerto Ricans either white or black, attitudes and culture make them neither white nor black, and our own resistance and struggle for survival places us between whites and blacks. . . . Historically, Puerto Ricans arriving in New York have found themselves in a situation of perpetual incongruence—that is, they saw themselves differently than they were seen. . . . Puerto Ricans, a culturally-homogeneous, racially-integrated group, find themselves opposed to the demand that they become racially divided and culturally "cleansed" of being Puerto Rican.[47]

Puerto Rican and Mexican-American writers also differ in their ambivalence about the "homeland." Few Chicano writers are preoccupied with the culture of Mexico per se. Their identity search is more complex and reflects the very long residence in the United States and the heterogeneity of the population itself. The Puerto Rican migration to the mainland is relatively recent, and most Puerto Ricans have strong roots in Puerto Rico. The heritage of a colonial relationship with the United States is deep and bitter. When the island was acquired by the United States, a literate and sophisticated intelligentsia found their culture and language devalued and threatened by the American educational system. As a consequence, for nearly a century, Puerto Rican intellectuals were preoccupied with nationalist themes—and with the preservation of a culture. Thus when Puerto Ricans began to move to the United States in large numbers, the first reaction of the island intellectuals was dismay. Rene Márques is a major Puerto Rican writer, and in his play *La Carreta* (1953), he saw the migration experience as abrupt moral and cultural deterioration. The only hope for salvation is in return to the island and to peasant life. The Puerto Rican oxcart (*carreta*) is the guiding symbol of the play, and it must be restored to its natural place in a world that is uncontaminated by inhuman modernity and incompatible foreign values. Tradition is the only hope for a life of decency on the

---

[46] Both Puerto Ricans and Mexicans cite the ideas of the Mexican philosopher José Vasconcelos that this typically Latin American racial mixture produces *la raza cósmica*—"the cosmic race." This ideology does not preclude racial prejudice on the island. Yet "blacks are not a distinguishable ethnic group" on the island and, for example, there are no taboos on black-white intermarriage as in the United States; see Samuel Betances, "Race and the Search for Identity," in *Borinquén* (New York: Vintage, 1974); and Clara Rodríguez, "Puerto Ricans: Between Black and White," in Rodríguez et al., eds., *Puerto Rican Struggle*.

[47] Rodríguez et al., *Puerto Rican Struggle*, pp. 25, 28.

sacred soil.[48] There must be no surrender to the Anglo-Saxon. In direct contradiction, Tato Laviera, a mainland poet, is proud of being a "Nuyorican." Instead of rural purity, Laviera identifies with the Puerto Rican roots that invoke the "popular culture of an Afro-Caribbean island, the birthplace of musical and poetic forms"— in short, an urban popular culture.[49] In this manner, some mainland Puerto Ricans see the positive side of a life that most Americans would view as degrading and miserable. At this point in time, it is a reasonable guess that the Puerto Rican ambivalence about the cultural consequences of a vast migration will not soon be resolved.

[48] J. Flores et al., "La Carreta Made a U-Turn," *Daedalus,* Vol. 110 (1981), p. 203. A different view of the migration experience is given in Barry Levine's *Benjy López: A Picaresque Tale of Emigration and Return* (New York: Basic Books, 1980). López hustles busily in New York, but "unlike the myth of immigrant success in the United States, López didn't go to the United States, and make it; rather, he went there, learned how to make it and . . . it was only when he returned to Puerto Rico and applied his street smarts . . . on his own turf that his story became one of ethnic success" (p. 200).

[49] Tato Laviera, *La Carreta Made a U-Turn* (Gary, Ind.: Arte Publico Press, 1979).

CHAPTER TWO
HISTORY:
THE HISPANICS APPEAR

Quite early in the American expansion, the Hispanics became a problem for native Anglo Americans. There was conflict and friction with Spain in Florida and with Mexicans in the Southwest, during the Texas Revolution, and through the ensuing war with Mexico in 1846.[1] Later, when contact became more frequent, something about the mixture of races so characteristic of the Hispanics, their poverty, and their Catholicism continued to generate friction. Perhaps the American horror at "mixed races" was carried over to the Southwest from the sharp distinctions drawn in the South between white and black. Mexicans were forced to endure the rough attentions of a rapidly expanding Anglo-American population quite convinced of its civilizing destiny. The supposed superiority of Anglo-Saxons was an ideology admirably suited to a variety of economic and political motives, some of them no more noble than simple greed.

The same themes of racial superiority dominated the Hispanic-Anglo "relationship" in the economic sphere. Imported laborers and thousands of Mexican immigrants were essential for the mines, factories, railroads, and fields of the Southwest. It was natural and convenient to assume a kind of racial inferiority. Later, when an expanding and aggressive United States annexed the island of Puerto Rico

[1]Probably these were the reasons for the appearance of an "Anglo-Saxon" ideology in the United States. For an interesting discussion of this idea, see Reginald Horsman, *Race and Manifest Destiny: The Origins of American Anglo-Saxonism* (Cambridge, Mass.: Harvard University Press, 1981).

the same racial bias was directed against the Spanish-speaking and mixed-blood Puerto Ricans. When they came to the mainland in large numbers after World War II, their poverty and racial mixture again provoked the same stereotypes. Cubans came to the United States later yet and, as refugees, added more overtones to the national perception of Hispanics.

Meanwhile, the flow of Mexican immigrants had grown to such proportions that many segments of American society felt threatened. Shifts and adjustments in immigration law became a prime concern. Chicano workers were essential, particularly in agriculture, but Anglo labor often felt abused. And because Mexicans now tend to live in large cities, the persistent problems of overburdened American institutions are a critical element.

This history of open conflict, economic deprivation, and racial prejudice is the background for the history of America's Hispanics. Mexican Americans, Puerto Ricans, and Cubans share this overall framework. Each will be treated separately, but with special emphasis on the Mexican Americans who were the first of the Hispanics, the largest Spanish-speaking segment, and whose problems in American society foreshadow those of all other Hispanics.

THE MEXICANS

The history of the Chicano minority is unlike that of any other American minority group. Perhaps this history most resembles that of the American Indians, but even there we can find only a few similarities. Mexican Americans *became* a minority not by immigrating or being brought to this country as a subordinate people, but by conquest. The process was somewhat different in each of the border states (Texas, New Mexico, Arizona, and California) but, nonetheless, it was conquest that set the stage for the reactions to large-scale immigration from Mexico in the early twentieth century. Later this background of subordination would be critical in the economic, social, and political roles of the Chicanos.

The Southwest before the Mexican War. In all the enormous reaches of the Southwest in the early nineteenth century, there were no more than a handful of non-Indian settlers. From Texas to northern California, most of the land was vaguely and ineffectively claimed by Mexico. The settlers, nominally Mexican and often the descendants of arrivals dating from the seventeenth century, lived in small, tight, defensible clusters in strategic areas. The "fan" of these settlements stretched more than 2,000 miles along the northern edge, but seldom extended more than 150 miles north of the modern Mexican border. Once we look at the approximate numbers of these early Mexican settlers, we can understand something of the very diverse experience of Mexicans in each area. There were perhaps 5,000 Mexicans in Texas, 60,000 in New Mexico, not more than 1,000 in Arizona, and perhaps 7,500 along the length of California.[2]

Imperial Spain and, later, the nation of Mexico gave these isolated citizens

---

[2] See Carey McWilliams, *North from Mexico* (Philadelphia: J. B. Lippincott, 1949), p. 52; and U.S. Bureau of the Census, *Historical Statistics of the United States, Colonial Times to 1957* (Washington, D.C.: Government Printing Office, 1960). The short history by McWilliams is still the best general history available.

virtually nothing, often not even the rudiments of defense or enough priests to administer the most basic of Catholic sacraments. The endless war with the Indians (who hugely outnumbered the first settlers) was actually being lost when the first Anglo Americans appeared early in the nineteenth century. From 1848 to 1886 (when the last hostile Apache were driven from the state), most areas of Arizona were impassable. American troops and most particularly a well-armed and efficient cavalry greatly impressed the resident Spanish Americans. No other government had ever been able to bring such a measure of security from the interminable massacres, attacks, and property damage.

In *Texas* the frontier of original Mexican settlement was quite limited and was kept small by the hostile Comanches. While there was considerable settlement even in the dangerous area between the Rio Grande and the Nueces rivers, most Mexicans (probably 80 percent) lived in the lower Rio Grande Valley and in the river cities, with El Paso the most westerly town of any consequence. Such present-day south Texas counties as Starr, Zapata, Cameron, and Hidalgo thus had thousands of early residents. Along the Rio Grande a series of mercantile towns grew up (Brownsville, Dolores, Laredo, Rio Grande City, Roma) to handle the commercial needs of this area. All these river towns had some Anglo and European residents in the early nineteenth century, but most residents were Mexican.

Conquest and its aftermath.   Friction with Anglo settlers pushing in from the East began as early as the 1820s and culminated in a short war with Mexico. In 1836 the Anglo settlers declared a Republic in Texas, leaving such resentment among the Mexicans that a second war was inevitable. In 1846, a rapid and successful American invasion of Mexico ended all Mexican claims to Texas, and after the war the Treaty of Guadalupe-Hidalgo ceded to the United States almost the entire modern Southwest. But it was not a treaty that ended disputes: the line of the Rio Grande was clear enough, but west of El Paso the treaty negotiators followed a faulty map. The ensuing arguments very nearly caused another war. Ultimately, James Gadsden was sent to Mexico City to negotiate a new acquisition. The original line would have followed the course of the Gila River across Arizona, but Gadsden managed to secure by purchase an additional 45,532 square miles. The new border ran south of the Gila and secured an area for a proposed railroad line to California. As it happened (and no Mexican thinks it accidental), the Gadsden Purchase of 1853 included some of the richest copper mines in the United States.

The Treaty of Guadalupe-Hidalgo guaranteed the rights of Mexicans in Texas and all other ceded territory. Nonetheless, the years after the treaty saw the rapid loss of most Mexican property interests in Texas and the slippage of Mexicans (as an economic group) into a segregated and despised working class. Anglo stereotypes were the ideology: certain almost irresistible economic changes were the immediate causes. Early cattle ranches in the border states were based on the ownership of livestock rather than land. When public land suddenly became private land, much of the Mexican livestock wealth disappeared in very short order. In one Texas example, between 1840 and 1859, by one means or another, all Mexican-owned land in Nueces County except one ranch passed into the hands of Anglo settlers.[3] Displaced

[3]Paul S. Taylor, *An American-Mexican Frontier* (Chapel Hill: University of North Carolina Press, 1934, 1972), p. 294.

ranchers and their descendants easily slipped into the ranks of the *peones,* badly needed by the new Anglo ranchers. The new ranches were soon fenced, after the invention of barbed wire in 1875. Enclosure and fencing tended to freeze out the smaller cattle and sheep ranchers who could not afford to buy land.

A few years later cotton plantations slowly moved into south Texas from east Texas, continuing a movement toward the west and cheap new land. Black slaves to cultivate the new crops were no longer available. The demand for cheap Mexican labor to "brush out" the new land and to cultivate cotton was so great that it fixed, very nearly in its modern form, the economic fate of the old Mexican settler and the new Mexican immigrant in a very few years. By 1900 the Mexican laborer in both rural and urban Texas had become defined as an inferior person and as a member of a distinctive race entitled to neither political, educational, nor social equality.[4] Remnants of Mexican equality survived only in some of the commercial towns of the Rio Grande Valley where Mexicans remained in the majority.

But economic dispossession was not the only heritage in Texas for the Mexican Americans. Mexican residents suffered periodically from lynch law and violent discrimination that often surpassed the Old South. Some measure of this conflict may be found in Walter Prescott Webb's history of the Texas Rangers, a group of Texas law enforcement officers formed in 1835 that survives to this day, proud of its history of quick "trail justice." Originally, the Rangers dealt with both Indians and Mexicans. When the Indians disappeared after 1886, the Rangers specialized in Mexicans. In 1935 the group merged into the Texas Highway Patrol and is still a fearsome name in Chicano folklore.[5] It is true that the early Rangers protected settlers from Indian raids, horse thieves, fence cutters, and other casual violence. But it is also true that the Rangers took an active interest in early labor struggles, particularly those involving Mexican labor. As late as 1963, *los rinches* (unfriendly nickname for the Rangers) were summoned by Anglo city officials in Crystal City when the officials felt threatened by a Mexican majority.[6]

It is hardly possible to exaggerate the amount of racial violence in Texas and the other border states from the earliest days until the end of the Mexican revolutions in 1925. Cattle raids, border looting expeditions, expulsions, deportations, lynchings, civil riots, labor wars, organized banditry, filibustering expeditions, and three formal wars occurred almost without respite. Some of these minor and almost unknown conflicts laid waste to entire counties and lasted for years. Conflict and racial violence are an essential part of the Chicano history in Texas—and in the border states in general.

In *New Mexico* and southern *Colorado,* the native Hispanics entered the period of Anglo settlement with its settlers centered in military and administrative

[4]See also Mario Barrera, *Race and Class in the Southwest* (Notre Dame, Ind.: University of Notre Dame Press, 1979).

[5]The standard history of the Rangers is that of Walter Prescott Webb, *The Texas Rangers* (Austin: University of Texas Press, 1935), although it is much less interested in the Rangers' anti-Mexican, antilabor role than are Chicano historians. A corrective view is given in detail by Rodolfo Acuña, *Occupied America: The Chicano's Struggle Toward Liberation* (San Francisco: Canfield Press, 1972), and Julian Samora, Joe Bernal, and Albert Peña, *Gunpowder Justice: A Reassessment of the Texas Rangers* (Notre Dame, Ind.: University of Notre Dame Press, 1979).

[6]John Staples Shockley, *Chicano Revolt in a Texas Town* (Notre Dame, Ind.: University of Notre Dame Press, 1974), p. 35.

towns (Santa Fe and Albuquerque), large ranches, and a considerable number of small villages. Agriculture and livestock were the staples of life. Isolation and constant warfare with the Indians meant that Anglo inroads came very slowly. In 1848, about 60,000 people lived in New Mexico territory, nearly all of them "Mexican" or, more precisely, Spanish American. Most, in fact, lived either within a 50-mile radius of Santa Fe or on the headwaters of the Rio Grande and Pecos rivers. Unlike the borderlands of Texas, the residents of New Mexico had developed a full range of classes with an established ruling group, able in every respect and interested in retaining political power. A small group of ruling families dominated the political, financial, and economic interests of the state and easily shared new and even more effective power with Anglo interests. For at least three generations, this alliance effectively dominated New Mexican life.

Most New Mexicans lived a considerable distance from the border and thus were spared much of the border warfare and violence so typical of Texas. Not until the coming of the railroads was movement easy in any direction, a factor that tended to keep the area peaceful and isolated. Nonetheless, economic changes were swiftly breaking down this curiously isolated society. By 1900 overgrazing and erosion; the consolidation of small holdings into larger ranches; the transfer of old land grant territories to loggers, railroads, and other exploitative interests; the steady division of lands among heirs; and the preemption of grazing land for various types of federal use doomed many small ranchers to extinction. Small herders and farmers were forced into wage labor to such an extent that by 1910 only 30 percent of the pre-Anglo landowners held their original land. At the same time, some immigration coming west from Texas swelled the labor pool and tended to reduce wage rates. Thus, long before 1900, the New Mexican traditional village was fighting a losing battle against pauperization. The decline of sheepherding meant the erosion of a form of social organization hundreds of years old.

But New Mexico was slow to develop the pervasive discrimination so characteristic of Texas. As Nancie Gonzalez writes, "Inter-marriage between American men and Spanish-American women was apparently quite common, and not restricted to any particular social class. Business and commercial mergers between Anglos and Mexicans occurred frequently, and in politics, coalitions of Anglos and Mexicans worked together in each of the major parties."[7] But there is evidence that this tolerant mood began to sour as early as 1900 as, inevitably, more and more American settlers and important American mining, ranching, and transportation interests took hold in New Mexico. Railroad lines broke down an isolation that had lasted for generations. The new rail services allowed dozens of isolated company towns to exploit the mineral resources. New markets for wool, meat, and hides opened by the railroads accelerated the growth of larger and more efficient ranches. Enclosure slowly cut off the livelihoods of smaller ranchers. The same forces that spelled economic opportunity to large Anglo enterprises were forcing a large portion of the resident Mexicans into the status of a dependent minority.

No state suffered more from Indian depredations than did *Arizona*. By 1856, nearly all of the Hispanic colonists in Arizona had been crowded into the single fortified city of Tucson. When it came, the shift to Anglo domination affected only

---

[7]Nancie L. Gonzalez, *The Spanish Americans of New Mexico: A Distinctive Heritage of Pride* (Albuquerque: University of New Mexico Press, 1969).

a very few Mexicans. These few could not satisfy the endless appetite for cheap wage labor. Thousands more were imported through the labor markets in the border towns of Laredo and El Paso. Thus the familiar pattern of a transition to wage labor appeared very early in Arizona and with it the dreary succession of lynchings, unsolved murders, and vigilante actions against a working-class population of what was defined as a different race, certainly as foreigners.

Arizona settlement patterns are notable for the large number of isolated mining towns, nearly all of them with a large majority of Mexicans. These company towns appeared in large numbers in the 1880s, nearly always in isolated areas such as Tubac, Miami, San Manuel, Walker, Dewey, Jerome, Morenci, and so on. Some still exist; others are ghost towns. Many were too small or too dominated by a single employer to provide any but the most rudimentary public services. There was rigid separation by occupation, which meant rigid segregation of the Mexicans from the Anglos in these tiny societies.

The story of Mexicans in *California* is much more complex. Here during the Mexican hegemony a handful of *rancheros* held an enormous area, separated almost completely from Mexican control.[8] Mexico generally ignored this westernmost province and even failed (beyond an occasional shipment of felons) to settle it in any substantial numbers. Most of the residents approved of the idea of annexation by the United States. Mexico was weak; there were endless quarrels with Mexican officials; there were serious troubles with Indians at times but little help from Mexico, and the ranchers were long accustomed to trade by clipper ship with the United States. Thus the "Bear Flag" rebellion of 1846 was a welcomed event, as was the succeeding military occupation by U.S. troops.

The early occupation was amiable enough, the new government fitting neatly into the administrative mechanism of a coherent and long-established society. But in 1848 gold was discovered in the interior, and suddenly northern California was being "settled" at tremendous speed by Anglo miners. At least 100,000 miners were arriving each year. Massive immigrations of Sonorans and Chileans (13,000 South Americans in 1849 alone) complicated the problem. The Anglo miner of midwestern or southern origin felt that "a greaser is a greaser" even if he owned 35,000 acres of land and was pure Castilian. In the mines, remote from any law, Mexicans and Chileans were taxed, lynched, robbed, and expelled in an endless series of incidents. Many of the Mexicans and Chileans then drifted into California towns and formed a substantial group of impoverished laborers. The mining troubles were an early and a bad precedent for American-Mexican relations in California.

Very soon the gold mines became less profitable, and the new arrivals turned to agriculture, squatting on the Mexican grants in large numbers and filling California courts with endless and complicated title litigation. Some of the Mexican grants were of dubious legality from their beginning, and others were often "floated" in court to cover all nearby improvements and sources of water. Within a few years, the *californios* had lost nearly all economic power in northern California.[9] Not all of the land claims were decided against them, but the steady and

[8]This account is based substantially on Leonard Pitt, *The Decline of the Californios: A Social History of the Spanish-Speaking Californians, 1846-1890* (Berkeley and Los Angeles: University of California Press, 1966).

[9]In 1849, state reports showed 200 *californio* families owning 14 million acres of California in parcels ranging from 4,500 acres to about 50,000 acres. Against this concentration, the American white settlers invoked the Jacksonian idea that a few men of immoderate wealth and special privilege wasted the land and denied industry its due. See ibid., p. 87.

growing influence of Anglo settlers left the *californios* in the position of a small, tightly knit group of overextended landlords, barely able to hold their lands, and hated by most of the communities. California became a state in 1850, and although the government was more decentralized, more powerful, and more responsive than in either Arizona or New Mexico, the land trouble in northern California was beyond the capacity of government to resolve.

In southern California, the situation was completely different. A generation after the Gold Rush, nothing much had changed. Mexican *rancheros* owned the land; the Indians did the work; the Anglo settlers were few and unimportant. Most of arable southern California was owned by no more than 50 men and their immediate families, including a group of about a dozen Mexicanized Yankees. Large supplies of Indian labor and cheap land worked against the development of a Mexican lower class, either on ranches or in the sparse towns. No economic enterprise in southern California needed large numbers of wage earners.

Although the ranchers shared power in local and state government and their economic base held firm, the generation after 1850 watched uneasily as racial tension grew noticeably. Los Angeles was inhabited by an explosive combination of lower-class Mexicans, Anglos, Indians, and Chinese, and it soon became almost impossible to maintain even a facade of racial harmony in an age of strong anti-Catholicism, nativism, and frequent violent crime. Even the state became less tolerant: taxes were imposed upon land, laws were no longer published in Spanish, and in 1855, a law was passed forbidding school instruction in Spanish.[10]

The *rancheros* hoped to split the state along a line near San Luis Obispo, but the issue became entangled with national questions of sectionalism and slavery. The final blow was economic. In 1862, a devastating flood was followed by two years of extreme drought, a disaster that very nearly destroyed California's Mexican wealth at its source. Mortgages, legal fees, taxes, and low cattle prices completed the ruin. A steady flow of Anglo immigrants meant that *californios* gradually disappeared from public life. By the early 1880s, there were no longer any Spanish names in the public offices of southern California.

The final blow (as in all of the border states) was the arrival of the railroad. In 1887 alone, two new railroads brought in more than 120,000 Anglo settlers, a year in which only 12,000 Mexicans lived in all southern California. The Mexican majority became a minority in just one year. A fierce land boom after the arrival of the railroads ended most of what remained of Mexican ownership of the great ranches.

This was roughly the condition of the Mexican Americans in the border states by the year 1900. In general, their first massive contact with Anglo settlements (usually when the railroads arrived) coincided with subordination, even if it did not immediately cause it. Everywhere except in New Mexico, this charter member minority (whose minority status is acquired by conquest rather than by immigration) was by 1900 hopelessly inundated by the tide of Anglo-American immigration, reduced to landless labor, and made politically and economically impotent. Socially, the older residents had become "Mexican"—a people indistinguishable to Anglos from the new immigrants arriving from Mexico. Perhaps more important, all Mexicans, whatever their isolation from other Mexican com-

---

[10] Albert Camarillo has written a fascinating and detailed account of the decay and "barriozation" of the California Mexican society. See Camarillo, *Chicanos in a Changing Society* (Cambridge, Mass.: Harvard University Press, 1979).

munities, had acquired a common heritage of racial conflict. Only in New Mexico did the natives retain numerical plurality and some degree of control in political matters.

Immigration from Mexico. By 1900 the basic Mexican settlements were well established in the border states. In nearly every city where there would be a sizable urban Mexican population, its rudiments had already appeared. Mexicans tended to settle together in distinctively "Mexican" neighborhoods or *barrios.* But the origins of these *barrios* often were different. One typical town plan in the border states was the settlement around a traditionally Mexican *plaza* (central area). When the railroads and highways brought growth of the Anglo population, it tended to center on the new terminals or nodes of transportation. The Mexican plaza area was bypassed and tended to deteriorate. In time (as in Albuquerque, Los Angeles, and dozens of other cities), the plaza area remained as the "Mexican downtown" or as a carefully reconstructed and often glamorized tourist center.

Still other Mexican enclaves are the residue of early labor camps. In southern California, such remnants as Santa Fe Springs and Pacoima in Los Angeles County are really new growth on the skeletons of old labor camps bypassed and isolated inside growing, spreading cities. Whole families of Mexicans emigrated or were imported into these camps to serve such functions as ranch work, railway maintenance, citrus harvesting and packing, and brick making. In yet other areas, the enclaves remain on the fringes of the metropolitan area and continue to serve as agricultural labor markets. Many such settlements have disappeared; some are in the process of urban renewal; some have been overwhelmed and displaced by a rapid rise in land values.

In some parts of the border states, Mexican Americans dominate the life of the community. This happened in small towns in northern New Mexico, southern Texas, and even in larger Texas border and near-border cities like Laredo. It is an extraordinary range of highly segregated to almost completely nonsegregated living patterns. In the large industrial cities of the Midwest and East, Mexican settlement is more traditional. Here, Chicanos are moving quite rapidly into low-cost rental areas, usually near the centers of the cities.

Feeding into these enclaves were groups of Mexican laborers brought for specific tasks. Albert Camarillo describes how the Southern Pacific railroad steadily imported laborers into Santa Barbara, California, and how the Mexican community on Quarantina Street near the railroad tracks steadily grew in size.[11] But most (or certainly a very high proportion) of the new arrivals brought themselves across the border simply to find greater opportunities.

Mexican immigration differs from the much better known European immigration in many ways. It may be well to abstract some of these distinctive features before proceeding with an account of this massive and ceaseless movement. There were at least six.

First, not until recently was it regulated by formal quota (see Chapter 8 for more details on immigration policy). Second, immigration from Mexico has been continuous, but it was massive only recently—and is the only recent prolonged heavy movement into the United States. Third, immigration from Mexico has

---

[11] Camarillo, *Chicanos in a Changing Society,* Ch. 6.

followed some very complicated patterns—some very informal (see Chapter 8). Fourth (and this is related to the third point), it is comparatively easy for Mexican immigrants to reach the United States. The large and economically attractive cities of the border states, especially those in Texas, are accessible by railroad, highway, and bus. It is relatively easy for both failures and successes to return home, and it has been relatively easy for a prospective immigrant to make a trial journey to the United States.

Fifth, no other minority was ever deported from the United States in such massive numbers as the Mexicans. And, sixth, no other minority except the Chinese has entered this country in such an atmosphere of illegality. A long, relatively unguarded border and recruiting by important economic interests ensured that in some years perhaps three times as many Mexicans entered illegally as legally. No accurate estimate is possible, but the consequence was inevitable. The Mexicans entering without papers and the communities sheltering them were peculiarly vulnerable to economic and social discrimination of all kinds.

Statistically it is impossible to analyze Mexican immigration earlier than 1910.[12] We know that an important movement took place after 1848 when thousands of Mexicans joined in the California gold rush. The chaotic condition of the border areas until 1886 prevented any government control whatever over population movements between Mexico and the United States. Arizona and its border areas were largely impassable. Not until 1907 was any form of control established. As late as 1919, the entire border was patrolled by only 151 inspectors, most of them confined to 20 regular ports of entry. It now appears that much of this laxness was deliberate so that the border states could retain a flow of cheap labor so badly needed in the economy.

By 1908 Mexican railroad connections could reach all 48 states. This made immigration much easier. Then the outbreak of the chaotic Mexican revolution after 1910 spurred even more movement. During this period, from 1910 to 1920, the immigrants apparently included a significant number of middle-class and upper-class Mexican refugees, many of whom hoped to return to Mexico. Meanwhile, American labor requirements were increasing. The Chinese were excluded in 1882 and the Japanese in 1907, and the supply of European immigrants waned with World War I. Special rules issued in 1917 admitted "temporary" farm workers, railroad maintenance workers, and miners. Many of the workers, perhaps as many as two-thirds, never returned to Mexico.

Changes inside Mexico were largely responsible for the heavy new immigration. Lawrence Cardoso thinks the primary cause was simply starvation. General Porfirio Díaz (president of Mexico from 1876 to 1911) and his advisors believed that immigration from Europe would solve Mexican problems and "have a favorable influence on a sluggish Indian and *mestizo* peasantry." To stimulate this change, Díaz granted public lands in enormous acreage to hacienda owners and colonization companies. These lands then were planted to export crops such as sugar cane to be

---

[12] Early immigration has attracted very little serious study. Until recently, there were only three studies of importance. See Manuel Gámio, *Mexican Immigration to the United States* (Chicago: University of Chicago Press, 1930); Leo Grebler, *Mexican Immigration to the United States: The Record and its Implications,* Advance Report 2 (Los Angeles: University of California, Mexican-American Study Project, 1966); and Julian Samora, *Los Mojados: The Wetback Story* (Notre Dame, Ind.: University of Notre Dame Press, 1971).

sold in the United States and Europe. The "public lands" were, in truth, communal lands that had been used as a livelihood by Mexican villagers for centuries. In the time of Díaz, it is estimated that perhaps 5 million *campesinos* lost their rights to the use of communal (*ejido*) land.[13] Yet other changes added to the misery and made revolution inevitable. Rapid increases in population strained Mexican agricultural capacity, and although wages actually decreased from 1890 to 1908, food prices nearly doubled. A series of world recessions and droughts also damaged the country.

Although destitution and civil disorder forced most of the immigrants into the long trek north, the feeling of expatriation, of desiring to return some day to Mexico was very strong. Middle-class Mexicans in particular resisted Anglicization and followed events in Mexico with great interest. In a sense, they imagined themselves as "*Mexico de afuera*" (Mexico outside Mexico).[14] *La Opinión,* a leading Mexican newspaper printed in Los Angeles, thought of the Mexican consul as the proper resort in disputes with Anglo law enforcement and Anglo society. The Mexican authorities were able at one time or another to impede the recruiting of Mexican labor inside Mexico. Official Mexican interest in the conditions of immigrant Mexican labor began as early as 1916, quite explicitly ordering consuls to do everything possible to aid the immigrants. The results (from a group of diplomatic representatives never larger than 51 consuls) were very mixed, although there were successful intercessions in a long list of labor disputes—meat packing plants in Kansas City, copper mines in Arizona, growers with *bracero* contracts in Arizona.[15] By contrast, because they were U.S. citizens, Puerto Rican workers never had even this rather faint help until after World War II.

Immigration continued quite steadily until 1929, prompted both by disruption in Mexico that followed the revolutionary wars and by an expanding demand in the United States for agricultural labor. The flow slowed markedly after 1929 when American agriculture fell into a prolonged decline even before the more general economic drop of the Great Depression. In the United States, other sources of cheap farm labor became available as the great migration from the Dust Bowl to the West began. A growing number of Anglo urban workers sought refuge in farm work. The drop in immigration also reflects the impact of massive efforts to send the Mexicans "home," where, it had always been assumed, they "belonged."

Meanwhile, there were some important changes in the destinations of the new arrivals. Typically, the immigrant of earlier years was bound for a company town, an agricultural work camp, or perhaps an urban enclave somewhere in the border states. From 1910 to 1929, Texas was the most popular destination. Slowly, California became more attractive. Figures from 1960 to 1964 show 55.7 percent going to California and only 25.1 percent to Texas. Arizona took 5.7 percent and New Mexico 2.5 percent. Only 10.6 percent of the newcomers intended to go outside this very limited area. Recent trends show that California still takes a very high

---

[13] Lawrence A. Cardoso, *Mexican Emigration to the United States, 1897-1931* (Tucson: University of Arizona Press, 1980).

[14] In a fascinating content analysis of *La Opinión,* the leading Mexican newspaper in Los Angeles, that covers 1926 to 1929, Francine Medeiros traces two dominant themes—criticism of Anglo society and cultural reinforcement: "*La Opinión:* A Mexican Exile Newspaper: A Content Analysis of the First Years, 1926–1929," *Aztlán,* Vol. 11, no. 1 (Spring 1980), pp. 65–87.

[15] Cardoso, *Mexican Emigration,* Ch. 4.

proportion, but some of the large midwestern cities, notably Chicago, are important goals. Very slowly, the Chicanos were escaping their historical residence in the border states and were becoming a national minority, not just an isolated regional group.

Mexicans become a national minority. In tracing the important changes since 1900, *the appearance of Mexican Americans on the national stage* is critical. A nation preoccupied with the dualism of black and white hardly noticed the Mexicans, isolated as they were, faraway inside the American Southwest. It was a process of recognition that would take generations and is not yet complete. By 1970, the word "minority" had expanded to include Chicanos; before that time, the tendency to think dualistically of urban minorities as simply American blacks greatly affected public policy.[16]

First, the Mexican population began, slowly but decisively, to "settle out" in cities rather than in rural areas convenient for a stream of agricultural workers. The importance of this *rapid urbanization* in recent decades cannot be overstated. As recently as 1950, a third of the total Chicano population lived in rural areas. By 1970 only 15 percent of the Mexican population lived in rural or rural nonfarm areas.[17] Those who still worked in agriculture were more likely to be foreign-born rather than natives. In California the shift to cities is nearly complete; approximately 90 percent of the Chicanos live in cities.

Second, *Mexican Americans gradually increased the range and quality of their participation in American economic life.* This happened very slowly—so slowly that in times of national hardship, it did not show progress at all. Yet since 1900, despite the almost endless flow of immigrants, there have been changes. In the early years, Texas served as a sort of collecting point for cheap Mexican labor for sugar beet harvesting in the North, the central states, and the West; electric railway construction and fruit harvesting in California; cotton harvesting in Arizona; and wage labor in the tanneries, meat packing plants, and steel mills of Chicago.[18] Mexicans appeared in the automobile factories in Detroit, the steel mills of Ohio and Pennsylvania, and the mines and smelters of Arizona and Colorado and in railroad maintenance everywhere.

Even with this base in heavy unskilled labor, we can watch the slow appearance of a middle class. It became customary to employ "reliable" Mexicans to hire and transport this vast flow. Straw bosses, supervisors, and labor recruiters grew out of the labor system. In the fields themselves, the workers sometimes moved into the operation and repair of equipment, the use of processing machinery, and even clerical tasks. The small "Mextowns" throughout the border states needed an array of small services: restaurants, rooming houses, small retail stores, and the personal services required by a flow of workers.

Substantial movement out of agriculture, railroads, and mining came with World War I. Wartime industries gave high wages for a few years to some Mexican

---

[16] Joan W. Moore, "Minorities in the American Class System," *Daedalus,* Vol. 110 (1981), pp. 275-299.

[17] See the *1970 U.S. Census of Population,* PC (2)-ID, Table 2.

[18] See, for example, Louise Año Nuevo de Kerr, "Chicano Settlements in Chicago: A Brief History," *Journal of Ethnic Studies,* Vol. 2 (1975), pp. 22-31.

Americans. Whenever possible the children of agricultural workers went to school and abandoned field labor. These gains were interrupted by the Great Depression. Problems in agriculture were part of the depression, and the resulting stagnation hurt Mexicans as much as any other minority group largely dependent upon wage labor. In the cities, the burden of Mexican welfare cases led to efforts at "repatriation" or massive deportations (see Chapter 8). Many of the cities in the border states were particularly vulnerable to the economic stresses of the depression because they lacked a well-diversified economic base. Agriculture suffered severely: in Texas cotton became so unprofitable that vast areas were returned to cattle, reversing a long and historic process. Falling prices hurt small farmers seriously and Mexican small farmers among them. Rapid mechanization (tractors, harvest combines) took even more jobs away. Then, as a final blow, when the famous Dust Bowl migrations began into the border states, particularly into California, Anglo workers began to displace Mexicans in the fields. Half of California farm labor in 1934 was native white; no more than a third of the field workers were Mexican.[19] Wage rates fell drastically as did farm prices. In New Mexico, to name just one area, wage labor almost disappeared, and the more traditional sources of income—farming and sheepherding—could not compete with modern techniques. Federal programs took up some of the slack, most spectacularly in New Mexico, where a *majority* of the Spanish Americans were directly dependent upon the federal government. A side effect of the misery in rural areas was a gradual speeding of the movement to the cities.

The gradual improvement in economic conditions between the end of the Great Depression and the beginning of World War II left the newly urbanized Mexicans in a much better position. The cities offered better education, even if it was often segregated. Cities offered more work opportunities and much greater contact with Anglo society and its varied institutions and agencies. Most important, it became clear that Mexicans were permanent residents, and this was an important realization for Anglo society.

World War II offered Mexican Americans new opportunities. Between 300,000 and 500,000 men served in the armed forces. Young men saw new areas of the United States outside their isolated five-state ghetto and also parts of the rest of the world where Mexicans had never been considered an inferior people. Others learned skilled trades and changed residence permanently. Mexicans with only a precarious grip on middle-class status were able to consolidate their gains, improve their housing, and send their children to better schools. A steady and accelerating migration began from Texas to California. The exchange of information, the broadening of experience, the increasing ethnic awareness, all meant a shift away from areas of more restricted economic and social opportunity. All this served as a catalyst to the development of new leadership in the community.

Third, *Mexican Americans gradually developed a sense of political self-awareness and involvement.* Mexican leaders frequently trace the beginnings of general self-awareness to the social changes brought on by World War II. But it is likely the beginnings occurred much earlier.[20]

[19] Carey McWilliams, *Factories in the Field* (Boston: Little Brown, 1939), p. 305.

[20] A new generation of Chicano historians and researchers has begun to explore the history. One of the interesting results of this exploration is the slow destruction of the myth of Mexicans as "docile" farm laborers. It appears now that the "docility" was perhaps a wise adaptation at certain periods and in certain places, particularly in Texas.

The violence and conflict between Anglo and Mexican is an important element of life in the border states. The northern Mexican provinces traditionally spawned revolutions. Inevitably, some of the conflict spilled over the border, particularly into New Mexico and Texas.[21] Mexican revolutions sometimes were plotted in the safety of American cities. A recent study of these *revoltosos*[22] living in the United States shows a range of ideology from the socialist and anarchist followers of Flores Magón (*magonistas*) to the reactionary, pro-clerical followers of Porfirio Díaz (*felicistas*). Both the American and Mexican authorities worked to suppress those movements considered dangerous, particularly if any threat appeared to American life and property either in Mexico or in the United States. For the Mexican Americans, the atmosphere of fear and suspicion of treason made their status in American life even less tolerable. It was an era when it was reasonable to expect a certain amount of docility from the Mexican *barrios.*

Yet there was actually a great deal of labor conflict involving Mexican workers. Some of these early strikes and protests were violent, although they were not frequent and usually they were not coordinated.[23]

Mexican labor organizations were active in many of the strikes. Later strikes in the fields and mines of the border states were both more frequent and more sophisticated. But these early demands were significant because Mexicans generally were denied normal political expression everywhere except New Mexico. The alien workers, of course, had no voice, but the settled and native-born citizens were also efficiently disenfranchised, either by means of the poll tax (as in Texas) or by simply being overwhelmed in numbers and by political manipulation (as in California).

On the West Coast, this consciousness of minority status was exacerbated by the famous "zoot suit" riots of the early 1940s. The disturbances discredited Anglo beliefs about Mexicans, nearly destroyed an older generation of Mexican advocates, and ended forever the convenient myth in the cities that the real Mexican leaders centered around the by now very conservative Mexican consul. The "zoot suit" or "*pachucho* riots" in Los Angeles left a deep residue of bitterness in the Mexican community, particularly in Los Angeles. Years later, the full story of the riots became known as well as the racist attacks of servicemen and police.[24] The Mexican American bitterness was particularly acute because there was so much pride in the

---

[21] Between 1908 and 1925 the Texas border was in nearly continuous conflict. Mexico herself enjoyed a deceptive peace only during the 35-year regime of Porfirio Díaz. After the downfall of Díaz in 1911, a full-scale revolution broke out, with fighting so continuous and so chaotic that the "Mexican government" (when it existed) could neither control border raids into the United States nor protect the lives and property of its own citizens from American reprisals. Raids by followers of General Pancho Villa on Columbus, New Mexico, Nogales, Arizona, and four towns in Texas prompted a full-scale invasion by the United States. An American "Punitive Expedition" commanded by General John J. Pershing entered Mexico in 1916.

[22] W. Dirt Raat, *Los Revoltosos: Mexico's Rebels in the United States* (College Station: Texas A&M University Press, 1981).

[23] Details of these strikes are available in Acuña, *Occupied America,* Ch. 8. During the more radical period following the Mexican revolution, Mexican consuls actively aided strikes, to the dismay of "Red" conscious American. See F. Balderrama, "En Defensa de la Raza: The Los Angeles Mexican Consulate and La Colónia Mexica During the Great Depression," Ph.D. dissertation, University of California at Los Angeles, 1978.

[24] See McWilliams, *North from Mexico,* for an account of the riots and other problems of Mexican Americans in Los Angeles.

record of soldiers in World War II. Returning veterans and a proud community felt that such patriotism justified some measure of political recognition.

The results of this feeling appeared quickly in Mexican communities. The organizations that formed at this time were much more aggressive in style, including such groups as the American G.I. Forum (see Chapter 10). The G.I. Forum conducted fact-finding investigations of the segregated school system in Texas and lobbied aggressively for changes. On many local scenes, there were protests against the more flagrant acts of discrimination practiced in the border states. In the Los Angeles area, the struggle centered on equal housing opportunities in suburban cities (such as Montebello and Whittier) and continued discrimination from governmental agencies, such as the police. Some of this discrimination is almost inconceivable in the 1980s. Yet it was so pervasive that successful Mexican Americans who *were* able to advance economically and socially tended to turn their backs on their ethnic heritage and proclaim their ancestry to be "Spanish."

The struggles for full participation in American life continued through the 1950s, even though this was the heyday of assimilationism. Discrimination continued: "Operation Wetback" in the mid-1950s deported hundreds of thousands of Mexicans and perpetuated the image that Mexicans were somehow different; in Texas, segregated bowling alleys, municipal facilities, and housing set the stage for the civil rights struggles of the next decade. The 1950s was a transitional decade for the Mexican Americans. Behind the apparent quietness of the barrios, community organizations were beginning to develop, presaging the ethnic mobilization of the 1960s.

Several factors converged during the 1960s to account for this ethnic mobilization. The *bracero* program, which had brought thousands of Mexican contract laborers to southwestern fields, was terminated, and Chicano agricultural laborers began to organize to improve their conditions. The impact of César Chávez's farm labor organizing efforts on the broader Chicano community cannot be overestimated. Chávez combined traditional American labor organization with religious and cultural symbols that appealed deeply to Mexican Americans. Another factor was the black civil rights struggle, and the turmoil about the 1954 Supreme Court decision that called for desegregation of schools and had many ramifications. Desegregation appealed to many Chicanos as one means to end discrimination in certain parts of the Southwest. Finally, the youth and counterculture movement gave legitimacy to Mexican-American youth to explore other ways to adjust to American society than "melting pot" assimilationism. Despite continuing Anglo indifference, it was during the 1960s that Mexican-American ethnic consciousness first emerged. Among Mexican Americans today there is still much diversity in outlook and in self-conception, the product of generations of isolation from other Mexican Americans as well as from the larger society. As more and more Mexican Americans achieve middle-class security, the strains between raw new immigrants and old residents grow more acute. The endless and vexing problem of heavy immigration and undocumented workers continued—in fact, up to the early 1980s, no substantial degree of control seemed possible. To some degree, this constant resupply of new, uneducated, unskilled Spanish-speaking Mexicans is balanced by recent gains in the *barrios* as a whole. Many of these gains became possible through federal programs of the 1960s and early 1970s, a late and grudging recognition of Mexican-American poverty.

THE PUERTO RICANS

Puerto Rican history has a much shorter period of contact with American society. The relationship began with an American war with Spain in 1898. It was a war that meshed neatly with the expansionist tendencies of a rapidly growing nation.[25] As the result of a quick victory, three new lands were acquired: Puerto Rico, Guam, and the Philippines. Cuba shortly became independent. Puerto Rico was particularly attractive to the United States: not only was it historically the richest coffee-producing island in the Caribbean, but its location also made it of strategic military importance. However, Puerto Rico presented certain dilemmas—primarily what to do with the nearly 1 million residents who could not speak English.

General Wilson, the first military governor, laid out an agenda that called first for:

> a military regime; then it will be declared an American territory; and later it will achieve the category of sovereign state within the Union. The duration of these periods will depend more or less on the merits of the territory.[26]

The first legislation to implement this program, however, left the islanders in limbo: they were neither citizens of the United States nor citizens of an independent nation. The measure was so universally disliked by Puerto Ricans that the Jones-Shafroth Act (called the Jones Act) was pushed through Congress in 1917, giving Puerto Ricans U.S. citizenship and making them eligible for military draft. Although a new constitution defined commonwealth status for Puerto Rico in 1947, the provisions of the Jones Act have basically established the status of residents of Puerto Rico ever since its passage. Residents of Puerto Rico are still U.S. citizens, subject to military draft, but they do not pay U.S. income taxes and do not fully participate in federal government social service programs.[27] The future of Puerto Rico—retaining commonwealth status, becoming the fifty-first state, or becoming an independent nation—remains a basic question for Puerto Ricans.

Americans have always tended to think of Puerto Ricans as a single coherent group. Nonetheless, Puerto Rican historians observed that the response to the American occupation in 1898 was as varied as the class elements of the *puertorriqueños* themselves. One historian notes the welcoming reaction of the *mulatto* workers, who felt that the victors of the American Civil War might bring some hope for black people. The *hacendados* and *commerciantes* were sure that the Americans would allow them to keep their power acquired under the Spanish. At first, supporters among the *criollo* professionals favored the change, but soon gave up all hope of equality within the American republic and began to work for independence. (The Spanish ruling group quietly departed for home.)[28]

[25] For the Spanish-American War, see David Healy, *U.S. Expansionism: The Imperialist Urge in the 1890s* (Madison: University of Wisconsin Press, 1970).

[26] Kal Wagenheim, *A Survey of Puerto Ricans on the U.S. Mainland in the 1970s* (New York: Praeger, 1975).

[27] Kal Wagenheim, *Puerto Rico: A Profile* (New York: Praeger, 1970).

[28] San Juan M. García-Passalacqua, "Yo Quiero un Pueblo: A Brief History of the Puerto Rican Masses," *The Puerto Rican Journal,* Vol. 1 (Fall 1982), pp. 1–23.

Politically speaking, the island and its people were left suspended, neither independent nor a state. Once the Spanish were driven from Puerto Rico and the excitement of the war subsided, dominant American thinking, particularly in Congress, was that the tropical location and the mixed Negro, Indian, and Spanish ancestry of the people made Puerto Rico incapable of self-government. As a leading historian remarks, "Thus one of the first fruits of American occupation was to bring to Puerto Rico a disdain for Negro blood."[29] Puerto Rico's status quickly got entangled in larger questions of free trade and, worse yet, whether or not the benefits of the U.S. Constitution were to follow the American flag. Meanwhile American commercial interests were rapidly changing Puerto Rican life. The most important was the growth of huge sugar plantations, possible now because of large infusions of American capital. In time, the growth of these enterprises created an economic and professional elite of *criollos* who were bound closely to American interests. Through the 1920s and 1930s, in the teeth of a growing economic depression, the monopoly control of sugar cane plantations cut down the number of small farmers, the *jíbaros*. As a result, Puerto Rico lost its subsistence economy. Without wage labor, Puerto Rican migration to jobs on the mainland was inevitable. At one time during the Great Depression, a third of the male population of Puerto Rico had no work. While the New Deal programs of Franklin Roosevelt eased the situation somewhat, high population growth continued to inject more people into the labor force.[30] Frank Bonilla and Ricardo Campos see the migration as an exchange of people for capital. More important, they feel the exchange process is still continuing in the series of federal efforts to "develop" Puerto Rico. Bonilla and Campos believe such development to be doomed to failure because the effect is always more poverty, forcing yet more people into migration.[31]

Other figures show that federal industrialization schemes did increase employment at the rate of about 3 percent per year (from 1960 to 1972). But the number of persons of working age increased at almost exactly the same rate—3 percent per year.

These efforts to improve living conditions in Puerto Rico began seriously in 1948 under the leadership of Luis Muñoz Marin. "Operation Bootstrap" was designed to introduce industry to Puerto Rico, particularly in pockets of unemployment. Tax benefits, labor training, and new industrial plants were part of the planning. Incomes did increase, but there were profound social and cultural changes as well. Most of these changes are familiar—rapid urbanization, suburbanization, a much larger middle class, and all the trappings of modern American life: supermarkets, housing projects, television, food stamps, highway complexes, and installment buying. It was a rapid industrialization that has since been considerably modified. Although successful in many ways, this capital-intensive industrialization

[29] R. F. Weston, *Racism in U.S. Imperialism* (Columbia: University of South Carolina Press, 1972).

[30] The island's population doubled between 1900 and 1940. Adalberto López, "The Puerto Rican Diaspora," in A. López, ed., *Puerto Ricans: Their History, Culture and Society* (Cambridge, Mass.: Schenkman, 1982), pp. 313–343.

[31] Frank Bonilla and Ricardo Campos, "A Wealth of Poor: Puerto Ricans in the New Economic Order," *Daedalus*, Vol. 110 (1981), pp. 133–176. Rita Maldonado, "Why Puerto Ricans Migrated to the United States in 1947–73," *Monthly Labor Review*, Vol. 22, (1976), pp. 7–18, demonstrates that wage and unemployment rate differentials between the island and the mainland explain migration flows between 1947 and 1967, but in later years, return migration was motivated by additional noneconomic factors.

failed to alleviate unemployment, a high birth rate, or the spread of some particularly noxious slums (*arrabales*). By 1970, the Martín Peña slum on marshland in San
Juan Bay was squalid and crowded enough to be famous. Puerto Rican poverty
continues to be a powerful impetus for migration to the mainland.

The migration out of Puerto Rico began on a small scale very early. In 1900, a
large group of sugar cane workers went to Hawaii. By 1920 at least 12,000 persons
in the mainland United States were migrants from Puerto Rico; in 1930, 53,000
persons; by 1944, an estimate of 90,000. (There are no controls or records on the
movements of Puerto Ricans, who are American citizens. Thus the only reliable way
in which to determine Puerto Rican origin until recently was to count the number
of mainland residents who were born in Puerto Rico.)

The opportunities offered Puerto Ricans were like those available for Mexican
nationals. In the beginning, it was an almost endless need for farm workers on a
seasonal basis, particularly after World War I when European immigration virtually
ceased. Puerto Ricans appeared in Arizona as workers in the new cotton fields in
the 1920s. Other crops were harvested in rotation throughout the Midwest and East.
In the 1940s, during World War II, a variety of industrial employers began to contract for Puerto Rican labor. On the railroads, Puerto Ricans replaced Mexican
workers; a contingent went to work in a soup company in New Jersey and another
to a mine in Utah. Contracting continued after the end of the war, with domestic
servants and laborers for the foundries and mills of the Midwest. Contracting of
agricultural workers was also expanded, and other crops were harvested in rotation
throughout the Midwest and East. Noticeable groups of Puerto Ricans began
"settling out" in New Jersey, New York, Massachusetts, and Detroit, Michigan,
sometimes joining the communities started by industrial contract laborers.[32] In New
York City they were cigarmakers and merchant seamen, and Puerto Rican women
worked in large numbers in the garment factories. All early records in New York
City show the islanders working at unskilled jobs—as operatives in factories and
most particularly in hotels and restaurants as a wide variety of service employees.
Small, dense *colonias* (or migrant settlements) formed near workplaces on Manhattan's Lower East Side, near the Navy Yards and a rope factory in Brooklyn, and
in parts of Manhattan that within a generation were to become major nodes of
settlement for the airborne migrants.[33]

Until about 1945, the high cost of transportation to the mainland probably
slowed migration more than any other factor. Then, after World War II, the sudden
appearance of surplus airplanes and low-cost airplane flights from Puerto Rico to
New York City provoked a burst of movement. Unemployment was rising on the
island. Unskilled jobs were plentiful, *barrio* communities were well-established in
the New York area, and transportation was cheap. The Puerto Rican population on
the mainland quadrupled between 1940 and 1950 and tripled again by 1960.[34]

[32] Edwin Maldonado, "Contract Labor and the Origin of Puerto Rican Communities in
the United States," *International Migration Review*, Vol. 13 (1979), pp. 103–121.

[33] V. Sánchez Korrol, *From Colonia to Community* (Westport, Conn.: Greenwood Press,
1983), especially Ch. 3.

[34] Clara Rodríguez, *The Ethnic Queue in the U.S.: The Case of the Puerto Ricans* (San
Francisco: R&E Research Associates, 1974); U.S. Commission on Civil Rights, *Puerto Ricans in
the Continental United States: An Uncertain Future* (Washington, D.C.: U.S. Commission on
Civil Rights, 1976); and A. J. Jaffe et al., *The Changing Demography of Spanish Americans*
(New York: Academic Press, 1980), pp. 188–189.

Most striking of all was the movement into New York City. The first settlements appeared in Harlem and the Brooklyn Navy Yard areas, but soon entered East Harlem and the South Bronx, areas even at that time among the most dilapidated in the city. The migration was well underway by 1930, but almost stopped during the Depression when the demand for cheap labor nearly disappeared. In the late 1940s, immigration became a flood. East Harlem became "Spanish Harlem" and closely identified with Puerto Ricans. The settlements spread rapidly.[35]

By the mid-1950s, it was becoming evident to some Puerto Ricans that the mainland was not offering the opportunities for economic mobility once envisioned. Even in a city housing an enormous black ghetto, the degree of poverty and misery among Puerto Ricans was remarkable. In a seminal study conducted by the Puerto Rican Forum in 1964, the following conditions were found:

50 percent of Puerto Ricans in New York City were living at below poverty levels.

Puerto Ricans had the lowest educational attainment of any minority group in New York.

87 percent of Puerto Rican children had dropped out of school.

In 1960 when unemployment was 4.3 percent for whites and 6.9 percent for blacks, Puerto Rican unemployment stood at 9.9 percent.[36]

Thrust into tenements constructed before 1900 and competing fiercely with poor blacks, Puerto Ricans somehow survived in a cold and hostile city. It is true and ironic that the newest immigrants arrived at a time when many urban experts pronounced the city of New York as being very near collapse. Perhaps even worse, many New Yorkers thought that the Puerto Ricans themselves were responsible. Jack Lait and Lee Mortimer, two New York newspapermen who should have known better, wrote in a best-selling book that Puerto Ricans are "mostly crude farmers, subject to congenital diseases . . . they turn to guile and wile and the steel blade, the traditional weapon of the sugar cane cutter, mark of their blood and heritage."[37] While the Puerto Ricans do not share the Chicano heritage of vigilante justice and border conflict, they face much the same prejudice and stereotyping. "English and Spanish language newspapers, all owned and controlled by non-Puerto Ricans, invariably sensationalized the crimes of Puerto Ricans and gave Puerto Ricans an image of their people as criminals," according to one observer at the time.[38] Like Mexican Americans in the 1950s, some light-skinned Puerto Ricans escaped into the middle classes by proclaiming their background to be "Latin American." But New York's Puerto Rican community in the late 1950s and early 1960s was strongly oriented to the island. In 1958 and 1959, almost as many children transferred

[35] See Joseph P. Fitzpatrick, *Puerto Rican Americans* (Englewood Cliffs, N.J.: Prentice-Hall, 1971), Ch. 5, for a description. See also C. Wright Mills et al., *Puerto Rican Journey* (New York: Harper & Row, 1950); and Elena Padilla, *Up from Puerto Rico* (New York: Columbia University Press, 1958). Patricia Cayo Sexton provides a good view of Spanish Harlem in the 1960s in *Spanish Harlem* (New York: Harper & Row, 1968).

[36] Antonia Pantoja, "Boricuas-The Puerto Ricans in the United States," in *Conference on Puerto Rican Studies* (San Juan: Papers on Puerto Rican Studies, 1970).

[37] Jack Lait and Lee Mortimer, *N.Y. Confidential* (Chicago: Ziff Davis, 1948), pp. 126–132.

[38] López, *Puerto Ricans,* p. 325.

from New York City's to Puerto Rican schools as transferred the other way, and it was not at all remarkable to see the 1960 candidate for Puerto Rico's governorship campaigning in New York for the 30,000 voters who were expected to return to Puerto Rico in time for the election.[39] As U.S. citizens, Puerto Ricans can return home as easily as can any other new New Yorker return to his or her family home in the Midwest or South.

By the mid-1960s Puerto Rican *barrios* began to be more ethnically self-aware. Organizations such as the Puerto Rican Forum (formed in 1957) and Aspira (formed in 1961) began to address the problems confronting Puerto Ricans on the mainland. In the mid-1960s, Puerto Ricans began to attain elective office, and with the civil rights movement, young Puerto Ricans began to emulate black and Chicano activists.

Outside New York, there are yet other important Puerto Rican settlements, nearly always in the poorest areas of these cities. By 1980, large concentrations lived in Chicago, Los Angeles, Miami, Philadelphia, northern New Jersey and in a number of smaller industrial cities. Often the Puerto Ricans are so mixed with other Hispanics that they lose visibility: Puerto Ricans are rapidly dispersing throughout the nation.

But the flow of Puerto Rican migrants into the continental United States continues. In some ways, their movement is similar to that of Mexicans across the border. For Mexicans, the complications of individual entry and reentry can be formidable. By contrast, Puerto Ricans are citizens who can (and do) return to visit or retire to the island. This back and forth flow is enormous, reaching in one recent year more than 2 million people. It is very difficult to measure net losses and gains.[40] Most experts believe that periods of high unemployment in Puerto Rico are the main factor in sending Puerto Ricans to the mainland.

The flow of returning people is profoundly important. It means, first, that the Puerto Ricans offer the larger society not only a new and burgeoning minority but also a close relationship to a small and overcrowded Caribbean island with serious economic problems. Second, the nearby island home gives Puerto Ricans themselves a sense of intactness, of closeness to an ancient home and reference group.[41]

THE CUBANS

Cubans are the third largest national origin group of Hispanic Americans. Like Puerto Rico, Cuba was acquired by the United States as a consequence of the Spanish-American War in 1898. But unlike the other Caribbean island, Cuba was

---

[39] N. Glazer and D. P. Moynihan, *Beyond the Melting Pot* (Cambridge, Mass.: M.I.T. Press, 1963), p. 100.

[40] For some informed speculation on the magnitude and causes of the returned Puerto Ricans, see Fitzpatrick, *Puerto Rican Americans,* p. 13; Eva E. Sandis, "Characteristics of Puerto Rican Migrants to, and from, the United States," *The International Migration Review,* Vol. 4 (Spring 1970), pp. 22–43; and U.S. Commission on Civil Rights, *Puerto Ricans,* pp. 25–31.

[41] "Restlessness" has been characteristic of Caribbean islanders for many years. Returning Puerto Ricans are put into this broader context in Wm. F. Stinner, K. de Albuquerque, and R. S. Bryce-Laporte, eds., *Return Migration and Remittances: Developing a Caribbean Perspective,* RILES Occasional Paper No. 3 (Washington, D.C.: Smithsonian Institution, 1982).

ruled by an American army of occupation for only three years. The Republic of Cuba appeared, in 1902, a close, independent, but dominated neighbor of the United States.

Even before the famous exodus from the Cuban Revolution, the United States received a steady trickle of Cuban immigrants. Cigar manufacturing brought many Cubans to Key West, Florida, and later to Tampa. An estimated 18,000 to 19,000 Cubanos were living in the United States in 1930; about 79,000 in 1960. This trickle suddenly became a flood when Fidel Castro took power in Cuba in 1959. Castro's revolutionary objectives directly affected professionals and managers, and many of them emigrated. Later, beginning in 1966, refugees from Cuba were airlifted regularly enough to bring 273,000 new immigrants to this country by 1973.[42] But this was not the end. In April 1980 more than 10,000 Cubans took refuge in the Peruvian embassy in Havana, hoping to leave Cuba. Eventually this group and many others were allowed to leave. At least 118,000 people came by boat from the Cuban port of Mariel. (These groups of refugees are more easily thought of as first wave, second wave, and the most recent third wave of *Marielitos*.[43] With births in this country, the total estimates of Cuban Americans now reach 800,000.)

This sudden appearance of Cubans is unusual in the history of Hispanic immigration for several reasons. First, the wealthy businessmen, government officials, professionals, and managers who left the new state of Fidel Castro, plus the poorer Mariel group, gave the United States a full range of the Cuban social class structure. Second, most of the new arrivals crowded into only one city—Miami, Florida. (There are smaller Cuban communities in Los Angeles and New York City and in the states of New Jersey and Illinois.)

Third, the *Cubanos* are the only Hispanic group to be systematically counted and observed. Not only are exact figures available, but it is possible to know that the first wave was 94 percent white, averaged 34 years of age, and was well educated (14 years of school). The second wave was less white (80 percent), younger, and poorer. And the third wave (*Marielitos*) was only 60 percent white, much younger, and even poorer.[44] The first two waves were notably conservative politically, as is probably inevitable among refugees from a socialistic revolution.

Fourth, unlike other new Hispanics, *Cubanos* exerted a considerable measure of political power from the days of the first wave. Jose Llanes describes these efforts in detail, noting that much of it was accomplished through personal contacts with a series of federal administrations. Most of the first wave refugees hoped to return and maintained contact with anti-Castro elements in Cuba. Thus, during the early 1960s, their hope of overthrowing Fidel Castro coincided nicely with American foreign policy. Cuban hopes and American objectives ended eventually in the bloody defeat of an invading force at the Bay of Pigs on April 17, 1961. This failure left the Cuban community in the position of patriotic freedom fighters, at least

---

[42] Jaffe et al., *The Changing Demography of Spanish Americans,* p. 248.

[43] P. Gallager, *The Cuban Exile* (New York: Academic Press, 1980), distinguishes two subgroups in Llanes's first wave (the purely political exiles and the upper bourgeoisie) and also identifies the trickle of "boat refugees" as a separate wave. These refugees came between what José Llanes calls the first and second waves. See Llanes, *Cuban Americans* (Cambridge, Mass.: Abt, 1982).

[44] A full-results sample survey including characteristics of race, income, sex, age, and education is available in Llanes, *Cuban Americans,* p. 216.

for a time. "They had CIA backing, unofficial government endorsement, and sharing the American belief that Cuba was on the path toward communism, they were ready to die in order to save their country from oppression."[45]

The city of Miami offered the exiles a closeness to home, a familiar climate, and a well-established community in which even monolinguals could survive. One expert on the Cuban migration believes that Cuban-American entrepreneurs had developed enough wealth and resources to sustain many of the poorer arrivals through their early adjustments. Studies of employment records of the 1980 immigrants show that many new Cubans actually were employed by earlier arrivals.[46] Furthermore, a substantial framework of public aid and private sponsors were available.

Yet the new refugees from Mariel arrived in the United States in an unpleasant atmosphere of resentment. Part of the negative national response to the third wave was created by the growing economic troubles of 1980; part was generated by the press and media accounts that sensationalized the Cuban felons, homosexuals, and mentally ill who were allowed to leave with the immigrants. The new arrivals also imposed a heavy burden on the resources of the city of Miami and on the Cuban community in particular (see Chapter 3).

[45] Ibid., p. 64.

[46] Robert L. Bach, "The New Cuban Emigrants: Their Background and Prospects," *Monthly Labor Review,* Vol. 103, no. 10 (October 1980), pp. 39–46.

CHAPTER THREE
THE DIVERSITY OF HISPANICS

There are yet other factors that divide American Hispanics—almost as much as does their history. History also divides other American immigrants. To take only one example, the Poles who entered the United States at the beginning of the twentieth century find it difficult to understand the Poles who immigrated after World War II. For each group, the meaning of ethnicity and the Polish-American experience were very different. But at least they shared a common concept of a national culture. Hispanics do not share national cultures. Nor do they share experiences in the United States. These factors disrupt communication between Hispanics and slow down the development of a strong sense of common destiny.

There is a great deal of regional diversity among Hispanics. Each of the three major nationality groups (Mexican, Puerto Rican, and Cuban) has been the dominant Hispanic group in a particular portion of the United States, even though all groups are spreading. Elsewhere, they are only subordinate. Mexican Americans live traditionally in the Southwest—and particularly in the border states of California, Arizona, New Mexico, and Texas. Puerto Ricans live in largest numbers in the New York metropolitan areas, and Cubans live in Miami, by and large. These "home areas" are different economically, socially, and politically—and these differences are important in understanding the special characteristics of each Hispanic group. When other Hispanics do appear in the "home areas," they are forced to adapt to local circumstances and to the dominant Hispanic group.

It is also unfortunate that most of the sociological theory about the absorption of ethnic and minority groups in the United States was developed from the immigrant experiences in northeastern and midwestern cities. European immigrants flooded these cities in the nineteenth and early twentieth centuries. Their fates were bound intimately with the social structure and the economic and political opportunity systems of the time. Hispanics were actually living elsewhere in the United States at the same time under entirely different circumstances. (They were, in fact, the natives and the Anglo Americans were the new arrivals.) Obviously, it is not possible to use generalizations for Hispanics that are based on newcomers' experiences in the industrial East of a hundred years ago.

More recently, the ironies in the statuses of Hispanics are compounded by the development of yet a new set of disparities implicit in the contrast between "Sunbelt" and "Snowbelt" states. The irony comes in that Hispanics are just entering the traditional older portions of the nation at a time when the generalizations about early ethnics do not apply any more. The decline of the older portions of the nation seriously affected the chances of incoming Puerto Ricans in particular, but also other new Hispanics in New York, Chicago, and other midwestern industrial cities. It is possible, however, that rapid development of the Sunbelt cities in recent years may not have benefited the Hispanics in any way. Then also, Miami is a special case with its huge proportion of new Cubans.

THE OLD SOUTHWEST

Some of the peculiarities of the border states tended to cause dispersal and isolation of the Spanish-speaking populations, most particularly the immigrants. Other and perhaps weaker factors tended to push the immigrants from Mexico and the "charter member" Mexicans into a common pattern.

Among the factors that tended to scatter enclaves of Mexicans, the vast spaces of the border states may have been decisive. Even today, the two most concentrated areas of Mexican-American population in the United States are more than a thousand miles apart, separated not only by sheer distance but by massive mountain ranges and desert lands hundreds of miles in width. Only a few highways and railroads connect these areas today. Before 1880, there was no east-west through passage whatever. It was inevitable that the small settlements, beginning in the latter part of the sixteenth century and continuing throughout the seventeenth and eighteenth centuries, would be effectively isolated: from each other, from the centers of population in Mexico, from the weak U.S. territorial governments—and even today, from the federal government in Washington.

The border states also offer comparatively easy access to the homeland—easier geographically for Mexican Americans than for Puerto Ricans. It is normal and natural today that all manner of social and economic interchange should easily cross the border. Most Chicanos still live within a short driving distance of Mexico.

Still another peculiar condition affecting the border states is their economic climate.[1] The economic development of these states lagged behind that of the rest of the United States—and, in fact, they retained until very recent years their reliance

---

[1] This account of the social, political, and economic milieu of the border states draws heavily upon Leo Grebler, Joan W. Moore, and Ralph Guzmán, *The Mexican American People* (New York: The Free Press, 1970). Ch. 4.

on agriculture and mining. This is an economy heavily oriented toward the exploitation of natural resources. It required much capital (which had to be imported from the East) and vast quantities of cheap and unskilled labor. There were few European settlers in these states in the nineteenth century. Accordingly, a succession of non-Europeans served as cheap labor, coming either as temporary contract laborers or as immigrants. Mexicans were recruited in large numbers following the Chinese (until 1882), Japanese (until 1907), Filipino, and even Hindu workers as the chief supply of labor. The housing and control of such workers in gangs or in groups of families meant the construction of labor camps and cheap housing near work sites but nearly always remote physically, socially, and politically from Southwestern life. A pattern of workers' enclaves, of pockets of isolation—the direct result of the economy of the border states—was firmly established and has left many traces.

Agricultural technology also tended to force the isolation of large groups of workers. Cattle ranching and dry farming were followed by a new technology of intensive farming based on irrigation. Irrigated farming is highly capitalized, with heavy labor requirements, year-round production, and crop specialization. No poor farmer or homesteader could possibly own or maintain such land. An acre of lettuce required more than 125 worker-hours of labor per crop and an acre of strawberries more than 500 worker-hours.[2] Melons, grapes, citrus fruit, sugar beets, cotton, and vegetables all required large investments for irrigated land, and then there were additional costs for brush grubbing, deep plowing, leveling and ditching, and extensive planting. For orchard crops, the new investor had a long wait for the first crop. Highly capitalized farms ("factory farms") would eventually dominate the conditions of life for Mexican Americans as decisively as the working patterns of coal mining once dominated wage labor in Appalachia. In turn, the absolute necessity for a steady flow of Mexican labor would soon define almost all relationships with the Mexican minority. Huge irrigation projects always brought the necessary Mexican workers, either as migratory workers or as seasonal workers who lived nearby—a pattern repeated in hundreds of towns in five large states, including a good portion of eastern Colorado.

The border states were much more slowly urbanized than was the rest of the United States. In 1900, 70 percent of the population of the American Southwest was rural, a proportion considerably higher than in the East or the Midwest. By 1940, the proportion of urban and rural residents approached equality, and surprisingly, since that date the process of urbanization throughout the border states has rushed ahead of that in the United States as a whole, although quite unevenly within the area. Thus the Mexican-American population was caught up quite late in one of the most significant national trends of this century.

The border states were also very slow to reach political maturity. All except Texas and California were territories for many years, and New Mexico and Arizona did not attain statehood until 1912. (The recency of these events is suggested by the fact that Arizona's first senator, Carl Hayden, still served in the U.S. Senate as recently as the mid-1960s.) Throughout the border states, political organization was late and relatively unstructured by what the East and Midwest define as normal

[2]Lawrence Leslie Waters, "Transient Mexican Agricultural Labor," *Southwest Social and Political Science Quarterly*, Vol. 22 (June 1941), pp. 49–66.

political party activities. There was never much opportunity for any ethnic group to duplicate the success of Irish, Italian, and Jewish immigrants in the urban areas of the East in influencing the objectives of local or state government. In fact, the Progressive reforms of the early 1900s, especially in California, were *meant* to avoid the political machines of northeastern cities. At no time has there been any counterpart of the urban ward system so characteristic of eastern cities. Thus in California there was no partisan training ground for the political game, no recruiting process for ethnic leadership as there has been for some other American ethnic groups. The heritage for Mexicans has been delayed entry into politics as well as parochialism and a sense of ineffectuality in organizational and political activity.

Furthermore, as indicated in the previous chapter, state governments in the border states were for many years dominated by relatively few economic interests.[3] The railroads, the powerful mining companies, the owners of the big "factory farms" and the big land development companies controlled border state governments for many years and are today a powerful influence. In the past, such an alliance between business and politics meant that a politically unsophisticated minority group could be easily manipulated. The late formal structuring of state and local government also has had unfortunate effects on border state law enforcement. All too often weak and understaffed local authorities became the arm of private interests, for example, in labor disputes. In recent years, the well-known Texas Rangers have been used in labor-management disputes and local political controversy involving Mexican Americans, an action quite in keeping with their historical record of violence against Chicanos.

The border states also present a remarkable and often bewildering social and economic diversity. Local social systems differ considerably, and the effect of a wide range of opportunity and of toleration for Mexicans has been enormous.[4] In California, a relatively rich and well-developed state, the variation ranges from the relatively open and industrialized society of San Francisco and Oakland to the social system of the nearby San Joaquin Valley, in whose large cities the Mexican minority is still quite rigidly segregated. Albuquerque is a world apart from the isolated villages in the northern valleys of New Mexico. Then, as an extreme range from either, the life of the Texas border cities of El Paso, Laredo, and the string of cities from Brownsville to McAllen is conditioned by the presence of nearby Mexico. In 1980 the percentage of Hispanics in El Paso was 61.9 percent; in Laredo, 91.5 percent; in the Brownsville-Harlingen-San Benito metropolitan area, 77.1 percent. Many smaller towns along the Rio Grande are almost all Mexican.

Demographic factors have also worked to create a peculiar climate in the border states: it is possible that they have significantly increased racial intolerance. First, through most of this century, these four states have had a higher proportion of native whites (as compared with foreign-born whites) than has the rest of the United States. This was true at each census date from 1910 to 1960. Texas and New Mexico tended to have the highest percentages of native whites.

Second, it is a demographic reality in the border states that Mexican Ameri-

---

[3]This account uses material prepared by Paul Fisher for the Mexican-American Study Project (Los Angeles: University of California, November 1967).

[4]For a description of several of these cities, see R. Bernard and B. Rice, eds., *Sunbelt Cities* (Austin: University of Texas Press, 1983).

cans share their minority status with several non-European groups. In all border states, except Texas and California, there have always been large numbers of American Indians. In Arizona's first census in 1870, Indians outnumbered whites 4 to 1. There are also very large numbers of Asians. To illustrate this point, 5 percent of California's 1910 population was nonwhite, with less than 1 percent black or Indian and 3.4 percent Asian. By 1980, the nonwhites had grown to 13.9 percent, of whom most were blacks (7.7 percent), only a few (0.9 percent) Indian, and a considerable number Asian (5.3 percent). In later years, the Mexican Americans increasingly found themselves sharing the bottom of the economic ladder with black Americans and Indians. The growth of California's present black population began only during World War II, and although the proportion of blacks in the Texas population has been declining, Texas was still 12.0 percent black in 1980. These demographic factors are important, first, because the Anglo population of the border states has faced several racial minorities (contact that preconditioned their relations with Mexican Americans) and, second, because the minorities themselves have been placed frequently and increasingly in competitive relations with each other.

Yet another factor in the border states population has been important to Mexican Americans. This predominantly Roman Catholic minority confronted an Anglo population that was substantially more Protestant than in most other parts of the nation. Of the non-Catholics, an extraordinary proportion, particularly in Texas, are oriented toward fundamentalist Protestantism. No other American religious group would be so likely to be hostile to the Catholic church, with its hierarchy, ritualism, and priestly control. (This stereotype of the Catholic church was not very accurate in the border states, as we shall discuss in Chapter 6.)

This uncongenial combination of population elements produced antagonism very early in the region's history. No other part of the United States saw such prolonged intergroup violence as did the border states from 1848 to 1925. Even the relationship between blacks and whites in the South offered less overt conflict. The extent of the violence—cattle raids, border looting expeditions, expulsions, deportations, lynching, civil riots, labor wars, organized banditry, filibustering expeditions, revolutions—can hardly be exaggerated. Some of these minor and virtually unknown conflicts laid waste to entire counties and lasted for years. Thus, the myth of broad, free, and easy frontier tolerance so cherished in the Southwest obscures the real fact of continuous and acute racial tension.

THE MODERN SOUTHWEST AND THE SUNBELT BOOM

In the 1970s, political and social analysts began to notice a dramatic shift in the comparative growth rate of cities in the so-called "Sunbelt." The new growth industries appeared to be locating in the southern part of the nation. It seemed that the new growth and the economic future of the nation would rest on aerospace, microchips, and other high-technology glamor industries.[5] The boom is real enough,

---

[5] A journalist, Kirkpatrick Sale, was one of the first to popularize the idea of the Sunbelt and Snowbelt. He identified "six pillars" of the Sunbelt economy: advanced technology, defense, agribusiness, oil and natural gas production, real estate and construction, and tourism and leisure. See his *Power Shift* (New York: Vintage Press, 1976). Federal monies were ex-

and people and jobs have increased disproportionately in the Sunbelt in general and in the Southwest in particular. Houston, Los Angeles, and Phoenix and other cities of the traditionally Mexican-American Southwest have become major growth centers.

But interestingly, the low wage rates that prevail in the region, low taxes, anti-union right-to-work laws in some of the states, and cheap land are important in encouraging the boom. Only a comparatively few people in the Hispanic population have the level of professional training necessary to enter high-tech industries. Nonetheless, the growing population of the region has also created many service jobs in restaurants, home construction and maintenance, retail sales, and so on, providing many jobs for Chicanos. Furthermore, the Sunbelt expansion was based not only on new glamor industries but also on low-wage enterprises that, like the garment industry, use large numbers of underpaid Hispanics. Los Angeles employers are notorious for consistent violations of laws concerning minimum wages, hours, and working conditions.

A final irony about the growth of the Sunbelt cities. These are states with typically low individual and property tax rates. As a consequence, the government services so important for a poor population lag far behind other states.[6] California once provided a high level of government services, especially in education. But at the height of the Sunbelt boom, when real estate prices were soaring, California voters passed a statewide referendum (Proposition 13) that would limit property taxes to a fixed (and low) proportion of the value of the home. This meant that far fewer funds were available for state services that were taken for granted in the past. In the early 1980s, at the same time that President Ronald Reagan began to cut back federal subsidies rather drastically, California saw serious cuts in the community college "open-door" admission policies, probation services, mental health services, and many other activities.

The typically low tax rate and the traditional hostility of many Sunbelt cities to government "intervention" led to a series of near scandals about conditions of life for the poor. Houston is the most notorious: sociologist Joe Feagin argues that living conditions have worsened in Houston for the low- and middle-income people—and especially for minorities. Housing shortages have pushed up rents and increased discrimination. Gentrification of older houses in the inner city brings middle-income families back to the city but tends to displace poor families. There is serious traffic congestion: the bus system is inadequate. Police malpractice toward blacks and Hispanics was a national scandal. Feagin argues that "from a . . . managerial point of view Houston's market-oriented growth looks extremely

---

pended directly not only in defense industries but in building an economic infrastructure of roads, water and power facilities, as discussed by Alfred Watkins and David Perry, "Regional Changes and the Impact of Uneven Urban Development," in Perry and Watkins, eds., *The Rise of the Sunbelt Cities* (Beverly Hills, Calif.: Sage, 1977).

[6] Medium-sized Sunbelt cities (with populations of between 200,000 and 500,000) tax their citizens a few dollars less than the U.S. average but spend substantially less. Public welfare expenditures for the United States as a whole were $11.88; for Sunbelt cities, it was $1.98, a tenth the amount. For public health the United States spent $2.96 versus $2.28 for Sunbelt midsized cities. As a whole, $15.80 was spent for municipal employment per 1,000 population in the United States and only $9.90 in the Sunbelt cities. See Peter Lupsha and W. Siembieda, "The Poverty of Public Services in the Land of Plenty," in Perry and Watkins, eds., *Rise of the Sunbelt*.

good. . . . But from the working-class point of view, the shining buckle of the Sunbelt has its tarnished side. . . . In good times and bad, Houston's huge poor and minority populations must limp along as the invisible victims of this socially costly pattern of private profitability."[7]

The Southwest, then, has been at the heart of growth in the United States in the 1970s and 1980s. Southwestern growth is particularly visible because of the nationwide recession and depression, and in particular, the recent slump in consumer demand that created an even more rapid decline of the "archaic" Snowbelt cities. For Hispanics, the growth has meant more jobs, to be sure, and possibly some improvement in their income and occupational status in the 1970s (see Chapter 4). But it is not a pure blessing. Some of the job opportunities are in exploitative industries. Some of the side effects of expansion have created yet more problems of quality of life for Hispanics in the Sunbelt cities.

MIAMI AND THE CUBANS: ANOMALY IN THE SUNBELT

Miami has become the mecca for most Cubans in the United States. Although Cuban refugees from the first, second, and third waves (see Chapter 2) were originally sent to sponsors (often organizations such as churches) throughout the United States and some remained in dispersed locations, many of the Cuban refugees drifted back to Miami. This anomaly of concentration in a single city is important to Cuban life and experience in the United States.

Miami is a Sunbelt city that has grown rapidly in recent decades. But Miami's growth is not a consequence of the relocation of industry away from the industrial North and Midwest. Nor is it a consequence of the growth of new kinds of industries, as in Dallas and Houston. Rather, Miami's growth is in specialties of the area—retirement communities, tourism, and the results of the Cuban influx, and a growing role in Latin American international trade. The Cubans began to arrive in the late 1950s, and a series of influxes continued until 1980, rapidly increasing the population.

Miami is a city of extremes—in 1970 it held the highest proportion of Spanish-speaking persons in the nation and the highest proportion of persons over 65, had the highest crime rate, and was the only major metropolitan area in the nation with an increase in overcrowded housing from the preceding decade. By 1980, more than 30 percent of the city's 580,000 residents were Hispanic. One consequence of the Cuban preeminence is that Miami is now "the hub of Latin America's international commerce."[8] Inside this city, the Hispanics in the Miami metropolitan area are by no means as tightly segregated as are the blacks, but have spread and dispersed from their central focus of settlement. This central area (the so-called "Little Havana") is

---

[7]Joe R. Feagin, "Sunbelt Metropolis and Development Capital: Houston in the Era of Late Capitalism," in L. Sawers and W. Tabb, eds., *Sunbelt/Snowbelt* (New York: Oxford, 1984), p. 125.

[8]Data on Miami are derived from David Longbrake and Woodrow Nichols, *Sunshine and Shadows in Metropolitan Miami* (Cambridge, Mass.: Ballinger, 1976). See also R. A. Mohl, "Miami: The Ethnic Cauldron," in Bernard and Rice, eds., *Sunbelt Cities*.

an 800-block community just west of the city's central business district and just east of the airport.[9]

Even though they are recent arrivals, Hispanics do much better in Miami than do blacks, both economically and politically, and this is a source of some resentment. (There were black riots at several points during the decades of Cuban settlement.) The first wave of refugees were overwhelmingly white, mature, and well educated. Many of them brought investment capital with them. At first the Cubans were welcomed by Miami. Even though good jobs were difficult to find during the 1960s, many Cubans started their own businesses.[10]

Shortly thereafter the Miami city fathers were less positive about the newcomers and began to refuse business licenses to persons who wanted to open enterprises north of 8th Street—that is, in Little Havana. The Cuban rush into businesses is remarkable: by 1970 almost a third of all businesses in Miami were Cuban-owned and operated. "These range from million dollar firms listed on the stock exchange to one-man or family-operated businesses."[11]

Significantly, a high proportion of Cuban Americans in Miami work for, or with, other Cubans. Some researchers speak of this as an "enclave economy" (see Chapter 4). To these observers, the self-contained nature of the Cuban-American economic community in Miami is in strong contrast to the subordinate position of Hispanics in other parts of the nation. Cuban entrepreneurs are especially strong in construction, real estate, clothing, tobacco, and restaurants, and the media of television and newspapers. Cuban immigrant professionals (heavily concentrated in the second wave of Cuban refugees) also have had some success in establishing themselves. This is particularly true of physicians, who, after meeting U.S. requirements, found a ready clientele.[12] Thus the three waves of immigration established a full-blown class structure in Miami, topped by a well-developed upper-status group, second to no other group in wealth and life-style. Miami has become "an international gateway to Latin America" and the Cubans are part of the gateway.[13]

But two more waves of Cuban refugees entered Miami (Chapter 2), and with these newcomers something of the pleasant image of a busy bilingual community faded. Problems with the third wave, or Mariel, immigrants persist, and the more established Cubans are upset by the ex-prisoners, street people, and homosexuals. Whatever the internal problems in the Cuban community, there is no doubt about the destruction of the Cuban image as members of a "Golden Exile."[14] There was a quick Anglo backlash in November 1980 when Miamians voted to eliminate Spanish

---

[9] Alex Stepick, "New Perspectives on Immigrant Adaptation," in M. Frank, ed., *Newcomers to the United States* (New York: Haworth, 1983).

[10] This material is based on José Llanes, *Cuban Americans* (Cambridge, Mass.: Abt, 1982).

[11] Longbrake and Nichols, *Sunshine and Shadows*, p. 50.

[12] Unpublished work by Alejandro Portes et al. compares the fate of Cuban with Mexican immigrants of the early 1970s. Cubans were able to cash in on their education and skills to a much greater extent than were Mexican immigrants thanks in large part (according to Portes) to this enclave economy. Cited in Stepick, "New Perspectives on Immigrant Adaptation."

[13] Ibid., p. 62.

[14] Alejandro Portes, "Dilemmas of a Golden Exile: Integration of Cuban Refugee Families in Milwaukee," *American Sociological Review*, Vol. 34 (1969), pp. 505–18.

language signs on streets and county buildings. Miami faced a strong reaction from its large black community and an immense, almost overpowering, crisis in its ability to provide services. In 1980, Ruth Shack, a Dade County commissioner wrote,

> Dade County today is literally a saturated community. The people poured in so fast, in such large numbers, that they soon occupied every available sofa, garage and porch in town. They were invisible from the streets, but in fact they hadn't really settled in at all. They were jammed in like passengers in a crowded elevator. . . . Now the community is saturated. The people are starting to overflow into the streets in a slowly rising flood of displaced humanity that is terrifying in its inevitability.[15]

But the Cuban refugees were not the only Hispanic problems in Miami. Nicaraguans, Salvadorans, and Colombians were also attracted by the Hispanic milieu in south Florida and arrived, often penniless, to press on the city's resources. Almost any political upheaval in Latin America produced a wave of immigrants—legal, illegal, or refugee—all of them complicating the survival of an overburdened city.

Perhaps the most important conclusion from this short history is that the Miami Cubans are an anomaly among the Hispanics. It is hard to call the earliest people "refugees" after such long residence and their high naturalization rates, but on the other hand, Little Havana is far from acculturated. Perhaps it would be more accurate to follow Jose Llanes and say that Dade County and the city of Miami have adapted to the Cubans. Meanwhile Miami and its Cubans form a complex community with severe internal strains.

THE DECLINING SNOWBELT

New York and the Puerto Ricans. Living conditions in New York City have decisively shaped the lives of Puerto Ricans on the mainland. These settlements first became important at about the time of World War II. There were several sites in Manhattan and Brooklyn and soon the infamous, burned-out South Bronx was to capture national attention as a New York slum of the worst kind. But Puerto Ricans were moving out of the five boroughs of New York as early as the late 1950s.

Virtually all the early community studies emphasize the shock felt by Puerto Ricans at the racial definitions imposed on them in New York (see Chapter 1). Furthermore, New Yorkers tended to see these newcomers as "foreigners," although the new arrivals are fully socialized into American history and into an expectation of being treated as citizens. "Puerto Ricans in New York come to realize in New York that American citizenship is a legal, not a social concept for them . . . you must become socially 'American,' that is nonethnic, to be privy to 'rights' of economic opportunity, political and legal justice and social equality."[16] In their

---

[15] Ruth Shack, "Dade County—Paradise Lost?" *Journal of Intergroup Relations,* Vol. 77 (Winter 1980-1981), pp. 23-31.

[16] Much of this material is derived from Clara Rodriguez, *The Ethnic Queue in the U.S.: The Case of the Puerto Ricans* (San Francisco: R&E Associates, 1974), pp. 90 ff.; and Marcus Ohlmann, "Drawing in the Reins: Political Responses to Fiscal Crisis in America's Cities," *Journal of Urban Affairs,* Vol. 4 (1982), pp. 51-64. For an excellent portrait of Dominicans in New York in the 1970s, see G. Hendricks, *The Dominican Diaspora* (New York: Teachers College Press, 1974).

home island, Puerto Ricans had no consciousness of being a minority; in New York it is impossible to avoid this status.

This is the background for Puerto Ricans in a city that almost classically demonstrates the dark side of the Sunbelt boom. Between 1960 and 1970, New York lost 173,000 jobs. Then the decline began to accelerate: between 1971 and 1976, New York lost an additional 450,000 jobs–half the manufacturing jobs in the city. This seriously hurt Puerto Ricans because in 1960 more than half of them were working in manufacturing. (Many of these jobs moved to the city's suburbs, but Puerto Ricans were unable to follow.) In the same period of time, the city lost more than a tenth of its total population, many of them middle-income people. This left a burden of older, poorer, minority people who remained. Meanwhile, New York had established itself as one of the most generous cities in terms of its provision of human services, especially to the poor. Along with Chicago, New York City paid the highest welfare (AFDC) and supported an elaborate mass transit system, a city hospital system, a large city college and university system, and many other expensive amenities unknown to most locales in the Sunbelt. By 1975, New York was spending nearly half its budget on social and welfare programs, a commitment that within a short time brought the city to the edge of bankruptcy. Stringent limitations were placed on city expenditures. This "crisis" became a prototype for other stressed Snowbelt cities during the coming decade. Cities–especially northern industrial cities–began to compete for corporations, offering more tax breaks and less government regulation. New York is comparatively disadvantaged, as are other Snowbelt cities, and this disadvantage is expected to continue well into the next century. Other nearby centers of Puerto Rican population have also suffered: Hoboken, New Jersey, lost a third of its stevedore jobs, and Bridgeport, Connecticut, was so disrupted by an unemployment rate of 50 percent in 1972 that it offered free one-way tickets back to Puerto Rico for its unemployed Puerto Ricans. Although the economy of many Snowbelt regions began to be restructured in the 1980s, the changes tend not to favor unskilled and semiskilled workers like the Hispanics.[17]

Chicago and the Hispanics. Mexicans were the first Hispanics to arrive in Chicago in large numbers. Just after World War II, large numbers of Puerto Ricans appeared as contract laborers. By 1983 the city held more than half a million Hispanics. But Chicago began to lose jobs in the 1970s, particularly in manufacturing. This loss greatly affected the Latinos because nearly two-thirds of the half-million Hispanics in Chicago held blue-collar jobs, primarily semiskilled and unskilled. (Slightly more than a third of the Chicago blacks held such jobs and less than a third of the Anglos.) Between 1979 and 1981, a period of only two years, 10 percent of the manufacturing jobs disappeared. In the same two years, Hispanic unemployment doubled. The largest number of jobs were lost in the steel industry, and it is here that Hispanics had made strong progress toward better positions. But Hispanics were not being hired in the Chicago growth industries. The degree of recovery from this dark side of the Sunbelt boom–and its effect on the Hispanic

---

[17]See B. Harrison, "Regional Restructuring and 'Good' Business Climates," in Sawers and Tabb, eds., *Sunbelt/Snowbelt,* for a discussion of New England.

population—is still very much in doubt. Meanwhile the entrapment of certain groups of Hispanics in economic problems is an important source of regional diversity.[18]

A PECULIAR BORDER AND AN INTERNATIONAL ECONOMY

Some experts argue that the shift of economic activity from the industrial centers of the Snowbelt to the new and expanding cities of the Sunbelt is part of a far more extensive shift. Critical in this process are the "runaway" low-wage industries. Even if such groups as the Puerto Ricans and Dominicans in New York are willing to work for very low wages, many employers will continue to search for even cheaper labor and for operating environments (including low corporate taxes) that will give them even higher profits. (The garment industry in New York City is probably kept in that city only because of the extremely low prevailing wages.) Some of these firms relocated to the Sunbelt. But some move to other nations—and important for this chapter is the peculiar relationship of American industry to cheap labor markets in Latin America. This relationship is most clearly seen in the economics of the U.S.-Mexican border.

The southern border of the United States is a land boundary between one of the world's most developed economies and one of the least developed. This border area has severe poverty, affecting most Mexican Americans. However, it is an economic situation not of two separate nations but, rather, of two interpenetrating nations, one dependent on the other in complex ways. This dependence is especially true in the many "twin cities" that string along the border—Nogales/Nogales, El Paso/Ciudad Juárez, and Laredo/Nuevo Laredo.[19]

The cities on the U.S. side provide many services for Mexican residents, including tourism, shopping facilities, and the routine use of superior health facilities in San Diego and El Paso. U.S. visitors also tour the Mexican side of the border towns, but the critical interdependence is industrial under the so-called "twin plant" or *maquiladora* program. Under U.S. tariff law, foreign-based subsidiaries of U.S. firms can assemble products in Mexico with components made in the United States. Then the finished products are returned to the United States with a minimal tariff. By the mid-1970s, some 200 American firms were using this border program with a work force of about 8,000 Mexican citizens, primarily women working for wages that run from $3.50 to $5.00 per day compared with $25.00 a day for U.S. workers. Many of these plants are truly runaways from the United States to an area of truly cheap labor. U.S. firms invested large sums of money to build twin plants in cities like Cuidad Juárez, across the Rio Grande from El Paso, but it is estimated that the *maquiladoras* spend about 40 percent of their wages in the United States.

[18] S. West and J. Macklin, eds., *The Chicano Experience* (Boulder, Colo.: Westview Press, 1979), contains a number of articles about Hispanic communities in the Midwest. See also, for Chicago, G. Orfield and R. Tostado, "Latinos in Metropolitan Chicago" (Chicago: Latino Institute, 1983), and various issues of *LIDER,* published by the Latino Institute.

[19] This section draws on Niles Hansen, *The Border Economy* (Austin: University of Texas Press, 1981); Ellwyn Stoddard, "Patterns of Poverty Along the U.S.-Mexican Border," University of Texas at El Paso, Center for Inter-American Studies, 1978; and Alejandro Portes and John Walton, *Labor, Class and the International System* (New York: Academic Press, 1981).

The different effects of this peculiar border economy are summarized by one researcher as follows: "In Mexico, the average family income increases as one approaches the bi-national border; in the U.S. family income decreases as one approaches the border—there is a levelling process."[20] Most of the poverty on the U.S. side is concentrated in the border towns of Texas. McAllen, Laredo, and Brownsville were among the poorest cities in the nation, with income per capita as low as $1,300 a year. Unemployment in the border regions of Texas is endemic; wages are very low by U.S. standards, and the region continues to supply many of the migrant farm workers who tour the midwest, Florida, and California each year to eke out their incomes in south Texas. The peculiar vulnerability of the border economy became painfully evident in the winter of 1983–1984. A severe frost devastated citrus and vegetable crops in the lower Rio Grande Valley and Imperial Valley of California, throwing some 25,000 farm laborers into unemployment; at the same time, two devaluations of the Mexican peso in a year meant that Mexicans no longer could afford to shop on the U.S. side of the border, and the local economies of dozens of border cities were thrown into depression. Four Texas counties were declared disaster areas in 1983.[21]

Political and cultural, as well as economic, interpenetration have been a fact of life on the border for a long time.[22] Increasingly, the shared nature of these border cities is being recognized. In the mid-1970s, a series of cooperative ventures began to solve certain common problems—air space, air pollution, water resources, and public health problems. The seriousness of these shared problems continues to grow. As a single example, in 1983 some southern California beaches were closed to bathers because of raw sewage from San Diego's neighbor, the city of Tijuana. Nearby La Jolla is an expensive and elegant beach city now threatened with the most obvious signs of untreated sewage. This situation rather aptly dramatizes how the periodic failure of a Mexican sewage disposal system is a shared concern. Disparities in public services and incomes affect both nations. The only surprise is that effective cooperation is so slow in developing.

Even the irritating problem of the runaway industries is a symptom of the ties that bind the United States, Mexico, and Puerto Rico. Most of these industries relocate in Mexico, Puerto Rico, and smaller Caribbean and Central American nations—just the sources of many undocumented workers who come to the United States for jobs. Usually they wind up working under sweatshop conditions in, for example, the garment industry. Thus immigrants add to the chances that low-wage industries can afford to remain in the United States. Perhaps even more important, the American consumer benefits from cheaper clothing, food, and many other items made possible by low-wage labor. The benefits and costs of this interchange of people is a subject of almost endless study and controversy. Whatever the conclusion, if such a conclusion is possible, social scientists along with policymakers are now forced to think in terms of the interdependence of Western hemisphere nations.

[20] Stoddard, "Patterns of Poverty," p. 20.

[21] National Council of La Raza, "The Border Economy: An Ongoing Disaster," News release, January 30, 1984.

[22] See S. Ross, ed., *Views Across the Border* (Albuquerque: University of New Mexico Press, 1978).

CHAPTER FOUR
PORTRAIT OF THE HISPANICS: I

Beyond the diversity and the history, there are the realities of Hispanic life in this country. To understand these realities, we must answer some important questions: How many Hispanics live in the United States? Where do they live? How many of the Hispanics are foreign-born? Are they predominantly rural or urban? What is their position in the labor markets? What are the opportunities open to them? What does poverty mean in the Hispanic context? What is the nature of Hispanic family structure? How much do they resemble other Americans? And, finally, how much do they share with each other?

PORTRAIT OF A POPULATION

It is characteristic of the Hispanic population that there has always been a certain degree of ambiguity about the basic facts—even how many Hispanics live in the United States. The U.S. Census is our primary source of information, but unfortunately, it has only recently begun to consider Hispanics worth counting as a separate group (as "persons of Spanish origin"). The oldest and largest segment is, of course, the Mexican Americans. They have been counted by different criteria ever since they were first noticed in 1930. This means that information collected in 1940 is never comparable with information collected in 1930 or 1950 and that it is impossible to trace changes from one decade to the next with accuracy. Recent censuses have depended upon self-identification. The respondents are given a choice of several different Hispanic "identifiers." For the 1980 census they could choose to be Mexican American, Mexicano, Chicano, Puerto Rican, Cuban, Central or South American, and other Spanish origin. In the past, the census has counted persons of Spanish surname in the Southwest, but this tactic proved to be seriously flawed.[1] Nonetheless, data from earlier years must be reported, even with all the known inadequacies. A more serious problem is created by the total absence of general information on matters as important as health and vital statistics.

As Hispanics became more and more a national minority, rather than a set of regional groups, community spokespersons began to realize the need for accurate statistics, most particularly because federal funds were often allocated on the basis of such figures. In 1976, after considerable pressure from Hispanic groups, Congress passed legislation (the Roybal Act) that required certain federal agencies to collect data relating to Hispanics. As a consequence, in recent years statistics on health, employment, and education (and some other data) have become more available. But there are still serious gaps in the statistical information. Responsibility for collecting some data (births and deaths, criminal justice figures) still lies with the states, and many states simply do not see any point in making expensive changes in their procedures. In addition, many of the data from government sources lump all Hispanics together, obscuring important differences between subgroups. All these problems reflect the complexity of the Hispanic population. There is also the question of race: many Hispanics refuse to fall into the categories comfortable to other Americans. Thus both the 1970 and 1980 censuses asked people to identify themselves by race. In both years, many Hispanics refused to call themselves either "black" or "white." In 1970, the census did not honor their choice of "other race," instead reclassifying such responses as "white," and only 1 percent of the population appeared as "other." The magnitude of error that is encompassed in this bureaucratic procedure became evident when it was revealed that in 1980 a full 40 percent of the Hispanics chose "other."

Complicating any analysis is the fact that even the U.S. Census consistently undercounted the Hispanic population by 27 percent in its *Current Population Surveys* during the 1970s.[2] As a consequence, historical analyses of Hispanic economic progress, such as levels of income, must be handled with care. Bearing in mind these difficulties, in this chapter we will deal as best we can with the size, growth, and distribution of Hispanic people, nativity, age patterns, and family

[1] Thus a Census Bureau study showed that about a third of the people who claim Spanish origin do not have Spanish surnames. About a third of those with Spanish surnames do not consider themselves to be of Spanish origin. U.S. Bureau of the Census, "Persons of Spanish Origin in the United States, March 1972 and 1971," *Current Population Report,* Vol. 250 (April 1973), p. 20. Many so-called Spanish surnames are shared with other ethnic groups, for example, the surname "Martin."

[2] The controversies about Hispanic statistics have a long history. A good summary is available in a 1974 U.S. Commission on Civil Rights report, *Counting the Forgotten.* One very special problem is that no reliable information is available on just how many undocumented Hispanics (from Mexico and the Dominican Republic in particular) live in the United States and to what extent they are included in any statistics. There may be millions of such persons, and they have good reason not to respond to government surveys like the census. Inevitably, therefore, there are great disparities in estimates of the total number of Hispanics. See also U.S. Bureau of the Census, *Coverage of the Hispanic Population of the United States in the 1970 Census* (Washington, D.C.: Government Printing Office, 1979).

structure. In the following chapter, we will discuss education, occupations, income, health, and housing—in general, the social realities that create the socioeconomic accomplishments of a group of people.

SIZE, GROWTH, AND DISTRIBUTION OF THE HISPANICS

As nearly as it is possible to estimate for 1980, the 14.6 million Hispanics formed about 6.5 percent of the mainland U.S. population. An additional 3 million were living in Puerto Rico. (By contrast, blacks were almost 12 percent, and American Indians were less than 1 percent.) We also know that the Hispanic population is growing at a very rapid rate, both through immigration and because of relatively high birth rates. The 14.6 million persons of Spanish origin counted in 1980 represent an average rate of increase of more than 8 percent in every year since the 1970 census, which counted about 8 million. By 1983, there were an estimated 16.9 million. Some estimates suggest that Hispanics will outnumber blacks by the year 2005. Of this total in the mainland United States, almost 60 percent (8.7 million) were of Mexican origin. Almost 15 percent (2 million) people were of Puerto Rican background. A smaller segment reported Cuban origin (about 5 percent of the total, or 800,000 persons). The remainder (3 million) entered from, or descended from, immigrants from other parts of Latin America or Spain.[3] (There are actually more of such persons than there are Cubans.) But there is an important caution: even government sources estimate that there may be as many as 3 million additional Hispanics not counted by the census. This estimate is based on some approximations of the number of uncounted undocumented persons and of the number of legal residents missed by the census (the undercount).[4] When these estimates are added in, the real 1983 total of Hispanics may be closer to 20 million people. Hispanic subgroups grew at different rates. People of Mexican origin nearly doubled during the decade; both Puerto Ricans and persons of Cuban origin grew by more than 40 percent (Figure 4.1).[5]

Why does the Hispanic population grow so rapidly? Demographers look at two sources of population growth. First, there is immigration, and, second, there is an excess of births over deaths. Unfortunately, both immigration statistics and fertility and mortality statistics are particularly unreliable for Hispanics. Immigration statistics are unreliable because of the large number of undocumented immigrants who cannot be counted or even accurately estimated. Fertility statistics are unreliable because birth and death statistics are among those kept by the states and many states do not report Hispanic origin. Even fewer states break down births in the Hispanic population to Mexican, Cuban, Puerto Rican, and so on. So, as best we can, we must piece the data together.

First is the question of fertility. Fertility refers, in a rough way, to the number

[3]There were 3,113,867 people choosing to classify themselves as "other Hispanics" rather than as of Mexican, Puerto Rican, or Cuban origin. Of these, 8 percent lived in Colorado and New Mexico—probably mostly traditional "Spanish-American" descendants of early settlers—leaving 2,855,854 more recent arrivals (PC 80 1C1, Table 233).

[4]For undercount, see J. Passel et al., "Coverage of the 1983 Census," and for estimates of the undocumented, see R. Warren and J. Passel, "Estimates of Illegal Aliens from Mexico," both papers presented at the 1983 Population Association meetings.

[5]It may be that all these figures overestimate growth because of the serious undercount in 1970.

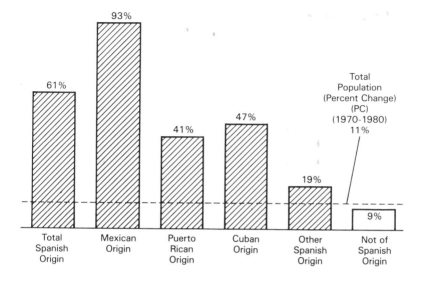

FIGURE 4.1   Growth of the Hispanic Population, 1970-1980 (percentage change)
Source: U.S. Bureau of the Census, "Condition of Hispanics in America Today," September 1983.

of children born. Obviously, fertility touches upon family structure, the role of women, and other social and psychological issues that we will deal with later (Chapter 6). We are concerned here simply with births. By 1980, 22 states kept records for Hispanics, and these states accounted for 90 percent of all Hispanic births in the nation. Without question, Hispanics are notably more fertile than are Anglos and are somewhat more fertile than are black Americans. In 1980, the Hispanic birth rate was 23.5 live births per 1,000 population compared with 14.2 for Anglos and 22.9 for blacks. Hispanic women have more children at every age than do Anglo women, and only among teenaged mothers is the black rate higher. There are, however, important differences among the Hispanic subpopulations. The Mexicans, the largest population, are also the most fertile (with 26.6 live births per 1,000 population). Thus, even without immigration, according to one demographer, the Mexican Americans were in the 1980s "perhaps the fastest-growing ethnic group." Cuban women by contrast, with an overall birth rate of only 9.6 per 1,000, were even less fertile than were Anglos. For all these groups of women, fertility declines as they achieve more education and as they take jobs outside the home. Nonetheless, the youthfulness of the Hispanic population means that more Hispanic women are in their child-bearing years, and this means continuing overall fertility.[6]

[6]S. Ventura, "Births of Hispanic Parentage, 1980," *Monthly Vital Statistics Reports,* Vol. 32 (1983). See also Frank Bean et al., "Patterns of Fertility Variation Among Mexican Immigrants to the United States," in Select Commission on Immigration and Refugee Policy, *U.S. Immigration Policy and the National Interest, Staff Report,* Appendix D, April 1981. (Washington, D.C.: U.S. Government Printing Office.) Analysis of earlier fertility patterns of Hispanic populations is provided in detail in A. J. Jaffe et al., *The Changing Demography of Spanish Americans* (New York: Academic Press, 1980), who also offer detailed analysis of the correlates of fertility for each subpopulation.

Second, immigration is a major source of population growth and Hispanic immigration has greatly accelerated in recent years. Thus a quarter of all Hispanics counted in the 1980 census were foreign-born. Of these, more than half were recent entrants—that is, had entered during the 1970s. (Country by country, the figures are startling: 77 percent of the immigrant Salvadorans, 57 percent of the Dominicans, 58 percent of the Mexicans, and 55 percent of the Colombians had arrived in the 1970s, for example.)[7] Immigration figures (Table 4.1) show that Hispanics are a steadily increasing proportion of all immigrants. By the late 1970s this proportion had reached 42 percent. For Mexicans, the first large-scale wave began from 1910 to 1920. During the next decade Mexican immigrants arrived in massive numbers. In the United States an expanding demand for agricultural labor helped to "pull" immigrants; in Mexico there was much disruption during the revolutionary wars. The influx from Mexico slowed markedly after the Great Depression of the 1930s and did not rise again until the 1950s, when Mexicans were imported almost continuously in a series of temporary worker (*bracero*) programs. And throughout this time many immigrants came without papers as undocumented aliens, possibly outnumbering the legal immigrants. Thus the total bulk of Mexican immigration (legal, contract labor, and undocumented) swelled during the 1950s. Several massive efforts to deport undocumented aliens during this period (see Chapter 8) slowed immigration somewhat. Then a steady rise continued during the late 1960s and 1970s.

The figures in Table 4.1 also show that the migration of Puerto Ricans to the mainland did not amount to much until the end of World War II. Then, new arrivals from Puerto Rico swelled to a peak in the 1950s, as with the Mexicans. This continued until, by the 1970s, about a third of all Puerto Ricans were living on the mainland. A great deal of return migration had begun by the 1970s, although there is also evidence that the mainland continued to gain Puerto Ricans (even if at a lower level than in the 1960s). Migration to and from Puerto Rico is shrouded in statistical mystery. Nonetheless, it is clear that there is much back-and-forth movement, a "permanent and restless traffic, a massive circulation of workers without fixed abodes or occupations, between Puerto Rico and a growing number of regional concentrations scattered throughout the United States."[8]

Fluctuations in migration from Cuba are even more obvious. Each wave of immigrants is a wave of refugees, carefully monitored and subsidized by federal refugee money. Before the arrival of these refugees, the United States held only a handful of Cubans and many of them were associated with the early growth of the cigar industry in south Florida.

Other countries of the Caribbean and Latin America are supplying substantial and growing immigration. There are many reasons for this influx of the last 15 years, both economic and political. Immigrants from Guatemala, El Salvador, and Nicaragua may consider themselves to be political refugees (like the Cubans) but do not enjoy official refugee status. Political instability (as well as economic underdevelopment) in Caribbean and South American nations is often reflected in movements of these "other Hispanics" into the United States.

[7]Unpublished tabulations, U.S. Census.

[8]Frank Bonilla and Ricardo Campos, "A Wealth of Poor," *Daedalus*, Vol. 110 (1981), p. 152.

TABLE 4.1 [Mexican, Cuban, and Puerto Rican] Immigrants to the United States Mainland, by National Origin and Immigration Status, 1910–1980

FISCAL YEAR	TOTAL IMMIGRANTS	LEGAL ENTRANTS				UNDOCUMENTED IMMIGRANTS (FROM MEXICO) APPREHENDED
		MEXICO	BRACERO	CUBA	PUERTO RICO	
1911–1915	4,459,831	75,821			4,139[a]	
1916–1920	1,275,980	131,124			6,368	7,575[b]
1921–1925	2,638,913	230,584			30,707	40,928
1926–1930	1,468,296	218,064			−7,677	49,449
1931–1935	220,209	8,517			15,824	45,180
1936–1940	308,222	9,419			23,120	104,562[c]
1941–1945	170,952	21,089	167,925[d]			1,217,580
1946–1950	864,087	54,835	261,520		155,037	3,226,632
1951–1955	1,087,638	122,654	1,298,163		253,572	213,982
1956–1960	1,427,841	196,058	2,067,592	19,400[f]	196,841	198,397
1961–1965	1,450,312	223,112	871,285	179,600[f]	45,085	828,796
1966–1970	1,871,365	220,189	16,350[e]		92,037	318,075
1971–1975	1,936,281	318,075	—	1,004,000[f]	85,556[g]	4,529,056
1976–1980	2,453,357	303,200	—	34,400[f]	N.A.	

N.A. – Not available.

[a] For 1920 only.

[b] For 1924 and 1925 only.

[c] For 1941 and 1943 through 1945 only.

[d] For 1942 through 1945 only.

[e] For 1966 and 1967 only.

[f] Figures for Cubans are cumulative and somewhat divergent from those for other immigrants. Thus "1956–60" includes Cuban aliens living in the United States in 1980 who entered before 1960; "1966–70" includes Cuban aliens living in the United States in 1970 who entered between 1960 and 1969; "1971–75" includes Cuban aliens living in the United States in 1975 who entered between 1970 and 1974; "1976–80" includes those who entered between 1975 and 1980.

[g] For 1971 through 1974 only. Later figures from the Puerto Rican Commonwealth Office are not compatible.

Sources: For data on total and Mexicans, see Annual Reports and Statistical Yearbook and unpublished data of the U.S. Immigration and Naturalization Service (INS) and its predecessor agencies. For data on Mexican braceros, see W. Cornelius, Mexican and Caribbean Immigration to the U.S. (La Jolla, Calif.: University of California Program in U.S.–Mexican Studies, 1979), pp. 37–38. Between 1979 and 1980, the number of undocumented Mexicans apprehended by the INS dropped substantially, because of decreased enforcement activity during the 1980 census. Figures remained lower in 1981, reportedly because Border Patrol personnel were diverted to manage the Cuban boatlift from Mariel.

For data on Cubans, see unpublished data from the Immigration and Naturalization Service.

For data on Puerto Ricans, see U.S. Commission on Civil Rights, Puerto Ricans in the United States, pp. 26–27, and Commonwealth Office. The figures are derived from statistics on passenger traffic to and from Puerto Rico and the U.S. mainland. The figures represent net migration to the mainland.

55

What are the prospects for future growth of the American Hispanics? Again, fertility and immigration are the major spurs to growth. Neither of these factors shows much evidence of leveling off in the near future. The largest Hispanic group, the Mexican Americans, also shows the highest fertility. Although educational attainment is associated with declining fertility, the process is very slow indeed (see Chapter 5). Immigrating Mexican women do not tend to be well educated and always have had many children. Yet in recent years fertility in Mexico itself has declined with amazing rapidity, and there is some reason to believe that new immigrants from Mexico are no more fertile than U.S.-born Mexican Americans.[9] With regard to immigration, there is no reason to expect a substantial decline. Economic conditions in the Spanish-speaking Americas are not very good. Population pressure is great in spite of efforts by such nations as Mexico to establish strong birth control programs. The borders of the United States are comparatively accessible both by land and by sea. A lively trade in forged documents and other smuggling of immigrants is well established. Even though policing of the border is a matter of considerable concern, there is little reason to believe much will change. It is therefore almost certain that the Hispanics will continue to grow much faster than the rest of the U.S. population. As they do so, the demographic realities that we discuss in the remainder of this chapter will steadily become more significant for the functioning of American society as a whole.

Where do America's Hispanics live? The most direct (and simplified) answer is that Hispanics still live in their traditional concentrations in seven states. Most Mexican Americans are living in the five southwestern states (California, Texas, Arizona, New Mexico, and Colorado) of their ancestors. Most Puerto Ricans live in New York and most Cubans in Florida (see Table 4.2). But these long-established patterns are beginning to change.

First, there are important changes in the residential distribution of Mexican Americans. There is a small but notable shift away from the states of Texas and Arizona, first toward California and, more significantly, toward the Middle West. Thus in 1970 Texas held 35.7 percent of the nation's Mexican Americans; by 1980, only 31.5 percent. In 1970, the state of Illinois contained 3.5 percent; by 1980, 4.7 percent. (In actual numbers there were almost a million more people of Mexican origin in Texas by the end of the 1970s, but the proportion had declined.) By 1980, Illinois had more Mexican Americans than did the traditional states of Arizona, New Mexico, or Colorado.

Second, the dispersal of Puerto Ricans from New York has been dramatic (although the state is still home for most). In 1970 almost two-thirds of all Puerto Ricans (64.1 percent) lived in New York; by 1980, slightly less than half (49.9 percent). Puerto Ricans were moving to New Jersey, Illinois, Pennsylvania, and Florida. Only Cuban Americans were becoming more concentrated in their traditional areas. In 1970 Florida had 46 percent of all Cubans in the United States, primarily in Miami. At the end of the 1970s, 58.6 percent of the *Cubanos* lived in Florida. The proportions of Cuban Americans living in more scattered locations had declined notably.[10]

[9]Dee Falasco, "Economic and Fertility Differences between Legal and Illegal Migrant Mexican Families," unpublished Ph.D. dissertation, University of Southern California, 1982.

[10]Data are from the 1980 U.S. Census, U.S. Department of Commerce, Bureau of the Census, Supplementary Report, *Persons of Spanish Origin by State: 1980*, August 1982, PC 80-S1-7.

TABLE 4.2   The Spanish Origin Population by State, 1980

| | | | PROPORTION OF EACH GROUP LIVING IN STATE | | | |
RANK	STATE	TOTAL HISPANIC	ALL HISPANICS	MEXICANS	PUERTO RICANS	CUBANS
1.	California	4,544,331	31.1%	41.6%	4.6%	7.6%
2.	Texas	2,985,824	20.4	31.5	1.1	1.8
3.	New York	1,659,300	11.4	*	49.0	9.6
4.	Florida	858,158	5.9	0.9	4.7	58.5
5.	Illinois	635,602	4.4	4.7	6.4	2.4
6.	New Jersey	491,883	3.4	*	12.1	10.1
7.	New Mexico	477,222	3.3ᵃ	2.7ᵃ	*	*
8.	Arizona	440,701	3.0	4.5	*	*
9.	Colorado	339,717	2.3	2.4	*	*
10.	Michigan	162,440	1.1	1.3	0.6	*

*Figures are not given for states in which there were fewer than 50,000 persons of Mexican origin or fewer than 10,000 persons of Puerto Rican or Cuban origin.

ᵃIt is notable that comparatively more "persons of Spanish origin" than of "Mexican origin" are reported for New Mexico, the state of traditional Spanish-American concentration. Many persons traditionally deny Mexican origin while they may acknowledge Spanish origin. This creates some amount of unknown distortion in these rankings.

Source: U.S. Department of Commerce, Bureau of the Census, Supplementary Report, Persons of Spanish Origin by State, 1980, August 1982, PC80-S1-7.

Third, the ancient patterns of concentration are still largely valid. In a manner of speaking, this is unfortunate for Hispanics because it is still much too easy for Americans to think of them as a group of regional minorities rather than a national minority. Yet half the people of Spanish origin still live in just the two states of California and Texas and are predominantly Mexican. New York still holds the third largest Hispanic minority (1.7 million people, about 60 percent Puerto Rican). The fourth largest concentration lives in Florida (see Table 4.2).

Four interesting points emerge from these patterns of geographical distribution. First, in the five traditionally Mexican southwestern states, Hispanics are the largest of the minorities. They considerably outnumber blacks and other non-whites (such as American Indians and Asians). In California, blacks are only 12 percent of the population and Asians are 5.3 percent; Hispanics are 19.2 percent (Figure 4.2). In Texas, blacks are only 12 percent, and Hispanics are 21 percent. These are patterns that reflect the special history of these states. In turn, these patterns will have consequences.

Second, not only are Hispanics concentrated in particular states, but inside these states, they concentrate in particular areas. In California, most Hispanics are in the southern part of the state. South Texas (especially the lower Rio Grande Valley and some of the larger border cities, notably El Paso) traditionally holds most of the Texas Chicanos. Recently, they have spread north to jobs in such cities as Houston that were once largely Anglo and black. In New York State, Puerto Ricans and other Hispanics are concentrated in the New York City metropolitan area.

Third, larger proportions of Hispanics are leaving the traditional areas of settlement. Puerto Ricans are appearing in large numbers in states bordering New

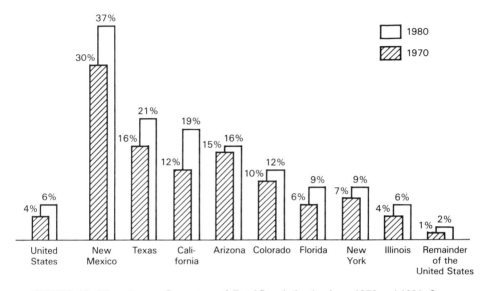

FIGURE 4.2 **Hispanics as a Percentage of Total Population by Area, 1970 and 1980.** *Source:* U.S. Bureau of the Census, "Condition of Hispanics in America Today," September 1983.

York (Massachusetts, New Jersey, and Connecticut). Cubans are found in New York, New Jersey, and California. Mexican Americans are showing a continuing shift from Texas to California. California tends to attract not only new immigrants from Mexico but Chicanos leaving the small towns and rural areas of the entire Southwest, especially Texas. Hispanic shifts into the Middle West build on a very old migration.

Fourth, Hispanics are highly urbanized. In 1980, a higher proportion of Hispanics (87 percent) lived in metropolitan areas (and in their central cities) than did the total American population (74 percent). (Mexican Americans are the least urbanized and Puerto Ricans the most.) This process of moving into cities is most obvious in California, where 93 percent of the state's Hispanics live in cities. Although Chicanos are often stereotyped as agricultural laborers, this segment of the Chicanos is rapidly shrinking: only 7 percent of the Mexican Americans lived in rural areas of California in 1980. Agricultural settlements still persist in the "old colonies" of Colorado and New Mexico and in south Texas. In contrast to California's 7 percent, 14 percent of Texas' and 28 percent of New Mexico's Hispanics were living in rural areas in 1980.[11]

There is one more important question about the living patterns of America's Hispanics: To what extent within the cities are Hispanics segregated into their own communities? In fact, in most large cities and many small towns, virtually any

[11] PC80-1-C33, C45. Mexican-American migratory farm workers tend to travel in families, in sharp contrast to Puerto Ricans, who tend to leave their families in Puerto Rico. Both Mexican and Puerto Rican agricultural workers are common in areas east of the Mississippi. See G. Thomas-Lycklama a Nijeholt, *On the Road for Work* (Boston: Martinus Nijhoff, 1980).

resident can point out the *barrio* or Little Havana quite readily. This is particularly true in the Southwest, where the Mexican part of town is well known and well established. Los Angeles has its East Los Angeles; Oxnard has its Colónia; and dozens of towns have *Sal si Puedes*, an ironic phrase that means, "Get out, if you can."

But the origins of many Chicano *barrios* contrast sharply to the more common and classical patterns by which European immigrant enclaves and those of other Hispanics were established in American cities. "Segregation" has a complex meaning. (The term *barrio* roughly corresponds to "neighborhood," although the connotations of the word "ghetto" sometimes are closer.) Typically, new immigrants settle into cheap housing in the older central areas of a big city. Such a pattern *was* followed by Puerto Ricans in "El Barrio" or "Spanish Harlem" on the upper east side of Manhattan—and with smaller settlements elsewhere. Most of these were in very poor slum housing once occupied by Italian or Jewish immigrants and blacks.[12] Similar enclaves were created by Chicanos settling in Chicago in an area named "Pilsen" after the Czech immigrants who preceded them. But most of the Mexican enclaves in the Southwest had very different origins. Some, for example, grew out of the reality that Mexicans were the original settlers of the town. The existing *barrio* is where Mexicans have always lived. A typical town plan in the Mexican colonies of the early Southwest is a settlement around a traditional *plaza* or central area. (One such *plaza* is carefully preserved in Los Angeles, complete with church, marketplace, and small park.) When railroads brought in Anglo settlers, the railroad terminus tended to be located near the center of the city—and to radiate out from that central area. The Mexican *plaza* area was bypassed and, typically, tended to deteriorate. In time (as in Albuquerque, Los Angeles, and dozens of other cities), the *plaza* area remained as the "Mexican downtown"—or as a carefully reconstructed and often glamorized tourist center.

Still other Mexican urban enclaves are the residue of early labor camps. In southern California, such remnants of past times as Santa Fe Springs and Pacoima in Los Angeles County and the Casa Blanca area of Riverside are really new growth on the skeletons of old labor camps and citrus packing shed areas. They were bypassed and isolated as the node of new Chicano settlement in the growing and spreading cities. Whole families of Mexicans were imported into these camps to serve such functions as ranching, railway maintenance, citrus harvesting and packing, and brick making. The ethnic population may remain, but it ceases to be employed in the old occupations. In other areas, the enclaves may remain on the fringes of the metropolitan area and continue to serve as agricultural labor markets, as in certain cities of the San Joaquin Valley of California. Many such settlements are being transformed by urban upgrading because they are located in parts of the city that become desirable for Anglos. Others have already been overwhelmed by a rapid rise in land values and the resident Mexicans displaced. Still other areas of the Southwest include cities where Mexican Americans are not found in ghettos or enclaves but, rather, dominate the life of the community. This is a pattern appearing frequently in the small towns of northern New Mexico and south Texas and in a

---

[12] See C. Wright Mills, Clarence Senior, and Rose Goldsen, *The Puerto Rican Journey* (New York: Harper, 1950), Appendix II, "The Sample," for a description of where Puerto Ricans lived before 1950 in the New York areas.

few large Texas border and near-border cities like Laredo. No other Hispanic group (and, indeed, no other American minority) shows such an extraordinary range of living patterns.

But beyond the question of the origins of Hispanic urban settlements, exactly *how* segregated is the Hispanic population? This information is important—first, because the degree of segregation indicates the degree of prejudice and of actual discrimination in housing and, second, because housing segregation has important social consequences, ranging from segregated schools to severely limited economic opportunities. This "degree of segregation" is a good measure of the extent of absorption of any group into American society. Thus, in general, when applied to the residences of ethnic groups, persons from southern and eastern Europe are still more segregated than are "old stock" immigrants from northern Europe. Blacks are consistently very segregated.[13]

The degree of Hispanic segregation has been studied only since 1960, but there are strong indications that Hispanic patterns are unlike the black-white pattern and more closely resemble those of European immigrants.[14] There is much more variation from one city to another in the degree of segregation of Hispanics from Anglos than of blacks from whites. For example, the segregation of Mexicans from Anglos is far higher in Texas cities than in California cities. (Black segregation in the same cities is much higher but much less variable.) Also, the segregation of Mexicans distinctly declined in most Southwestern cities between 1960 and 1970. At the same time, Mexicans are becoming more segregated from blacks than from Anglos. (In Texas, especially, there is a greater degree of separation from the black community.) However, things were different for the racially mixed Puerto Ricans. By 1970 Puerto Ricans were more separated from whites than from blacks in Boston and in New York. This is ironic, because in 1960 Puerto Ricans were seen as a sort of bridging group connecting black and white areas. Now the darker Puerto Ricans are tending more to live with blacks. "Black Puerto Ricans are especially concentrated in areas of intense black settlement . . . and not in areas of high Puerto Rican concentration."[15] The discovery of this racial shift within the Puerto Rican

---

[13] See Stanley Lieberson, *Ethnic Patterns in American Cities* (New York: The Free Press, 1963), for an analysis of segregation patterns of various foreign-stock populations. (Lieberson excludes Hispanics.) The segregation of blacks from whites has been monitored over time by Karl and Alma Taeuber, beginning with their book, *Negroes in Cities* (Chicago: Aldine, 1965). The Taeubers find some slight decline in the degree of black segregation from whites between 1970 and 1980, but it is still high.

[14] The first study of segregation in 1960 of Spanish-surnamed persons (Mexican Americans) from Anglos and from blacks was done for cities in the five southwestern states by Joan Moore and Frank Mittelbach and is condensed in Leo Grebler et al., *The Mexican American People* (New York: The Free Press, 1970). This study was replicated with data from the 1970 census by Manuel Mariano López, "Patterns of Interethnic Residential Segregation in the Urban Southwest, 1960 and 1970," *Social Science Quarterly,* Vol. 62 (1981), pp. 50–63. Longitudinal data on Hispanic groups other than Mexican American, however, are scarce, although inter-Hispanic comparisons are now being conducted. An example is Douglas Massey, "Hispanic Residential Segregation: A Comparison of Mexicans, Cubans and Puerto Ricans," *Sociology and Social Research,* Vol. 65 (1981), pp. 311–22, and Anne M. Akulicz de Santiago, "Residential Segregation of Spanish Origin Populations: A Study of Recent Trends in a Sample of U.S. Cities," unpublished Ph.D. dissertation, University of Wisconsin-Milwaukee, 1984.

[15] Peter Jackson, "Paradoxes of Puerto Rican Segregation in New York," in Ceri Peach et al., eds., *Ethnic Segregation in Cities* (London: Croom Helm, 1981).

population strongly suggests that Hispanics in general will be more acceptable to American society than will blacks.

It is also interesting that in cities with relatively large numbers of different Hispanic groups (for example, the Mexicans and Puerto Ricans in Chicago), the Hispanic subpopulations may be as segregated from each other as from Anglos. In Chicago, for example, Mexicans entering the city in the 1920s to work in the steel industry established small colonies near their workplaces. When the Puerto Ricans arrived in the 1950s, closeness to the job site was less important. The core areas of Puerto Rican settlement were built up far from Mexican settlements in this very large city (except for a very few locations). But this is not true in Detroit, Washington, D.C.; and West New York, N.J. By 1980 the large influx of Hispanics into American cities seemed to bring an increase in residential segregation in 14 out of 25 large cities studied. Hispanic *barrios* throughout the United States were becoming more densely settled, and ethnically mixed areas were becoming all-Hispanic.[16]

NATIVITY AND GENERATION

The nativity patterns of Hispanics are also changing. In the nineteenth century, most Mexican Americans were U.S. citizens because they were incorporated by treaty in 1848. Then the great waves of immigration in the early part of the twentieth century tipped the scales toward foreign-born. Since then the proportion of native-born Hispanics increased until very recently, where immigration tipped the scales again. In 1980, 75 percent of the Spanish origin persons counted by the census were born in the United States. Mexican Americans were 75 percent native-born, and by contrast, only 25 percent of the Cubans and about a third of the persons of Central and South American background were native-born. Forty-five percent of the Puerto Ricans living on the mainland were born there in 1970.

Immigration during the 1970s continued to be heavy, and by 1980 the proportion of Hispanics who were native-born had dropped to 71 percent. Florida contained the highest proportion of foreign-born Hispanics—60 percent. Both California and Illinois held a 37 percent segment of foreign-born Hispanics.

New York has many non–Puerto Rican Hispanics, 27 percent of whom were foreign-born. Two states with traditionally high Hispanic populations (Texas and New Mexico) had very low percentages of foreign-born in 1980—19 percent and 6 percent, respectively. Thus New Mexico with the highest percentage of Hispanics also had the least number of foreign-born, a proportion that reflects the long history of New Mexican Hispanics. The continuing presence of large numbers of foreign-born Hispanics underscores the importance of immigration for continued population growth.

In general, the differences between nativity classes or "generations" follow the patterns we have learned to expect from other American immigration populations. Typically, third- or later-generation Hispanics tend to be better educated and to make more money in their occupations than do the foreign-born. Yet it is

---

[16] Santiago, "Residential Segregation of Spanish Origin Populations."

notable that the third generation tends not to receive higher incomes than do the second-generation Hispanics (native-born of foreign parentage).[17]

AGE PATTERNS AND FAMILY STRUCTURE

One of the most remarkable characteristics of the American-Hispanic population is its comparatively low median age, implying that there are many children. Based on 1979 figures, the median is only 22 years of age. By contrast, the median age of the total population is 30. Youngest of all the Hispanics are the Puerto Ricans, with a median age of 20. Mexican Americans were close at 21 years of age. Both median ages rose slightly from 1970, when the median age of Puerto Ricans had been 19.8 years and Mexican Americans, 20.2 years. This very slight change probably reflects changes in immigration. (Central and South Americans were close to the U.S. norm in age, but still young, with a median age of 26 years (up from 24.9 in 1970). Cubans not only cannot return to Cuba, but they have very low fertility, so the population is steadily aging. The median age of the Cuban population in 1980 was 36 years (up from 31.3 in 1970).

Most immigrants are of working age, usually young adults, and of child-bearing age. There are few children among immigrants and few older people. Thus the constant flow of immigrants can produce some deceptive statistics in age patterns. As an illustration, in 1970 the median age of Puerto Ricans born in the United States and living in New York was only 9.3 years; Puerto Ricans born in Puerto Rico were 30.0 years on the median. The immigrants who had come to New York in the 1950s were getting older, of course, but others were coming, still in their child-bearing years. Meanwhile, in New York, most New York–born Puerto Ricans were children.

Further distorting the figures is the unknown factor of Hispanic return migration. Both the Mexican-American and the Puerto Rican populations show comparatively few older people. (See Figure 4.3 for comparison with the general U.S. population.) Although there are no reliable figures, it is possible that older Hispanics may be leaving the United States in considerable numbers. The proportion over 65 years of age was slightly less than 5 percent for Hispanics, compared with 11 percent for the total population. The proportion of aged actually declined among Mexican Americans and Puerto Ricans after 1970, falling to only 3.7 percent of the Mexican Americans and 2.3 percent of the Puerto Ricans. Yet these proportions should not obscure the fact that Hispanic elderly (like the rest of the Hispanic population) are increasing in absolute numbers.

The other and obvious consequence of high fertility is large families. In 1980, Hispanic families contained one more person than did the average Anglo-American family. Mexican-American families were the largest, with 4.07 persons. Puerto Ricans were next with 3.67 persons, Cubans next with 3.58 persons, and then fami-

[17]1970 data. Similar nativity breakdowns were not available in 1980 census data. In an interesting article, P. Garcia and L. Maldonado present data on differences between various Spanish heritage groups and among nativity classes of Mexican Americans. Their analysis underscores the hazards of using "Spanish-origin" data uncritically: see "America's Mexicans: A Plea for Specificity," *Social Science Journal,* Vol. 19 (1982), pp. 9–24.

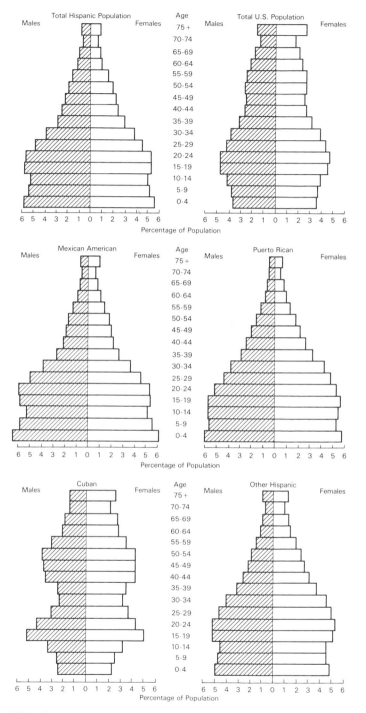

FIGURE 4.3 Age-Sex Composition of the Hispanic and Total U.S. Population, 1980. *Source:* Hearings Before the Subcommittee on Census and Population, September 13-15, 1983, 98th Cong. (Washington, D.C.: U.S. Government Printing Office, 1983).

lies of other Spanish origin with 3.37. Yet all these figures represent a slight decline in family size from 1970. Some of the decline reflects a drop in fertility that accompanies the changing position of women. In the next chapter we shall see that many more Hispanic women are entering the labor force. As a consequence, there is a reduction in their fertility.

But there is another and unhappy factor at work. There is an increase in the proportion of households headed by women. Thus in 1970, 16.9 percent of all Hispanic families with children were headed by women, against only 10.8 percent of all American households. By 1981 the Hispanic figure had grown considerably, to 21.8 percent, compared with 18.8 percent of all American families with children under age 18.[18] Puerto Rican families were most likely to be headed by a woman (40 percent) and Mexican families least likely, at 15 percent. Female-headed households are a growing tendency among all households in the United States, not just Hispanics. Nonetheless, the tendency represents a problem, and some of its implications will be developed later when we discuss Hispanic families (Chapter 6). In 1980, 72 percent of Hispanic children were living with both parents, as compared with 84 percent of white and only 43 percent of black children.

These figures on age distribution and family structure have some important consequences. We noted, for example, that the Hispanics have more children and the Anglos have more old people. These disparities show up in the age pyramids given in Figure 4.3. Just at this time, the schools and other youth-serving agencies are competing for tax funds that must also be used for new services to an aging population. In the 1980s, the tax dollars for both the young and the old are being cut back substantially. It appears most graphically in the deteriorating support for public education (particularly in the minority-dominated cities). In short, there is competition based on ethnicity for these tax dollars. The chances are high that both Hispanics and the other city-based minorities (most especially blacks) will not be the winners.

The age figures also imply a high rate of future population growth. This is inevitable unless young Hispanics depart substantially from the fertility patterns of their parents—and at a rate greater than the fertility shown in the 1970 and 1980 figures. The long years of inflation during the 1970s made it particularly hard for low-income Hispanics to support large families, so there is a general incentive to have fewer children. Per capita income (income per person) is much lower than the reported family income because, of course, a family income must be divided among more people.

Yet another consequence of the Hispanic age figures is a high "dependency ratio." This ratio is a statistical method of comparing two fractions of a population. Only part of a population is of working age; the other parts (the very young and the old) are not likely to work and, therefore, are dependent. Thus the dependency ratio accurately expresses the actual economic burden of the dependents on a working population. The burden is higher for Hispanics than for either Anglos or nonwhites—92 dependents in 1980 for every 100 Hispanics between ages 20 and 64 compared with only 74 for every 100 in the white population.[19] Yet this ratio has

---

[18] U.S. Commission on Civil Rights, *Disadvantaged Women and Their Children, 1982.* For comparison, 30.6 percent of black American families were headed by females in 1970 and 47.5 percent in 1981.

[19] *Statistical Abstract of the United States, 1981,* Tables 28 and 29, unpublished 1980 census data.

declined slightly for Hispanics between 1960 and 1970—and, again, between 1970 and 1980, as Hispanic fertility had declined slightly, indicating that this high dependency ratio is due almost entirely to the large number of dependent young people rather than a large number of old people.

CHAPTER FIVE
PORTRAIT OF THE HISPANICS: II

All the population realities that we have described in Chapter 4 affect the socio-economic status of American Hispanics. Some of these consequences can be traced quite accurately. They include education, income, occupations, health, housing, and crime.

TO GAIN AN EDUCATION

In a society that is steadily demanding ever more education in the form of high school and college diplomas, the Hispanic educational status is sobering. By most measures, Hispanics lag behind other groups. We see this vividly in the most common measure of educational achievement—the median number of school years completed (see Table 5.1). For those persons 25 years of age and over (normally at the end of the college years), Anglo Americans had completed a median 12.5 years of school. Blacks trailed by a margin of less than a year, completing 11.9 years of school—or slightly less than all of high school. Hispanics, by contrast, were nearly two years behind blacks, with a median completion of 10.3 years.

These figures cover the entire group and conceal some important intragroup differences. Among Hispanics, Mexican Americans were the least educated, achieving only 9.9 median years. Puerto Ricans were close with 10.2 years. Other Hispanics (which includes Cubans) gained 12.1 years, a figure higher than that of blacks and approaching that of the Anglo population.

TABLE 5.1   Median School Years Completed by Ethnic Group for Selected SMSAs, 1970 and 1980

SMSA	1970			1980		
	TOTAL	SPANISH ORIGIN	BLACK	TOTAL	SPANISH ORIGIN	BLACK
Albuquerque	12.5	10.7	12.1	12.8	12.2	12.6
Chicago	12.1	8.8	11.0	12.5	9.3	12.2
Corpus Christi	11.5	6.7	10.2	12.3	9.2	11.9
Denver	12.5	9.9	12.1	12.9	12.1	12.7
El Paso	12.5	8.0	12.2	12.3	9.7	12.7
Fresno	12.1	7.7	9.4	12.5	9.0	12.1
Los Angeles/Long Beach	12.4	10.0	12.1	12.7	10.2	12.6
Lubbock	12.2	5.3	9.9	12.6	8.0	11.4
Miami	12.1	9.8	9.8	12.5	12.1	11.9
Newark	12.2	8.7	10.9	12.6	11.2	12.2
New York	12.1	9.1	10.9	12.4	10.5	12.2
Phoenix	12.3	8.3	9.8	12.7	10.6	12.4
San Antonio	11.5	7.4	10.9	12.4	10.0	12.5
San Francisco	12.5	11.4	11.7	13.0	12.3	12.6

Sources: U.S. Census of Population, 1970 data are from PC (2)-1C, Table 13, and PC (1) C-1, Tables 83 and 91; U.S. Census of Population, 1980 data are from PC80-1, Tables 119, 150, 132.

There are also important variations between states and metropolitan areas. Table 5.1 shows some of these differences between the years 1970 and 1980. From this table, it appears there was much improvement for Hispanics. In fact, between 1970 and 1980, the average increase was more than 1.5 years of schooling in all metropolitan areas combined. Yet only four areas were able to educate Hispanics to the point where more than 12 years of school (or a high school education) were achieved. These were Albuquerque, Denver, Miami, and San Francisco. Yet each of these four cities is unusual in some way. Albuquerque and Denver have many native-born Hispanics. Miami has many highly educated Cubans, and San Francisco has an unusual number of "other Hispanics." None of these cities has many recent arrivals from Mexico or Puerto Rico.

Texas cities are notable for the large gains between 1970 and 1980. California (despite its reputation for strong public education) showed the least improvement. In fact, the Los Angeles/Long Beach Standard Metropolitan Area gained only two-tenths of a grade increase for Hispanic students. This poor performance may stem from the fact that Los Angeles/Long Beach is an important "port of entry" community for many Mexican and Central American immigrants. In Los Angeles proper, 48 percent of all students in the school system are Hispanics. Many of these are new immigrants who, in many cases, have completed fewer years than their Anglo counterparts. High school graduation rates sharply picture the differences between states. In California, 43.6 percent of Hispanics 25 years of age or older graduated from high school. In New York, the figure is somewhat lower: only 42 percent of a similar group graduated from high school. Illinois achieved a much smaller percentage with approximately one-third (36.7 percent) finishing high school. Florida does much better with a very large percentage of 54.6 percent. But these four states lag

TABLE 5.2   Individuals 25 Years and Older with Less Than Five Years of School

	NATIONAL	NORTHEAST	WEST	SOUTH[a]
White	2.7%	2.1%	2.4%	4.1%
Black	9.6	4.7	4.5	14.0
Hispanic	17.6	12.6	17.3	21.0

[a]Includes Texas and Florida.

Source: American Council on Education, *Minorities in Higher Education, Second Annual Report* (Washington, D.C.: ACE, 1983), p. 4.

greatly behind Anglo high school graduation. The gap is greatest in California (33 percent) and lowest in Florida (15 percent).

Fortunately, there are signs of improvement for the younger Hispanics who now are graduating from high school. In the 20- to 24-year-old group, the rates of graduation are California, 55 percent; Florida, 75 percent; New York, 58 percent; and Illinois, 48.7 percent. Yet, in spite of this improvement in high school graduation, the figures are still grim. The national rates for functional illiteracy among Hispanics are very high, as we see in Table 5.2. (The term "functional illiteracy" is used to describe a person with less than five years of elementary school or no school at all.) Hispanics show twice as many people with this handicap than among black Americans. Hispanic functional illiteracy is six times that of Anglo Americans.

School retention is also used to measure educational success and shows yet another depressing story. Hispanic dropout rates (Table 5.3) are nearly double those of blacks and Anglos between the ages of 14 and 25 years. Stated another way, for every 100 Hispanic children who enter kindergarten, only 55 graduate from high school, 25 enter college, and 7 complete college. Only 4 will enter graduate school and 2 will finish. The situation is most acute in certain states. In California, the Hispanic dropout rate from high school averaged 45 percent during the 12 years from 1971 to 1983.[1] Not only do Hispanic children drop out in large numbers, but they are far more likely than Anglos to lag behind in grade level. This gap increases in later years. Thus we find that 24.2 percent of the boys of Spanish origin are below grade in the early years of elementary school (ages 6 to 9) compared with 17.9 percent of Anglo boys. By the high school years (ages 14 to 17), the Hispanic boys are 45.7 percent behind in grade level. A much smaller 26.3 percent of the Anglo boys are below grade level in performance.[2]

But these figures cannot be taken uncritically. Two factors must be taken into account. The first is that there are major differences between native- and foreign-born Hispanics. For example, a survey taken in the middle of the 1970s showed that 45 percent of Puerto Ricans and 55 percent of the Mexican Americans between the ages of 14 and 30 who were born outside the mainland United States were not enrolled in school and were not high school graduates. This contrasts to 16 percent of the Puerto Ricans and 18 percent of the Chicanos born in the United

[1]Robert Montemayor, "Latino Students Advance, Only to Fail," *Los Angeles Times,* August 1, 1983.

[2]U.S. Bureau of the Census, "Characteristics of American Children and Youth, 1980," *Current Population Reports,* P-23, no. 114, 1982.

TABLE 5.3   Percentage of High School Dropouts, by Age and Race/Ethnic Group (Weighted Averages), 1974-1978

GROUP	AGE						
	14	15	16	17	18	19	20-25
Whites	1%	2%	6%	10%	13%	16%	17.8%
Blacks	1	2	6	12	20	27	29.4
Mexican Americans	2	6	16	23	31	41	49.7
Puerto Ricans	2	4	12	19	36	42	52.5

Source: American Council on Education, *Minorities in Higher Education, Second Annual Report* (Washington, D.C.: ACE, 1983), p. 6.

States who were neither in school nor high school nor high school graduates.[3] In other words, birth in this country creates a 30 to 40 percent difference. Obviously, U.S. schools are better able to educate young people born in the United States. Yet the Hispanic population contains a high percentage of immigrants—and it is very likely that this trend will continue. Undereducation will continue to be a significant problem, reflecting as it does a long history of educational discrimination and neglect (see Chapter 9).

A second factor that is closely related to the nativity of children is their language background. The use of Spanish as a native language greatly affects educational achievement. As one report states, "Hispanics with a monolingual English language background were almost as likely to complete high school as whites."[4] Yet many Hispanics live in communities where English is not the only language. Hispanic *barrios* from East Los Angeles to East Harlem characteristically use both Spanish and English. Some educators feel that children from these areas have special educational problems. The problem is compounded by the fact that Hispanic children may be native-born monolingual English speakers, foreign-born Spanish speakers, and native-born children exposed to both languages.

As might be expected, college enrollment reflects these many problems. Hispanic youth of college age (20 to 24 years) were only one-third as likely to be attending college as were Anglo young people in the states of California, New York, and Texas. Only in Florida was the ratio more favorable, and even in Florida, Hispanic college enrollment trailed Anglo enrollment. Figure 5.1 offers a visual summary of the relative position of Hispanics in the educational pipeline.

TO EARN A LIVING: INCOME AND OCCUPATION

Demographic patterns profoundly affect the share of income that is available to each Hispanic individual. In fact, the median income of Hispanic families reported in the 1980 census was only $14,700, a big step below the national median of

[3] George Brown et al., *The Condition of Education for Hispanic Americans* (Washington, D.C.: U.S. Government Printing Office, 1980), p. 102.

[4] *The Condition of Education for Hispanic Americans* (Washington, D.C.: Government Printing Office, 1980), p. 105.

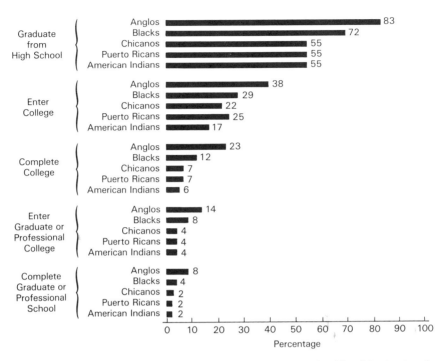

FIGURE 5.1   The Educational Pipeline. *Source:* Alexander Astin, *Minorities in American Higher Education* (San Francisco: Jossey-Bass, 1982).

$19,900 for non-Hispanic families. Hispanics on the average earned slightly more than blacks, but only about three-fourths as much as other Americans. The poorest of the Hispanics were the Puerto Ricans, who earned only 46 percent as much as did non-Hispanics, and the best off were the Cubans, who earned 85 percent as much as did non-Hispanics. Mexican Americans, the largest group, earned 72 percent as much as did non-Hispanics.

Disturbingly, the Hispanics were not able to improve their relative standing between 1970 and 1980. In fact, during these 10 years, the Mexican Americans lost slightly; Puerto Ricans dropped from 70 percent of white income in 1970 to 46 percent in 1980, and even the relatively well off Cubans declined from 95 to 85 percent of white income. Female-headed households fared even worse. By the middle of the decade, for example, Mexican-American households headed by women were earning only 30 percent as much as Anglo households; Puerto Rican female-headed families earned 29 percent, and both figures represented declines from the census year of 1970.[5] In the recession of the early 1980s, the Hispanic median income fell 6.8 percent compared with a drop of 1.7 percent for Anglo families.

[5] For 1970, data are taken from U.S. Census of Population PC(2)-1C, Table 10, and PC (1)-C1, Table 83. The later year is 1978, and figures are derived from data presented in D. Bailey, "Status of the Hispanic Population in the United States," *The Hispanic Population of the U.S.: An Overview* (Washington, D.C.: Congressional Research Service, March 1, 1983).

TABLE 5.4 Occupational Distribution of Employed Males and Females Aged 16 and Over, by Ethnic Group, 1980

OCCUPATIONAL CATEGORY	ANGLO	SPANISH ORIGIN	BLACK
1. Males			
Executive, administrative, and managerial	12.4%	5.7%	4.7%
Professional specialties	10.6	4.6	4.9
Technical, sales, and administrative support	18.0	13.0	12.8
Service	7.7	11.9	14.9
Precision production, craft, and repair	20.4	18.5	13.5
Operators, fabricators, and laborers	21.0	29.9	33.5
Handlers, equipment cleaners, helpers, and laborers	5.7	9.5	10.8
Farm laborers	0.9	3.8	1.2
Other farming, forestry, and fishing	3.0	2.3	2.1
2. Females			
Executive, administrative, and managerial	7.5	4.4	4.2
Professional specialties	14.0	6.9	10.6
Technical, sales, and administrative support	45.9	35.9	33.2
Service	16.0	19.5	27.7
Precision production, craft, and repair	2.2	3.7	2.2
Operators, fabricators, and laborers	10.7	21.8	16.2
Handlers, equipment cleaners, helpers, and laborers	2.0	4.0	3.0
Farm laborers	0.4	1.6	0.3
Other farming, forestry, and fishing	0.6	0.6	0.2

Source: Calculated from U.S. Bureau of the Census, *Detailed Occupation and Years of School Completed by Age, for the Civilian Labor Force by Sex, Race and Spanish Origin, 1980* PC80-S1-8, Table 1.

The data on female-headed households are from U.S. Commission on Civil Rights, *Social Indicators of Equality for Minorities and Women,* August 1978, p. 50. (The data for 1975 are taken from the substantial *Survey of Income and Education.* Those for 1979 are taken from the U.S. Census. The sample size makes estimates for subpopulations other than Mexican and Puerto Rican unreliable.)

But beyond the bald numbers, what lies behind these very low incomes? First, the numbers reflect the occupational pattern of Hispanics. This disadvantageous pattern is illustrated in Table 5.4. Hispanics, along with blacks, were substantially underrepresented in the better paid occupations (such as executive-level jobs and professional specialties). This was true for both men and women. In the 1980 census, the most common occupation was semiskilled work in factories (operators, fabricators, and laborers). Almost a third of the Hispanic men and a fifth of the women worked in such jobs. Skilled work (precision production, etc.) was performed by about a fifth of all male Hispanic workers. Hispanics were far more likely than Anglos to work as unskilled laborers (handlers, etc.)—and the Mexican history of farm work is still reflected in their higher than average tendency to hold jobs as farm laborers. Only Cuban men approached an occupational profile that resembled that for Anglo men. Cubans held more professional jobs, and there were more men who were managers and proprietors of businesses. Correspondingly fewer Cubans held jobs as laborers, semiskilled workers, and service workers. Puerto Rican men were underrepresented among skilled workers, as were Mexican Americans, to a lesser extent.[6]

Hispanics have improved their position only very slightly in recent years. In general, Hispanic women are gaining ground in white-collar occupations. (This is especially true for Puerto Rican women.) But such an improvement should not obscure the fact that Hispanic women were still overrepresented in semiskilled jobs, typically factory jobs.

A second factor tends to pull down Hispanic income. This is the rate of unemployment. Unemployment varies with economic conditions. (The United States endured a notable recession between 1973 and 1975 and an even sharper drop in the early 1980s.) Unemployment for Hispanics tends to follow these cyclical swings. But Hispanic unemployment is *always* higher than Anglos' and for some segments, much higher. In general, over time, the Hispanic unemployment rate is about 40 to 60 percent higher than is that of the total U.S. population. Although this is generally somewhat lower than black unemployment, the Puerto Ricans consistently suffer unemployment equal to blacks—that is, at a rate almost double that for all American workers. Cubans have the lowest unemployment rates, but then, not so many Cubans are young people and the young always have higher rates of unemployment. Young Puerto Ricans suffer extremely high unemployment.[7] Thus the unemploy-

---

[6] In the 1980 census, occupational categories were changed so completely that they are not at all comparable with 1970 occupational categories. The 1980 changes were implemented to reflect changing American industrial and occupational structures. Joan Moore, *Mexican Americans* (Englewood Cliffs, N.J.: Prentice-Hall, 1976), presents comparisons between 1950 and 1970 for Mexican Americans that show some trends. For changes in census classifications, see M. Riche, "The Blue Collar Blues," *American Demographics,* Vol. 5 (1983), pp. 20–23. In these discussions, the statements about Cuban, Puerto Rican, and Mexican-American peculiarities are derived from Bureau of Labor Statistics data presented by the Congressional Research Service.

[7] U.S. Department of Labor, Bureau of Labor Statistics, "Employment and Earnings," March 1982, cited in D. Roth, "Hispanics in the U.S. Labor Force," in *The Hispanic Population of the U.S.: An Overview* (Washington, D.C.: Congressional Research Service, Library of Congress, March 1, 1983). Roth's essay is a major source for this section on unemployment, along with the U.S. Commission on Civil Rights, *Unemployment and Underemployment Among Blacks, Hispanics and Women,* November 1982. José Hernández, *Puerto Rican Youth Employment* (Maplewood, N.J.: Waterfront Press, 1983), covers these issues in sophisticated detail for Puerto Ricans.

ment and occupational experiences of Hispanics accurately reflect their generally disadvantaged position in the American labor force.

The search for explanations for this disadvantage involves two very different approaches. *Individual factors* are one explanation. Another approach emphasizes *structural factors* in which certain hard-to-change features of the economy and the society are emphasized. There is little doubt that neither explanation is sufficient by itself. Both must be considered.

First, the individual factors. These include education, language proficiency, vocational training and experience, immigrant status, and health.[8] These characteristics are clearly associated with both lower earnings and lower occupational status for Hispanics. To state the case another way, if Hispanics were American-born and English speaking, had education comparable to that of Anglos, held jobs that involved longer training, and enjoyed a health status comparable to Anglos, then they would be more competitive in the job market.

It would appear that all these factors could be remedied. In fact, much of the effort of policy that is designed to improve the work status of Hispanics is directed at these individual factors. But, in general, these statistical analyses show very plainly that, even when Hispanics exactly match the characteristics of Anglo workers, they would still earn up to 20 percent less. It is suggested, therefore, that not all individual factors have been isolated: we have not measured the motivation of the individual—or the quality of his or her education. But a more productive approach is to look for features in our economy and society that explain the disadvantage.

The feature that is most likely to attract attention is discrimination. But discrimination is very difficult to measure. It is true that some organizational requirements are discriminatory. Thus height requirements for firefighters in Los Angeles County were found to exclude 45 percent of the otherwise eligible Mexican-American applicants.[9]

Language discrimination has been detected and protested successfully, but more subtle forms of discrimination that do not rely on bureaucratic rules are virtually impossible to assess. Any effort to measure discrimination must then rigorously remove all measurable factors. The residue can usually be accepted as discrimination. We will return to this later. But what are these measurable factors?

Some of these factors are related to characteristics of the Hispanic population. Age is an example. Young people earn less, and the Hispanic working population includes a relatively large group of young people. Participation in the labor force is a factor. If fewer Hispanics are in the labor force, then comparatively fewer are earning any money. We might expect that Hispanic participation would be low, but in fact that is true for only one segment—the Puerto Ricans. Taken as a whole,

---

[8] Studies of these factors include those summarized by the National Commission for Employment Policy, *Hispanics and Jobs: Barriers to Progress* (Washington, D.C.: NCEP, 1982); Richard Santos, "Earnings Among Spanish-Origin Males in the Midwest," *Social Science Journal,* Vol. 19 (1982), pp. 51–59; U.S. Commission on Civil Rights, *Social Indicators;* James Long, "Productivity, Employment Discrimination, and the Relative Economic Status of Spanish Origin Males," *Social Science Quarterly,* Vol. 58 (1977), pp. 357–373; and Marta Tienda, "Nationality and Income Attainment Among Native and Immigrant Hispanic Men in the U.S.," *Sociological Quarterly,* Vol. 24 (1983), pp. 253–272.

[9] C. V. Dale, "National Origin Discrimination Against Hispanics in Employment," in *The Hispanic Population of the U.S.: An Overview* (Washington, D.C.: Congressional Research Service, Library of Congress, March 1, 1983).

Hispanic participation is actually *higher* than is that of Anglos or blacks.[10] Hispanic women, however, are notably less likely than Anglo women to be in the labor force.[11] (See also Chapter 6 for detailed discussion of women and work.)

Other factors include certain *characteristics of the jobs* that are held by Hispanics. Hispanics are more likely to be "underemployed"—a term that describes persons who hold jobs that are available only part time or seasonally. As a consequence, fewer people are actually working full time, even though they may wish to do so. Many of the jobs held by Hispanics (especially women) are "marginal." A marginal job has a combination of low wages, poor working conditions, high turnover, and few (or no) fringe benefits. (Unemployment insurance and Social Security may also not be contributed by marginal employers.) A job is not necessarily an opportunity. It may be meaningless and dead end as well as badly paid. Some careers are nothing but a lifelong succession of bad jobs. The essential question is: Exactly how does the job market really work for Hispanics? And this question brings us to structural factors, to the mechanism of the job market itself.

What is the *labor market* really like? Until recently, most labor economists assumed that the job market was simply a mass of job seekers who were lined up for employment in the exact order of their individual qualifications. This lineup is called a "queue." The first best qualified person in the queue, regardless of ethnicity, sex, or other factors irrelevant to performance, would be selected for the best job. Prejudiced employers who insisted on discrimination would, in the long run, pay for their taste for discrimination by being forced to pay more for less productive white male workers. This is a comfortable belief in the rationality of employers. It is crumbling away now in the face of a great deal of evidence that something quite different happens in the labor market. In fact, there is not just one labor market but several. In technical words, the labor market is "segmented."

Theorists who study labor markets argue that the labor market actually works differently for different types of employers.[12] Employers who offer "good" jobs (relatively high wages, good working conditions, fringe benefits, security, a chance for advancement, and due process for grievances) recruit in labor markets different from those used by the more marginal employers. The better employers (in the "primary" sector) are enterprises that are heavily capitalized and concentrated and tend to be unionized. On the other side of the labor market, the marginal employers of secondary labor run highly competitive businesses, particularly in terms of labor costs. Not only do they pay the lowest possible wage, but they may structure their work force as they please, systematically evading wage and hours laws, as proved to be the case with 78 percent of a group of garment manufacturers recently inspected in California.[13]

[10] This is particularly true for men of Mexican origin. Puerto Ricans (especially in the island of Puerto Rico) have very low (and declining) rates of participation, probably because of discouragement with long-standing and high rates of unemployment.

[11] This is particularly true for Puerto Rican women, only a third of whom are working or looking for work. The labor force participation of Mexican-American women is higher and is increasing, although it is still lower than that of Anglo or black women.

[12] David M. Gordon, *Theories of Poverty and Underemployment* (Lexington, Mass.: D. C. Heath, 1972).

[13] These employees were overwhelmingly Hispanic. See U.S. Department of Labor, "Strike Force Finds $658,173 Due 1,372 Los Angeles Garment Workers," *Noticias de la Semana,* July 14, 1980.

Marginal employers seek employees who make minimal demands. Teenaged workers in the fast-food chains will work for minimum wages and are happy with an occasional free Saturday night as a "reward" in the weekly negotiations for a work schedule. Undocumented aliens will work in sweatshops. But many adults actively reject such jobs, and this leads to continual complaints by low-wage employers about labor shortages.[14]

Employers have actively recruited Hispanic workers for many decades—from rural Texas, Puerto Rico, Latin America, and the Caribbean. These workers accept the wages and working conditions that make them attractive to marginal and exploitative employers.[15] The problem appears with the children of these workers. Second-generation Hispanics tend not to be so easily convinced that such jobs are attractive. The newcomers were exploitable and docile workers; their American-born (or urban-born) children are likely to be demanding and skeptical. Yet there seems to be little doubt but that a high proportion of Hispanic workers are in the "secondary labor market" and have no better options. When a study by the U.S. Commission on Civil Rights attempted to measure the extent to which Hispanics and other minority workers were concentrated in such jobs, their data showed that in 1980, 11.2 percent of Hispanic men and 18.5 percent of Hispanic women held such jobs. Only 5.3 percent of Anglo men and 13.9 percent of Anglo women held such jobs.[16] It is surprising to find that these rates change very little over the years—in good times and in bad.

The stable pattern of marginal jobs over time strongly suggests that such jobs are a permanent feature of the labor market—that is, a segmented market is a structural factor. Furthermore, the labor market is not uniform between regions, as we have seen in Chapter 3 in our discussion of Sunbelt/Snowbelt differences. To recapitulate, Puerto Ricans have been hurt by the loss of manufacturing jobs, especially in New York, and Mexican Americans have profited indirectly, at least, by the expansion of jobs in their traditional Sunbelt states.

The greatly increased number of Hispanics is critical in the slow emergence of a middle-class Hispanic (and heavily Chicano) group. Unfortunately, the *rate* of growth of middle-income Hispanics is well behind what one would expect from the overall boom in the Southwest. Even within the Sunbelt states, substantial disparities in Hispanic income from one state to another still indicate great differences in the taste for discrimination against them.

An important exception is the Cubans, who have done very well in Miami. Wilson and Portes believe this remarkable success to be the result of an "enclave" economy in which thousands of immigrant Cubans were able to establish their own businesses. As a result, an extremely high proportion (half) work for other Cuban employers. The Cubans who emigrated to Miami in the 1960s were relatively well off. Many were business people or professionals in Cuba before the Castro revolution and thus brought with them substantial managerial skills. Many were able to

---

[14] In the spring of 1982 the Immigration and Naturalization Service arrested some 5,000 undocumented workers in nine cities to permit native-born workers to take the jobs (which averaged $4.41 per hour). However, native workers refused the jobs, which were considered too hard and too demeaning. The undocumented workers soon returned. See *The Wall Street Journal,* December 6, 1982.

[15] Michael Piore, *Birds of Passage* (Cambridge: Cambridge University Press, 1979).

[16] U.S. Commission on Civil Rights, *Unemployment and Underemployment,* pp. 8-9, 20.

bring some capital. Thus Wilson and Portes argue that the Cuban immigrants were able to avoid the marginality of most Hispanic arrivals.[17] Another factor generally overlooked is the amount of federal assistance given Cuban refugees during the 1960s and 1970s. But this is not to say that the Cubans totally avoided the "bottom of the ladder" position of other Hispanics. More general evidence suggests that this thriving enclave economy is somewhat lower paying than the mainstream. Cubans living outside the Miami area were less likely to be managers and administrators than were their Miami cousins, but they were likely to be earning somewhat more.[18]

Yet another structural factor is the possible shift of jobs away from the central cities and toward the suburbs.[19] Most Hispanics live in the central areas of cities, and it is clear that the cities are much more stricken by unemployment than are suburbs and rural areas. Hispanic youth unemployment in particular is heavily concentrated in the cities. More than half the unemployed young Hispanics live in urban areas.[20]

These are the major social and economic structural factors that are associated with the poor showing of Hispanics in the American labor market. When statistical analysts add up these structural factors and the individual factors, the combination usually explains much if not all the income disparity between Hispanics and the competing Anglos.[21]

But there remains a perplexing residue. Even if all Hispanic males were exactly matched with Anglo males, they would still earn between 8 and 15 percent less than Anglos. (Hispanic women, like Anglo women, earn only about half as much as Anglo men.) It is this residue that implies the existence of a factor that cannot be identified and measured. Many analysts are confident that the disparity is prejudice and discrimination. It is this factor that has been the target of various affirmative action programs. In appraising them, it appears that the programs indeed had some effect, although apparently less for Hispanics than for blacks.

Welch, Karnig, and Eribes examined government employment in more than 80 southwestern cities, examining changes in the proportion of Hispanics hired between 1973 and 1978. There were substantial changes in hiring Hispanic men, particularly in cities with a large Hispanic population.[22] Many of the occupational gains made by Hispanics have occurred in the public sector, although Hispanics tended to gain less than did blacks. Analysis of 1976 data shows that half of the

[17]K. Wilson and A. Portes, "Immigrant Enclaves: An Analysis of the Labor Market Experience of Cubans in Miami," *American Journal of Sociology,* Vol. 86 (1981), pp. 296–318; and A. Portes et al., "Six Years Later, The Process of Incorporation of Cuban Exiles in the United States, 1973–1979," *Cuban Studies,* Vol. 11 (1981); Vol. 12 (1982), pp. 1–24.

[18]A.J. Jaffe et al., *The Changing Demography of Spanish Americans* (New York: Academic Press, 1980), p. 273 ff.

[19]See Joan Moore, "Minorities in the American Class System," *Daedalus* 110 (1981) 275–298, for a summary. Rodriguez argues convincingly that such a shift has hurt New York Hispanics; see Rodriguez, "Economic Survival in New York City," in Clara Rodriguez et al., eds., *The Puerto Rican Struggle* (New York: Puerto Rican Migration Consortium, 1980), p. 30.

[20]For adult employment, see U.S. Commission on Civil Rights, *Unemployment,* p. 30. For youth unemployment, Bureau of Labor Statistics, 1978 annual averages.

[21]U.S. Commission on Civil Rights, *Social Indicators,* p. 54.

[22]S. Welch, R. Karnig, and R. Eribes, "Changes in Hispanic Public Employment in the Southwest," unpublished manuscript.

Chicano professionals were working for government agencies. The most common profession was that of teaching. There were similar patterns for the higher-level clerical occupations.[23]

Of course, there is much controversy about the effectiveness of affirmative action programs. But certainly there is convincing evidence that without affirmative action and public hiring the growth of a Hispanic middle class would be greatly cut down. Recent cutbacks (late 1970s and early 1980s) in these programs are important for minorities that are slow to develop a substantial middle class. Proposals by the Reagan administration to weaken the programs brought a storm of protest from Hispanic groups.[24]

A recent study suggests, furthermore, that private employers have been greatly affected. A massive study in 1983 by the U.S. Department of Labor showed that between 1974 and 1980, firms with affirmative action programs increased their minority employment by 20 percent. Employers without programs increased their minority hiring by only 12 percent.[25]

Finally, there is still a local impact on wages that may reflect a combination of all these structural factors, including discrimination. By one indicator, the differences between localities may be declining, but not to the advantage of Hispanics. Thus, the 1970 census reported that in Texas, Spanish-surnamed males over 16 earned 60 percent of the income earned by Anglo male Texans, whereas in California Hispanics earned 75 percent of the median earned by Anglo males. By the 1980 census, the difference had all but vanished: in California, Spanish origin males earned 67 percent of the median earned by non-Spanish origin males, and in Texas they earned 63 percent.

The large-scale immigration of the 1970s and 1980s compels us to look especially hard at the role of immigrants in the overall economic situation of Hispanics. A careful study of immigrants to Los Angeles shows several interesting features:

> First, most Mexican immigrants to California settled in Southern California—half in Los Angeles County—and thus their impact is very localized. Most (72 percent) were undocumented, and thus very vulnerable.
>
> The second important finding is that Mexican immigrants to this expanding metropolitan labor market followed a classic immigrant pattern. They were heavily concentrated in low-wage manufacturing jobs (constituting 47 percent of all such workers in 1980).[26]

[23]Tabulations by Joan W. Moore from unpublished computer files, *1976 Survey of Income and Education.*

[24]Antónia Hernandez of the Mexican American Legal Defense and Educational Fund aired some of these concerns in testimony before the House Subcommittee on Employment Opportunities of the Committee on Education and Labor, on April 18, 1981.

[25]The report does not contrast Hispanics to other minorities, but comments that the gains are especially notable because total employment in affirmative action companies grew less during the period than the others. Some 77,000 employers were studied, for a total of 20 million workers; see *The New York Times,* June 19, 1983, Section 1, p. 12.

[26]Thomas Muller, *The Fourth Wave: California's Newest Immigrants: A Summary* Washington, D.C.: Urban Institute Press, 1984), pp. 11, 12.

The author notes that "the immigrant influx was not accompanied by job losses for other workers"[27] because in this expanding labor market the more skilled older residents could find better paying jobs. Thus the immigrants functioned to push resident workers up the job ladder. In particular, the often-voiced concern about whether Hispanic immigrants displace black workers was proven groundless. Blacks clearly moved up—and especially into public employment—and this was true in other southwestern cities in addition to Los Angeles.

The third major finding is that immigrant workers depress wages. Those industries in which they are concentrated lagged well behind. The author concludes that "these workers themselves [immigrants], and, to a lesser extent, Mexican Americans absorbed much of the adverse impact of the depressed wages."[28] More important from the economist's point of view, the low wages paid to immigrants had distinctly positive effects elsewhere: "the depressed wages in low-skill jobs caused more such jobs to open up. . . . Beneficiaries of the lower wages for unskilled work included business, consumers, households using domestic help, and nonproduction workers in highly competitive industries."[29]

To put this analysis in human terms, let us quote José Hernández' summary:

> No matter what causal explanation may be proposed for continued poverty among Puerto Ricans, there is general agreement on the consequence for human resource development. . . . One's survival and that of kin and significant others becomes a fundamental career goal. . . . Puerto Rican teenagers seem to find limited meaning and economic value in completing a secondary school curriculum. They compare "staying in" with such options as . . . learning the normative aspects of making it at the bottom of society, exploring conventional and other ways of earning a living; marriage, military service and similar institutionalized evasions; getting a head start on the jobs open to Puerto Ricans, and investing the time and energy demanded by schooling into finding out how they fit in a world of lifelong uncertainty and very modest aspirations.
>
> The common features of these options is a quest for luck . . . and the realization that formal instruction has little to do with success . . . in a field of odds set against them. The major question should not be why Puerto Ricans continue submerged in poverty, but how they manage to survive and achieve some degree of advancement in a world of continually negative conditions.[30]

THE CONSEQUENCES OF POVERTY

All the available materials from the U.S. Census and other reliable sources show the deep poverty of American Hispanics (Figure 5.2). But will this poverty endure? And what are the consquences? Regrettably, the best evidence is that poverty will dominate the lives of many Hispanics for years to come.

[27] Ibid., p. 13.
[28] Ibid., p. 16.
[29] Ibid.
[30] José Hernández, *Puerto Rican Youth Employment*, pp. 56–57.

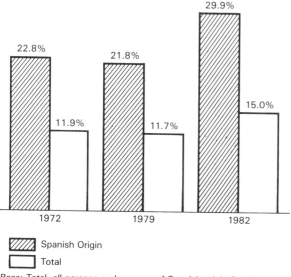

Spanish Origin

Total

Base: Total, all persons and persons of Spanish origin for whom poverty status is determined.

FIGURE 5.2   **Poverty Rates of Total and Spanish Origin Persons, 1972–1982.** *Source:* U.S. Bureau of the Census, "Condition of Hispanics in America Today" (Washington, D.C.: U.S. Government Printing Office, September 1983).

Summarizing this material, we find that in the late 1970s almost a quarter of all Mexican-American families and almost a third of all Puerto Rican families were living in poverty. Furthermore, the poverty is increasing. In 1981, 26.5 percent of Hispanic families were poor, and by 1983 the percentage had increased to 29.9 percent.[31] Households headed by women were in worse shape. The 1981 figures show that more than half (53 percent) of such Mexican-American and Puerto Rican families were poor.[32] These rates were almost identical with those of blacks—and in all instances, almost double those for white female-headed households.[33]

This meant (in simple terms) that Mexican-American families were two and

[31] Summarized in *The Wall Street Journal,* August 3, 1983. About 15 percent of all U.S. families were poor in 1982.

[32] "Poverty" is defined in terms of living costs for families in different circumstances. Thus, in 1980, a male-headed nonfarm family with two children was defined as "poor" if the household income fell under $8,418. *Statistical Abstract of the United States,* 1982, p. 417.

[33] U.S. Bureau of the Census, *Money Income and Poverty Status of Persons in the United States,* 1981 (Advanced Data) Series P-60, No. 134, p. 21, cited in U.S. Commission on Civil Rights, *A Growing Crisis: Disadvantaged Women and Their Children* (Washington, D.C.: U.S. Government Printing Office, 1983), p. 8.

one-half times more likely to live in poverty than were Anglo families. Puerto Rican families were three and a half times more likely to be in poverty. Female-headed families of Puerto Rican, Mexican, and black origin were more than five times more likely to be living in poverty than were Anglo families.

When we try to project the future, it is obvious that there will be steady immigration of very poor Hispanics. In the early 1980s, it appears there was some slackening in inflation, but a serious recession was cutting into the occupational gains of Hispanics in the Southwest and in the Northeast. There were also serious cutbacks in many of the federal programs designed to help the Hispanic population.

This prevailing poverty greatly affects the quality of life that is available to Chicanos, Puerto Ricans, and other Hispanics. It also creates certain problems that go beyond the poor themselves and creates, in effect, a problem for all of us. Or perhaps the best phrase is a "community problem." We will look in turn at housing, health, and crime.

Housing.   Poor housing is a direct consequence of poverty. Fewer and fewer Hispanics are able to own their own homes, despite very strong cultural values in the Hispanic communities about homeownership.[34] In 1970, a total of 63 percent of all American households lived in their own homes. By 1980 (in spite of years of high mortgage rates), the total had risen to 66 percent. In 1980 only 43 percent of America's Hispanics owned their own homes (see Figure 5.3). A majority of the Hispanics live in rental housing; a majority of other Americans live in their own homes.[35] Poorer Hispanics (with incomes under $15,000) were even more likely than poor blacks and whites to be renters.[36]

Hispanics pay a higher proportion of their incomes both for mortgage payments and for rents. There are also some interesting differences between Hispanic subgroups. Cubans and Central and South Americans pay close to the national average for their housing, while Mexicans pay slightly more and Puerto Ricans pay much more for their housing. (Puerto Ricans apparently are the victims of high costs in New York City. Possibly the Mexican figures reflect inflated real estate costs in California.)

Quality is an important factor in housing, not just the cost. Hispanic housing is four times more likely to be overcrowded; Hispanic families are larger. Finally,

[34] This section is derived from Richard Eribes and Albert Karnig, "Hispanic Housing," a paper written for the Department of Housing and Urban Development (White House Conference on Families), and Dorothy Bailey, "Housing of Hispanics," in Congressional Research Service, *The Hispanic Population* (Washington, D.C.: Congressional Research Service, March 1, 1983). The basic data are derived from *Annual Housing Surveys* conducted for the Department of Housing and Urban Development. Data from surveys conducted in 1975 and 1976 were published by HUD's Office of Policy Development and Research, *How Well Are We Housed?: 1. Hispanics* (Washington, D.C.: U.S. Government Printing Office, 1978).

[35] The rate of homeownership varies from area to area as does the ratio of homeownership of Hispanics to Anglos. The lowest ratio of homeownership of Hispanics to Anglos is in New York, where only 47 percent as many Hispanics own their own homes as do Anglos. The highest ratio is in Denver. Here 85 percent as many Hispanics as Anglos own their own home. But the rates and the ratios are always lower for Hispanics. U.S. Department of the Census, *Annual Housing Survey, 1980: A. General Housing Characteristics* (Washington, D.C.: U.S. Government Printing Office, 1981).

[36] U.S. Department of the Census, *Annual Housing Survey: 1980: C. Financial Characteristics of the Housing Inventory* (Washington, D.C.: U.S. Government Printing Office, 1981).

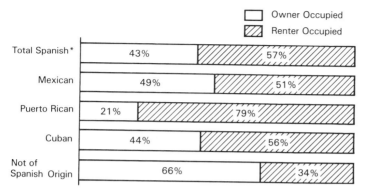

*Includes "Other Spanish" not shown separately.
Base: Total all housing units with householders of respective origins.

FIGURE 5.3 **Percentage of Households Owner or Renter Occupied, 1980.**
Source: U.S. Bureau of the Census, "Condition of Hispanics in America Today" (Washington, D.C.: U.S. Government Printing Office, September 1983).

Hispanics are twice as likely to live in housing that is physically inadequate—especially in terms of heating. It may not seem important that homes in warm climates are not properly heated; yet poor Chicano areas in the Southwest still suffer outbreaks of home fires in the wintertime. Puerto Rican housing is most likely to suffer from poor maintenance, and in such areas as New York City, "poor maintenance" means garbage, rats, and dilapidation.

Housing has improved for Hispanics since 1960, possibly because of a "trickle-down" or "filtering" process. As Americans in general move into better homes, and the worst housing is destroyed in the process of urban upgrading, the poor can move into better housing. But much of the hand-me-down housing is in the Anglo part of town, and there is clear evidence that housing discrimination hurts Hispanics.[37] Many landlords refuse to rent to families with children, a form of discrimination that hurts Hispanics particularly.

The process of "urban upgrading" in the form of public improvements is also often destructive to the supply of Hispanic housing. In Los Angeles, a set of freeways built east of the downtown area cut wide swaths through Chicano neighborhoods, destroying many acres of homes. In New York City, the lower East Side of Manhattan is rapidly replacing century-old slums with rehabilitated units far beyond

[37]Thus a 1979 HUD study showed that "dark-skinned Chicanos encountered blatant forms of housing discrimination much more often than light-skinned Chicanos in Dallas." Further, "light-skinned Chicanos appear to encounter discriminatory treatment about as often as blacks, while dark-skinned Chicanos appear to encounter discriminatory treatment more often than blacks." U.S. Department of Housing and Urban Development, Office of Policy Development and Research, J. Hakken, *Discrimination Against Chicanos in the Dallas Rental Housing Market* (August 1979), cited by Dorothy Bailey, "Housing of Hispanics," p. 142.

the means of displaced occupants—Puerto Ricans and Dominicans. The old *barrio* can expect a very short life.

Health. Because of the absence of national health, birth, and death statistics on Hispanics, it is hard to say much about the effect of poverty on Hispanic health. Many of the existing studies are seriously flawed.[38] And the very rare careful studies of the causes of death deal with Texas Hispanics, who may not be representative because of more poverty in Texas and poorer health services.

But considering the Texas data nonetheless, we find that in Houston (1950 and 1960) and San Antonio (1950), Mexicans were considerably more likely to die at an early age. Black Texans also died earlier than did Anglos—and at about the same rate as Chicanos. Standardized mortality ratios indicate that in 1950 Chicano males had an observed mortality rate 1.6 times greater than did Anglo males. Chicanas had a mortality rate 2.4 times greater than did Anglo women. But these differences had fallen rather sharply by 1960, as had the differences between blacks and Anglos.[39] In the later years there were notable differences in the rate at which degenerative diseases cause death. Anglos (especially women) were more subject to death from cancer; Mexicans were far more likely to die from diabetes. (Hispanic problems with diabetes have appeared in studies elsewhere, including in New York.)[40]

The absence of systematic, large-scale data on the health status of Hispanics is a serious deficiency in the nation's ability to monitor changes in health status. The deficiency obscures effective policymaking. For poverty-level populations, public funding for health care may have a major impact. Thus a substantial increase in funding for maternal health care in south Texas brought a dramatic decrease in deaths over a ten-year period (65 percent).[41] Ironically, there has been a great deal of research into Hispanic attitudes toward health and mental health care because such research is easily designed and easily accomplished (see Chapter 8), but the more consequential national statistics on health problems are still missing in the 1980s.

Crime. Poverty is also clearly associated with Hispanic crime. Fighting youth gangs have been a feature of poor Mexican and Puerto Rican neighborhoods in many cities for many decades.[42] Thus the Hispanic rates of juvenile delinquency

[38] As an example, a study in Alameda County, California, reported no health differences between Anglos and Chicanos in 1974 and 1975, but these data were self-reporting surveys with an unknown bias due to nonresponse and distorted responses. See R. E. Roberts and E. S. Lee, "The Health of Mexican Americans," cited in Bailey, ed., *The Hispanic Population.*

[39] Robert Roberts, "Mortality and Morbidity in the Mexican American Population," given to the Mexican American Population Conference, Austin, Texas, 1973, provides a useful overview and bibliography. A. T. Moustafa and G. Weiss, *Health Status and Practices of Mexican Americans* Advance Report 11 (Los Angeles: University of California, Mexican American Study Project, 1968), provide a useful, though dated, view.

[40] Jose Oscar Alers, *Puerto Ricans and Health: Findings from New York City,* Monograph No. 4 (Bronx, N.Y.: Fordham University, Hispanic Research Center, 1978).

[41] Antonio Zavaleta, "Federal Assistance and Mexican American Health Status in Texas," *Agenda,* Vol. 11 (1981), pp. 19–25.

[42] See Joan W. Moore et al., *Homeboys* (Philadelphia: Temple University Press, 1978), for a description of Los Angeles gangs; and Patricia Cayo Sexton, *Spanish Harlem* (New York: Harper, 1965), and Alfredo López, *The Puerto Rican Papers* (Indianapolis: Bobbs-Merrill, 1973), pp. 165–175, for Puerto Rican gangs in New York.

tend to be higher than for Anglos. Puerto Ricans in New York have a rate twice that of New York Anglos.

There have been a number of attempts to "explain" the higher rates in terms of inherent characteristics. The first prevailing explanations were racial. These were evident during the attempts by Los Angeles sheriffs' deputies to explain the violence during the zoot suit riots of 1943:

> the criminality of teenage Mexican Americans is due to inferior genetic and cultural factors. . . . Mexicans are more prone to kick an adversary who has been knocked down in a fight whereas an Anglo youth would be more inclined to fight fair.[43]

In large measure these explanations reflect a biological approach to Mexican crime patterns dominant in the criminology of the early twentieth century. Later, cultural explanations superseded them and tend to persist both as "commonsense" explanations and scholarly explanations. The notion that Hispanics come generally from "cultures of violence" is particularly strong. In the 1930s this was applied to Mexican-American culture:

> Aggravated assault is common among Mexicans, not because they are inherently aggressive but because they live in a certain cultural stage, where fighting is approved.[44]

And more recently, it has been applied to Puerto Ricans as well.[45] There were even scholars who argued that delinquency was normal in Mexican-American communities:

> The excess of juvenile delinquents among Mexican Americans is not composed of deviants from the cultural pattern but rather of boys who overconform to this pattern. In this view, the most striking "deviants" among Mexican American youth are not those delinquents but the youngsters . . . who aspire to or who do attend college.[46]

Such views are now seen as ethnocentric. More recent sociological views (particularly with regard to youth gangs) tend to emphasize a minority context of poverty and hopelessness that encourages a subculture. Gangs are a grouping through which adolescents can control some portion of their own fate and express their own sense of courage and dignity.[47] Some authorities also argue that the very

[43] Quoted in Carey McWilliams, *North from Mexico* (Boston: Little, Brown, 1948), p. 250.

[44] Max Handman, "Preliminary Report on Nationality and Delinquency: The Mexican in Texas," *Report on Crime and the Foreign Born*, Vol. 2 (1932), cited in Larry Trujillo, "La Evolucion del 'Bandido' al 'Pachuco': A Critical Examination and Evaluation of Criminological Literature on Chicanos," *Issues in Criminology*, Vol. 9 (1974), pp. 43–67.

[45] Jaime Toro-Calder, *Personal Crimes in Puerto Rico*, unpublished M.A. thesis, University of Wisconsin-Madison, 1950, cited in Peter L. Sissons, *The Hispanic Experience of Criminal Justice*, Hispanic Research Monograph No. 3 (Bronx, N.Y.: Fordham University, 1979).

[46] Celia Heller, *Mexican American Youth: Forgotten Youth at the Crossroads* (New York: Random House, 1966), pp. 76–77.

[47] Moore et al., *Homeboys*.

age structure of Hispanics (high birth rates and large numbers of young people) will continue to generate high delinquency rates, because it is overwhelmingly young people who commit crimes.

But crime does not stop with adolescence. Even though some areas stereotyped as crime ridden actually have rather low rates, like East Los Angeles, Hispanics throughout the nation are considerably overrepresented among men and women who go to prison for narcotics offenses—especially those involving heroin. Again, cultural explanations are often advanced for the patterns of drug use, just as they are for delinquency.[48] And there is much evidence to suggest that narcotics use permits Hispanic men to "substitute one big problem for a lot of little problems," according to one study of Puerto Rican addicts in New York City.[49]

Narcotics addiction is also almost invariably connected with a way of making a living and sometimes substantial income. While many addicts burglarize or rob to support their habits, many are also involved in "dealing for profit." Observers believe quite generally that the involvement of Mexican Americans in the Southwest in heroin sales is outside the channels of Mafia-style organized crime. This appears to be less true for Puerto Rican and Cuban American drug traffickers. Puerto Ricans tended to settle into cities in which organized crime was well established. At least some writers argue that Hispanics in such cities (more slowly than blacks) are moving into more powerful positions in organized crime networks.[50] Hispanic crime networks are more likely to be based on kinship and youthful gang affiliations than are black networks. Cubans in both Miami and New York are reputedly involved in drug trafficking and in other forms of organized crime. Francis Ianni sees the Cubans as being much more "sophisticated" than other Hispanics:

> Like the Italians before them, they keep crime out of their communities even while organizing it elsewhere in the city. They do not allow drug pushing or prostitution in their neighborhoods. . . . A likely reason is the close working relationship Italian-American and Jewish gangsters maintained with pre-Castro Cubans in Havana. . . . The Cubans are moving rapidly upward in organized crime and are rarely found on the street level for very long. Again, like the Italians, most Cuban organized crime figures have legitimate fronts to cover and augment their crime activities.[51]

Yet with the possible exception of drugs, most observers do not think there has been Hispanic penetration of the stable criminal networks.

As in many other poor communities, crime is a difficult and painful aspect of life in Hispanic *barrios*. Hispanics are significantly more likely than non-Hispanics to be victims of robbery, personal theft, burglary, and petty household larcenies. Weapons are more likely to be involved when crimes are committed against His-

---

[48] E. Casavantes, *El Tecato: Cultural and Sociologic Factors Affecting Drug Use Among Chicanos* (Washington, D.C.: National Council of Spanish Speaking Mental Health Organizations, 1976).

[49] E. Preble, "Social and Cultural Factors Related to Narcotics Use Among Puerto Ricans in New York City," *International Journal of the Addictions*, Vol. 1 (1966), pp. 30–41.

[50] Francis Ianni, *Black Mafia: Ethnic Succession in Organized Crime* (New York: Simon & Schuster, 1974).

[51] Ibid., 203–204.

panics than when crimes are committed against Anglos.[52] This difference may help to explain the high level of fatalities associated with Hispanic crime in New York City. Almost a fifth of the Puerto Rican deaths of persons aged 15 to 44 were homicides. Hispanics were 22 percent of the homicide victims in the state, although only 5 percent of the population.[53]

Life history accounts give some idea of the importance of an illegal economy in New York City—affecting many Puerto Ricans. Money is spent and earned in the numbers racket; family members may be involved in drug addiction and low-level narcotics dealing, and "hot" or stolen merchandise makes desired goods readily available.[54] Lest the portrait generate too much disgust, it should be recalled that penny gambling is fairly widespread in the United States; that low-level dealing in illegal drugs can be found in most high schools in the nation, and that stolen goods are openly peddled in many middle-class and Anglo settings as well as in poor Hispanic communities. Poor families in the large cities often manage to combine several sources of income to eke out an existence. Work in the secondary labor market does not provide enough income to sustain families, and often minimum wage labor is all that is available to a Hispanic household head. Family income may be supplemented if a member receives Social Security payments, or disability or unemployment compensation, and is further stretched by participation in the illicit economy. Life in the *barrios* does not lead people to think in terms of lucrative careers in the world of work; rather, the emphasis is on survival and making do through a variety of expedients. Petty property crime expands the Hispanic populations in the prisons and is tightly linked to poverty.[55]

[52] U.S. Department of Justice, *The Hispanic Victim*, Advance Report (Washington, D.C.: Bureau of Justice Statistics, June 1980).

[53] Sissons, *The Hispanic Experience*, p. 31.

[54] Susan Sheehan, *A Welfare Mother* (Boston: Houghton Mifflin, 1976).

[55] See Moore et al., *Homeboys*, Ch. 1, for a discussion of this economy. See also Paul Bullock, *Aspiration vs. Opportunity* (Ann Arbor, Mich.: Institute of Labor and Industrial Relations, 1973), for an analysis of the importance of the illegal economy in the calculations of poor Chicano and black adolescents in Los Angeles, and Bettylou Valentine, *Hustling and Other Hard Work* (New York: The Free Press, 1979) for an analysis of parallel processes in a black urban community.

CHAPTER SIX
THE HISPANIC COMMUNITY: STABILITY AND CHANGE

Families, communities, and churches are the most important social structures of the Hispanics, just as of any other ethnic group. Families, communities, and churches of immigrants have preoccupied social scientists for a very long time. This interest stems from the idea that America is a nation of immigrants, each group with its distinctive culture and its own institutions. There was also an assumption: economic opportunity would expand forever, and there would always be mobility up the ladder to a better life. In the process, all but the barest traces of non-American origin would vanish. So inevitable was this process (according to the model) that in the 1940s, it was possible to outline a detailed timetable for its happening. The class system would dissolve ethnic institutions. Who would want to be ethnic if it also meant being poor?

This timetable for assimilation was based on a "measurable" similarity between the larger American society and the institutions of the immigrants. The closer the match, the faster the process. Thus, the quickest to assimilate would be the Western Europeans, particularly English-speaking Protestants. Next in speed would come the immigrants from southern and eastern Europe. Then the Latin Americans—the Hispanics who were racially mixed but somewhat resembled the Mediterranean Catholics.[1]

Even in the 1940s there was one nagging exception to the timetable: Ameri-

---

[1]W. Lloyd Warner and Leo Srole, *The Social System of American Ethnic Groups* (New Haven, Conn.: Yale University Press, 1945).

can-born blacks. It was obvious that the timetable was not working for them. To account for this exception, blacks were seen as a group of people locked into a castelike system, and for a time, at least, the idea of caste seemed adequate. But the trouble came when it was realized that too many exceptions were showing up. American Indians were an exception. Then, when Puerto Ricans began to arrive on the mainland in large numbers, they, too, became an exception. But the exception approach used for Indians and for Puerto Ricans was much less excusable for the millions of Mexican Americans living in the Southwest. It was perfectly obvious from the most superficial observation that Chicanos were not a caste, nor did they fit into the assimilation timetable. Among other discrepancies, there were Spanish-American settlements holding firmly to their own way of life since their arrival in the seventeenth century.

It was obvious that Hispanic and other minorities' social structure and culture were persistent enough to call for new theories. One set was based on the experiences of former European colonies. The situation of Mexicans and Puerto Ricans, in particular, seemed to be similar to those of colonial and postcolonial societies. It had some flaws, this "internal colonialism" model, but the resemblance to reality was striking. Internal colonialism was an analogy that drew attention to old structures and to emerging social structures that were otherwise easy to overlook if one focused exclusively on assimilation. The race and caste analogy was too narrow a conceptualization.[2] In particular the "internal colonialism" model called attention to the critical role of Anglo institutions (see Chapter 8) and stopped the easy practice of blaming the culture.

Almost all discussion and research into Hispanic social structures and cultural forms is now controversial. The very idea of "persistence" of structure and culture seemed to imply that such persistence was hampering social mobility. It is seen as a tendency to blame Hispanics for their failure in the class system. This has been most particularly a concern, for example, in studies of the Hispanic family. Many are interpreted as being critical of the Hispanic family. The often vehement defense of Hispanic family structure (usually by Hispanic social scientists) has its uses. It serves to identify aspects of family functioning that may be concealed from ethnocentric, Anglo-oriented social scientists who are not directly familiar with Hispanic family dynamics.[3] A similar defensiveness is sometimes found in studies about culture, especially *machismo,* about the persistence of the Spanish language, and other features of distinctively Hispanic institutions and cultural practices, if they seem to be viewed solely as a handicap.

Hispanic institutions can also be viewed as social and moral units that stand in

[2] For more details of this interesting controversy, see Joan Moore, "Internal Colonialism: The Case of the Mexican Americans," *Social Problems,* Vol. 19 (1970), pp. 463–72; Robert Blauner, *Racial Oppression in America* (New York: Harper & Row, 1972); and Edward Murguia, *Assimilation, Colonialism and the Mexican American People* (Austin: University of Texas Press, 1975). For a critique, see Joan Moore, "American Minorities and 'New Nation' Perspectives," *Pacific Sociological Review,* Vol. 19 (1976), pp. 447–67.

[3] A good example is Jaime Sena Rivera, "Extended Kinship in the United States: Competing Models and the Case of La Familia Chicana," *Journal of Marriage and the Family,* Vol. 41 (1979), pp. 121–129, which explicitly criticizes the notion that extended kinship can be measured by household composition. Such a measure is easy to obtain, but fails to recognize the complex bonds that unite members of large-scale Chicano kin networks.

symbolic opposition to the dehumanization and depersonalizing demands of the dominant society. Thus family, community, language, and culture are a source of pride for many Hispanics. Often, they are explicitly contrasted to an Anglo culture and an Anglo family structure that is seen as cold, shallow, and uncaring.

In the material that follows in this chapter, we must guard against any tendency to stereotype in a negative fashion when we compare Hispanic structures and ideals with an equally stereotyped (and idealized) Anglo middle-class norm. It is almost as important to be on guard against romanticized positive stereotypes. Yet another precaution. It must be remembered that the institutions of Hispanic communities are changing. Some changes are the consequence of urbanization. Some changes result from the class status of Hispanics. And there are changes simply because many young people move closer to the dominant society and new migrants continue to come in. Thus when Hispanic family life or Hispanic community life is discussed, we are forced to capture and to dissect a cross section of a condition that is living, changing, and anything but uniform.

COMMUNITY, GENERATION, AND CLASS

Communities and "the community."   There are two ways of thinking about the "Chicano community" or the "Puerto Rican community." Most people immediately think of the most dense settlement of Hispanics in their city, usually a mixture of poor people and people with relatively modest incomes. But the word "community" also has another implication, especially for Hispanics, and evokes the sense of all Hispanics who identify with *la raza* no matter where they might live—or what their class status may be. Furthermore, there is no doubt but that in every large city Hispanics live in far more widely dispersed residential settlements than do other minorities (see Chapter 4).

Let us consider one of the largest Hispanic communities in the United States as an illustration of the two concepts of community. This is Los Angeles with some 2½ million Hispanics. (More people of Mexican descent live in Los Angeles than in any other city except Mexico City and Guadalajara. New York City also has more Puerto Ricans than any city, even in the island of Puerto Rico.)

First, the territorial communities. Los Angeles has grown enormously since the late 1920s when its citizens of Mexican origin first began to appear in large numbers. (Los Angeles was founded by a Mexican expedition and remained a Mexican city until the late nineteenth century, but there were few inhabitants of any ethnicity until much later.) In the 40 years from 1928 to 1968, Los Angeles grew with great speed. A regional trading center became an economic center of national and international importance. Slowly, and with many setbacks, Mexicans were caught up in its expansion. Two of these setbacks were the Mexican repatriations of the early depression years and the serious and recurrent clashes with police highlighted by the "zoot suit" riots of the early 1940s. The original Mexican settlements appeared around the downtown Plaza and in a variety of work camps scattered throughout the metropolitan area. As the *barrios* expanded, Mexicans moved both into new housing built in agricultural lands and sometimes into areas where old residents were displaced. Sometimes the movement resembled the traditional "invasion-succession" cycles familiar to students of ethnic ecology in Eastern cities. Mexican settlements were consolidated, leaving a scattered residue of non-Mexican people and non-Mexican institutions.[4] But in some parts of the Los Angeles area, the *barrios* were isolated by a huge influx of new Anglo residents. This happened on a large scale shortly after World War II when the opening up of the San Fernando Valley to thousands of tract homes swamped the old *barrios* of the fruit workers. The *barrios* became completely surrounded by the new cities of Los Angeles suburbia. The San Fernando *barrios* have not yet merged into one massive settlement. "East Los Angeles," the enormous extension of the original Mexican settlement near downtown, represents such a merger of separate *barrios.*

Yet another contrast appears in some of the Chicano settlements near the Pacific Ocean. As time passed, this land became increasingly valuable. Now expensive homes and condominiums have virtually squeezed the smaller *barrios* out of existence. The Hispanic residents sell their homes, often at very good prices, and move elsewhere.[5] But *barrios,* as distinct areas of concentration, are only part of the story of Hispanic communities in Los Angeles. As long ago as 1960, almost a third of the Mexicans in Los Angeles lived in neighborhoods that were predominantly Anglo (85 percent or more). Another third lived in neighborhoods of mixed ethnic composition—from 55 to 84 percent Anglo. Only about a third lived in concentrated *barrios.*[6] Virtually any large city will show the same concentration of Hispanics in an identifiable area, mostly poor and working class. Here will be found Hispanic food stores, restaurants, *bodegas, farmacías,* and other ethnic supplies and services. But many, if not the majority of, Hispanics in these cities will live outside those concentrated areas. A terminology to describe the two kinds of people comes from the sociologist Alex Simirenko.[7] He used the word "frontier" for the predominantly nonethnic areas and "colony" for the predominantly ethnic areas. He noted that the Russian colonists lived in the area immediately around the Russian Orthodox church: here remained most of the traditionalists. Using census data, José Hernández documented this kind of pattern for Puerto Ricans in the 1950s.[8] But choosing to remain in the colony does not mean that an ethnic person is not occupationally mobile. Nor are the ethnic frontiersmen necessarily mobile. Middle-class people may live in colonies and poor people in frontiers, although generally there is a close association between poverty and the colony and higher income and the frontier. (This is an important reason why Hispanics are likely to be seen as predominantly poor. Many of the poor are concentrated in a visible community, and the middle class are dispersed.)

[4] For more details of this process, in three communities, see Joan W. Moore et al., *Homeboys: Gangs, Drugs, and Prison in the Barrios of Los Angeles* (Philadelphia: Temple University Press, 1978), and Ricardo Romo, *East Los Angeles: The History of a Barrio* (Austin: University of Texas, 1983) for a general history of this massive Mexican American concentration.

[5] In 1983, the *Los Angeles Times* printed a series of vignettes of Latinos in the Los Angeles metropolitan area, which captures this range: *Southern California's Latino Community, 1983.*

[6] Leo Grebler, Joan Moore, and Ralph Guzmán, *The Mexican American People* (New York: The Free Press, 1970), p. 305.

[7] The terms were used in a study of second-generation Russians in a midwest city. See Alex Simirenko, *Pilgrims, Colonists, and Frontiersmen* (New York and London: The Free Press and Collier-Macmillan, 1964).

[8] J. Hernández-Alvarez, "The Movement and Settlement of Puerto Rican Migrants Within the United States, 1950–1960, " *International Migration Review,* Vol. 2 (1968), pp. 40–52.

Research in Los Angeles and San Antonio in the 1960s showed that Chicanos living in the colonies or *barrios* are more likely to use other Mexican Americans as both a membership group and as a reference group. Those living in the ethnic frontiers are more likely to use Anglos. The value of the phrase "more likely" varies from city to city. The deciding factor apparently is the openness of the Anglos in the city to involvement with Hispanics, along with certain historical features of the Hispanic communities. In Los Angeles, for example, 66 percent of the frontier respondents reported that the friends of their children were predominantly or all Anglo, compared with 34 percent in San Antonio. Many fewer residents of the colonies reported that either they or their children were close to Anglo friends. The work environment for people in the colonies is heavily fellow ethnics. The ethnicity of the boss was more likely to be Anglo in Los Angeles (73 percent) than in San Antonio (29 percent). Hispanic adults and children in the dense *barrios* in all cities are less likely to have predominantly Anglo friends and workmates, but the differences between cities are very important. If involvement with Anglos is a measure of assimilation, then we can see how importantly assimilation depends on the nature of the larger system, with all of its important regional and local variations. The final measure of assimilation is, of course, intermarriage, and we will see shortly how this varies by city.

Now let us consider the symbolic community. This great involvement of Hispanics in the frontiers does not mean they cease to identify with the local and national Hispanic "community," although there are Hispanics who see their ethnicity as purely a private matter. (There are also Hispanics in any large city who immigrated as middle-class individuals, some of whom vehemently reject identification. This is especially true if the immigrants are from white nations, like Argentina, and the largest local Hispanic community is darker Mexican or Caribbean.) On the other hand, it is almost impossible for a *barrio* resident to deny identification as a Hispanic. Indeed, some are so strongly attached to their local *barrio* that they may even refuse a good job if it requires relocation. Regardless of these variations in self-concept, it is important to understand that a "Hispanic community" does transcend local residence and stretches to include many people far outside the *barrios* (see Chapter 1 on identity).

Generation. In most American ethnic groups, the term "generation" refers to nativity in reference to the homeland. Thus "first-generation" people are immigrants from the homeland; the "second generation" refers to their children, and so on, and each successive generation is more acculturated. For the Hispanics of the United States, there are important reasons for not always assuming that successive generations show ever-increasing acculturation and assimilation into the larger society. Because Hispanics are one of the few American ethnic groups still immigrating in large numbers, the relationship of Hispanics to their community is far more complex in terms of legal status, age, and class than with most other ethnic groups. Italians, for example, by now are nearly always old people. Also (and most different from European ethnics), there are Hispanics who were living in the United States long before Anglos, are tenth-generation Americans, and are still largely unacculturated.

First-generation immigrants are complex in terms of *legal status*—and this is confounded with national origin. There are four major types of legal status: island-born Puerto Ricans (who are American citizens), refugees, legal immigrants (tempo-rary and permanent), and undocumented immigrants (temporary and permanent). Legal status can make a great deal of difference to the communities. Neither island-born Puerto Ricans nor Cuban refugees have any fears about deportation, while one recent study found that many Mexican immigrants are "fearful of deportation even when they have legal status in this country."[9]

There is substantial controversy about the impact of undocumented Hispanics on the Hispanic communities. One argument is that they retain strong ties to their homeland—and do not try to adapt to the United States because they have no stake in the country. (They are "sojourners.")[10] One study in San Francisco supporting this view found a community of immigrants (legal and undocumented) from a small agricultural community in Jalisco. Continuous migration and visiting back and forth to the home village, combined with an enormous contempt for Anglos, Chicanos, other Hispanics (and even other Mexicans), built strong social-cultural walls around the community, which the researcher calls "what is in many respects an extraterri-torial extension of their home village."[11] A somewhat greater degree of accommo-dation to U.S. society was found among undocumented Mexicans in southern California, in a pattern called "binationalism." These people may work for years in the United States and maintain residences in both countries; they may still think of their sojourn in the United States as temporary, oriented to the needs of an ex-tended family, and largely economic.[12] There are also undocumented workers who come to the United States to establish themselves permanently. Temporary immi-grants often live in truly miserable conditions, with six or more male workers living in a tiny two- or three-room apartment in a slum hotel near downtown Los Angeles.[13] Immigrant workers with families tend to share rents with other families or boarders, a compound household arrangement that makes it possible for even undocumented persons to have their families with them.[14]

We know very little about the role of immigrant Hispanics in the *barrios*. Yet there is no question that such a concentration continuously reinforces home-land patterns. The continuing large volume of Hispanic immigration makes this im-

[9]Daniel Ramirez, "Legal Residents and Naturalization: A Pilot Study," report prepared for the Mexican American Legal Defense and Education Fund, Davis, California (Davis: Uni-versity of California Press, 1979), p. 8. This report, along with many other published and unpublished studies, is cited in Wayne Cornelius, Leo Chávez, and Jorge Castro, *Mexican Immi-grants and Southern California: A Summary of Current Knowledge* (La Jolla: University of California, Center for U.S.-Mexican Studies, 1982). See also G. Hendricks, *The Dominican Diaspora* (New York: Teachers College Press, 1974) on the role of undocumented Dominicans in New York.

[10]The term "sojourners" is used especially for Chinese patterns of settlement and is also useful for many Latin American immigrants.

[11]Laura Zarrugh, "Home Away from Home: The Jacalan Community in the San Fran-cisco Bay Area," in S. A. West and J. Macklin, eds., *The Chicano Experience* (Boulder, Colo.: Westview Press, 1979), pp. 145–165.

[12]Reynaldo Baca and Dexter Bryan, "The 'Assimilation' of Unauthorized Mexican Workers: Another Social Science Fiction?" *Hispanic Journal of the Behavioral Sciences*, Vol. 5 (1983), pp. 1–20.

[13]See Michael J. Piore, *Birds of Passage* (New York: Cambridge University Press, 1979), pp. 55, 62.

[14]Cornelius et al., *Mexican Immigrants and Southern California*, p. 51.

portant. One result is that a second or third-generation Hispanic who lives in the *barrio* is virtually forced to speak Spanish. This has always been true for Hispanic communities. Undocumented Hispanics who gain a foothold in the United States (most are discovered and expelled very shortly after entry) are occupationally mobile. Several studies find that almost half of them gain semiskilled jobs.[15] The undocumented are thus not a permanent drag on the Hispanic communities nor do they move into welfare dependency, but unquestionably they add to cultural maintenance in the *barrios*.

The meaning of "generations" in the Puerto Rican communities also departs from the conventional categories based on the European immigrant experience. Puerto Ricans move back and forth to the island quite freely, and there is no simple move toward acculturation at home or on the mainland. However, the symbolic value attached to identification with the mainland versus the island means that the "Nuyorican" (while he may often visit Puerto Rico) is much more accepting of his mainland culture and identity, regardless of his appearance to an Anglo observer. Puerto Ricans in both New York and Puerto Rico are not candidates for assimilation in the traditional sense. Some observers of the Puerto Rican community argue that it is more accurate to say that Puerto Ricans live as a colonized minority in both New York and Puerto Rico[16] or that acculturation has affected Puerto Ricans on the island as much as on the mainland. Thus Puerto Ricans are different from other Hispanic immigrants.

The question of generation is even more irrelevant in dealing with the history and legal status of the preconquest Spanish Americans of northern New Mexico and southern Colorado. These Hispanics follow traditional rural occupations, often speak English with difficulty if at all, and appear to be more traditional than some of the new immigrants from Mexico. In this area, generations mean changes, but not adoption of an urban American life-style. These are a people who adjusted first to a colonial society hard-pressed by hostile Indians and then to an isolated and alienated minority status under the first American governments. Economic circumstances are now threatening their very livelihood. These changes and adaptations do not by any means imply "acculturation" in its conventional meaning, even though these earliest settlers in the Southwest have lived in the United States for many generations.[17] Spanish Americans in New Mexico and Colorado are conscious of

---

[15] Ibid., pp. 81–82. Maurice Van Arsdol, Joan Moore, David Heer, and Susan Haynie compared occupations in Mexico and the United States for undocumented workers and found that only 20 percent of Mexican white-collar workers held similar jobs in the United States but that 60 percent of the undocumented who had blue-collar jobs in Mexico obtained jobs at comparable levels in the United States—largely skilled and semiskilled workers. See their *Non-Apprehended and Apprehended Undocumented Residents in the Los Angeles Labor Market* (Los Angeles: University of Southern California, Population Research Laboratory, 1979).

[16] Juan Flores, John Attinasi, and Pedro Pedraza, Jr., "La Carreta Made a U-Turn: Puerto Rican Language and Culture in the United States," *Daedalus*, Vol. 110, no. 2 (Spring 1981), pp. 193–218; E. Seda Bonilla, "Que somos: puertoriqueños, neoriqueños, o nuyoriqueños?" *The Rican*, Vol. 2 (1975), pp. 81–107; and D. Lindorff, "The New Wave from Puerto Rico," *New York*, Vol. 15 (1982), pp. 12–13, for a recent "flood."

[17] See Florence R. Kluckhohn and Fred L. Strodtbeck, *Variations in Value Orientations* (Evanston, Ill.: Row, Peterson, 1961), for an account of traditional life in a Spanish-American village. Note especially Kluckhohn's account of the changes she observed in the village culture between her first research trip in the late 1930s and her later visit in the 1950s.

generational differences in a different form. Here people can distinguish between families that entered the Southwest with the first wave of Mexican immigration after the Oñate expedition of 1598 and the "late" waves of the seventeenth and eighteenth centuries. These are distinctions that are recorded, memorized, and passed along from generation to generation.[18] For a New Mexican, a name like Baca, Chávez, Roybal, or Montoya evokes a particular lineage. These charter member *manitos* are proud to distinguish themselves from the newer immigrants from Mexico, using clear-cut criteria of "generation."[19]

Class differences.   But, still, it is true that generations are associated generally with upward mobility in the class system. Further, generations are associated with dispersal to the ethnic frontiers and away from the colonies. There is only a modest degree of occupational mobility, to be sure, particularly for the sons and daughters of laborers. Yet the movement into white collar and professional occupations is strong enough to mean a strong middle-class element that is always found in cities with relatively large concentrations of Hispanics. However, a fairly high proportion of the middle class may be the children of middle-class parents.[20]

As we discover in dealing with questions of generation, class is very complex among Hispanics. In New Mexico the middle-class persons may have been "middle class" long before any U.S. settlers arrived, because this state had a fully established Mexican class system. New Mexico has always had Hispanic political and business leaders who often intermarried with Anglos but who nonetheless remained firm in their old upper-class lineage. Yet another example is provided by the "Canary Islanders" of San Antonio. Shortly after San Antonio was founded in 1691, one group of settlers from the Canary Islands was given the equivalent of a patent of nobility and declared *hijos dalgo* (aristocrats) by the Spanish Crown.[21] Ever since, the Canary Islanders distinguished themselves from the "Mexicans" around them, and they became a significant segment of the upper-status "Spanish" in San Antonio. In every major city of the Southwest, there are remnants of this seventeenth- and eighteenth-century colonial Hispanic aristocracy.

In Santa Barbara, California (to name only one of many cities), an elaborate fiesta is staged every year that pays homage (as do the names of the streets) to the

---

[18] See Fray Angélico Chávez, *Origins of New Mexico Families* (Santa Fe: The Historical Society of New Mexico, 1954), for a compilation of family histories arranged by "wave." Tourists may still see graffiti with Spanish names from these early expeditions carved deeply into a rock on the trail in western New Mexico.

[19] When the U.S. Census began to use self-enumeration and mailed forms, these distinctions became important. As noted in Chapter 4, many New Mexicans refuse to identify themselves as "Mexican origin" persons on 1980 census forms, preferring "other Spanish," even though many refer to themselves in Spanish as *Mexicanos*. A. J. Jaffe et al., in *The Changing Demography of Spanish Americans* (New York: Academic Press, 1980), are among the few scholars who discuss this group apart from Mexican Americans, although there are many problems with their identifiers.

[20] Matthew Snipp and Marta Tienda, "New Perspectives of Chicano Intergenerational Occupational Mobility," *The Social Science Journal*, Vol. 19 (1982), pp. 37–50. Male and female workers were combined for purposes of this analysis.

[21] Sister Frances Jerome Woods, *Mexican Ethnic Leadership in San Antonio, Texas* (Washington, D.C.: Catholic University of America Press, 1949), p. 12. She gives an interesting historical analysis of the social structure of the Mexican-American community of San Antonio.

original Spanish settlers. Los Angeles is reverential to its del Valles, Ortegas, and descendants of the Dominguez-Watson families—only a few names from an elite group calling itself "First Century Families." In general, however, outside New Mexico the descendants of the elite Hispanic families intermarried so heavily with Anglo families that an Hispanic elite is never a separate element of any local upper-status group. It is considered rather a nice seasoning to the mystique of the pre-dominantly Anglo upper class in San Francisco, Santa Barbara, and Los Angeles.

Outside this relic of early colonial days in the Southwest, the Hispanic wealthy and powerful are few and far between. But they do exist. Bebe Rebozo, the friend of President Nixon, and D. Tirso de Junco, head of California's Republican Party, are reminders that many wealthy and professional Cubans came during the exodus to Miami and that they continue to exert influence and to make money in the United States. In New York, upper-status Hispanics (like the Dominican designer Oscar de la Renta) form part of the fashionable scene. But much of the limited wealth gained among Hispanics comes out of the ethnic base. A well-established doctor with a successful *barrio* clinic in East Los Angeles operates a million-dollar ranch. A successful auto dealer invests heavily in urban real estate and does very well. A successful manufacturer of Mexican foodstuffs becomes treasurer of the United States under President Nixon. There are successful film actors, recording stars, sports figures, television actors—and so on. There are few fortunes made in mainstream corporate America. In fact, there are virtually no Hispanics on the boards of large American corporations, but Hispanic entrepreneurship is so lively that by 1983 the top 100 Hispanic businesses were outgrossing the top 100 black businesses, and for small businesses as well as large, the picture generally is one of vigorous growth.[22]

All the older Hispanic elites reflect the racist tendencies of the colonies of old Spain and the United States. "Pureblood" aristocracies means no admixture of Indian blood. One of the long-standing consequences was a pattern for social acceptability that for a century kept many upwardly mobile Texas and California Mexican Americans resolutely claiming "pure" Spanish ancestry, denying any association with Mexicans. However, the recent decade of the Chicano movement had a considerable impact on such attitudes. The movement quite consciously attempted to legitimate stereotyped lower-class and *cholo* cultural attributes. (There were parallels among Puerto Ricans.) It was no longer necessary to be "pureblooded" or to talk of "pure" culture. (Many established middle-class Hispanics found such ideas repellent, and occasionally, even now, a "respectable" Mexican American will express outrage at being called by the despised term "Chicano.") This period also brought many young Hispanics to college—far more than ever before. At a time of heightened social awareness among all college youth, class distinctions began to lose some of their nastier edges.

Social concerns were reflected in occupational choices. Like blacks, Hispanic professionals and white-collar groups work disproportionately in service occupations. Hispanics work somewhat more for private industry than does the black middle class. Thus they probably depend somewhat less than do blacks on jobs

---

[22] Jesús Chavarria, testimony, Hearings Before the Subcommittee on Census and Population, September 13–15, 1983, 98th Cong. (Washington, D.C.: U.S. Government Printing Office, 1983, p. 163).

created in the public sector by affirmative action.[23] Yet this involvement in the community is important for the people in the *barrios*. Organized Hispanic mental health workers, social workers, and other human service professionals reflect not only the "new" middle class but also pressure to improve services for Hispanics.

But there is another element in the Hispanic middle class that is much more ambivalent. These are the middle-class immigrants, Latin Americans who arrive in this country as mature, middle-class adults and often want little to do with the poor masses of *la raza*. Latin and Central Americans have been involved in most Hispanic organizations on the East Coast and on the national level. But all too often there is mutual rejection—that is, the local poor Hispanics will reject the local middle-class Chilean, and vice versa. A poignant illustration occurred in the Puerto Rican community in the 1980s. A series of setbacks—including the serious recession of the early 1980s, acute economic problems in Puerto Rico, and a heavy influx of Cuban refugees and other middle-class Caribbean immigrants to Puerto Rico—shut down many college opportunities for Puerto Rican college graduates. Middle-class Puerto Ricans began to leave the island in relatively large numbers—large enough to create concern about a "brain drain." Stateside recruiters were drawing trained people away, and a large number of professionals were migrating not just to New York City and its immediate area but to other job opportunities throughout the nation. But they did not, in general, live in the *barrios* or even near them. And they had little or no sense of identification with mainland-born Puerto Ricans who had struggled a very great distance to obtain professional degrees. One journalist reported on the contrary that there was much competition between the two groups. Further, the incoming Puerto Rican professionals were rather pleased to be taken for nationalities other than Puerto Rican. In commenting on this migration, Angelo Falcón, director of the Institute for Puerto Rican Policy said, "All we can conclude at this point is that the 'new' migration may only serve to increase Puerto Rican frustration with the American experience."[24]

The Cubans in Miami represent yet another peculiarity in terms of class. As successive waves of refugees entered the United States (Chapter 2), "Little Havana" came more and more to replicate the class structure of pre–Castro Cuba, from the very top down to the street people, with accompanying racial variations.

THE HISPANIC FAMILY: DIVERSITY AND A COMMON THEME

The analysis of Hispanic family life is quite generally centered on the question of change and whether the Hispanic family (as a distinctive institution in the community) has helped or hindered the Hispanic community's well-being and develop-

[23] Thus, 45.7 percent of Puerto Rican professionals, 50.4 percent of Chicano professionals, and 58.6 percent of black professionals were employed in the public sector. Among clerical workers, 33.5 percent of the Puerto Ricans, 35.6 percent of the Chicanos, and 40.6 percent of the blacks were employed in the public sector. (Unpublished tabulation of data from the *1976 Survey of Income and Education* performed by Joan Moore).

[24] Howard Bray, "The New Wave of Puerto Rican Immigrants," *The New York Times Magazine,* July 3, 1983, pp. 22, 26, 33–34, and Angelo Falcón, letter to the editor, *The New York Times Magazine,* August 7, 1983.

ment in the United States. Both questions take for granted the rather doubtful assumption that there is such a thing as *the* Hispanic family. This assumption is rooted in an idealization of the Latin American origins, and we will discuss this, first, using some research findings from Latin American countries. Then we will examine contemporary variations found in the United States. The evidence for change and for stability will be considered, focusing on the role of women, the position of the aged, and intermarriage.

Background for the Hispanic American family.   Substantial research is available on family structure and characteristics in Puerto Rico. More limited research has been done in Mexico, particularly with village families.[25] The studies do show some common themes, but there are substantial differences when class and national background vary.

First, consider the common themes, stemming from the Spanish colonial period. Hispanics are familistic: that is, they value family relationships so highly that family well-being takes priority over individual well-being. But the word "family" means not only the nuclear parent-child family, but an extended family of several generations, including cousins. These relationships are supposed to be emotionally and financially supportive. Familistic feelings go beyond blood kin to the godparents of the family's children. Godparents are chosen not only for baptism, but for other rites of passage as well and are drawn from a pool of friends of the family (or from relatives or superiors, depending on the situation). Godparentage (*compadrazgo*) in this traditional system is a method of knitting the community together and of formalizing informal ties of friendship. A man and the godfather of his child become *compadres*. *Compadrazgo* is more important as a tie between two age peers than it is as a religious belief or as a tie between godparent and godchild. (As a religious act, it formally symbolizes a promise by the godparent that the child will be brought up as a Christian should anything happen to the child's parents.) The practice is universal throughout many Christian denominations and is elaborated in similar fashion in Mediterranean as well as Hispanic countries.

Another common theme: the Hispanic family is patriarchal; that is, authority is vested in the male head of the family. There are several corollaries. The complex of values known as *machismo* is perhaps the best known. *Machismo* is a particular cultural definition of masculinity, with implications for women as well. *Machismo* has been associated with a strong double standard of sexual morality, with masculinity to be demonstrated through displays of physical and sexual prowess, even

[25]The studies of Mexican families include N. S. Hayner, "Notes on the Changing Mexican Family," *American Sociological Review,* Vol. 7 (1942), pp. 489–497, and "The Family in Mexico," *Marriage and Family Living,* Vol. 16 (1954), pp. 369–373; Norman Humphrey, "Family Patterns in a Mexican Middletown," *Social Service Review,* Vol. 26 (1952), pp. 195–201; and Rogélio Diaz-Guerrero, *Psychology of the Mexican Culture and Personality* (Austin: University of Texas Press, 1975). For Puerto Rico, see the sources cited in the summary by Sidney W. Mintz, "Puerto Rico: An Essay in the Definition of National Culture," in F. Cordasco and E. Bucchioni, eds., *The Puerto Rican Experience* (Totowa, N.J.: Littlefield, Adams, 1973). Particularly interesting are the studies that compare Mexican and island Puerto Rican family values as did R. Fernandez-Marina, E. D. Maldonado Sierra, and R. D. Trent, "Three Basic Themes in Mexican and Puerto Rican Family Values," *Journal of Social Psychology,* Vol. 48 (1958), pp. 167–181. This study found that Puerto Rican middle-class families were closer to those of Mexico than to those of the United States.

outside marriage.[26] (This practice is by no means confined to lower-class men. It has been common among upper-class Latin Americans, even to the point of maintaining a separate household—the "outside family.") "Good" women are to be kept chaste until marriage, and their sexuality (and much of their other activity) is restricted to the marital role. It is felt that women's most meaningful relationships should be within the family. Ideally, women's social relationships and recreation should consist solely of visits to cousins and other relatives. "Bad" women, on the other hand, are available for sexual pleasure, not for marriage.

This common theme with regard to the status of women differs slightly in Mexico and Puerto Rico. But there are still strong common threads. For the Mexican;

> A contemporary [feminist Mexican] writer, Juana Armando Alegria, asserts that the vast majority of Mexican women, now and in the past, accept and have accepted without protest their role as "champions of suffering" at the hands of demeaning and domineering men. Undoubtedly *machismo* ("extreme male dominance") and its counterpart *hembrismo* ("extreme female submission") have been pervasive in Mexico, in part because of the Aztec subordination of women and even more because of the Spanish colonial experience. . . . Yet, women in pre-Columbian and Spanish colonial society played a crucial role in the economy, ran large households, and participated actively in religious life. In addition, women found emotional support from the network of female relationships with the extended family that mitigated feelings of subordination and victimization.[27]

Tolerance for masculine infidelity is common to both national cultures. In Mexico, such tolerance is built into the late nineteenth century laws in Mexico.

Macias argues that *machismo* was especially pronounced in Mexico, compared with other Hispanic countries. There is also some evidence that Puerto Rican women are allowed substantially more freedom for independent achievement. More women than men now attend the University of Puerto Rico, for example.[28]

The question of *machismo* is one of the major sources of controversy about the Hispanic family. Some researchers condemn it as close to pathological, and the traits associated with *machismo* are seen as compensation for feelings of inferiority.[29] On the other hand there are experts who claim that such a view of *machismo* is a caricature and that "an important part of . . . *machismo* . . . is that of using authority within the family in a just and fair manner."[30] Neither side of the contro-

---

[26] Maria Lucero Trujillo summarizes the positive and negative aspects of *machismo* in "The Terminology of *Machismo*," *De Colores,* Vol. 4 (1978), pp. 34–42.

[27] Anna Macias, *Against All Odds: The Feminist Movement in Mexico to 1940* (Westport, Conn.: Greenwood Press, 1982), p. 3.

[28] Edward Christiansen, "The Puerto Rican Woman: A Profile," in Edna Costa-Belén, ed., *The Puerto Rican Woman* (New York: Praeger, 1979).

[29] These traits include (in addition to an emphasis on sexuality and physical aggressiveness) a stress on emotional detachment. Analogously, the mother becomes involved and self-sacrificing. See O. Giraldo, "El Machismo como Fenómeno Psicocultural," *Revista Latino-Americana de Psicologia,* Vol. 4 (1972), pp. 274–309.

[30] Nathan Murillo, "The Mexican Family," in N. Wagner and M. Haug, eds., *Chicanos: Social and Psychological Perspectives* (St. Louis: C. V. Mosby, 1971).

versy denies that the traditional Hispanic family is one in which women are considered not only appropriately subordinate but also emotional, rather than rational. Furthermore, the segregation of males and females is important: they live in separate realms with little communication.

Machismo is also related to the Hispanic emphasis upon respect (*respeto*), which implies that a man with certain qualities of *machismo* is a man who can command respect. Elders also should command deference. The man of respect (*hombre de respeto*) can therefore be contrasted to *relajo*—a vulnerability to shame or being put down. All these are components of manliness.[31]

It is argued that Mexican family structure is influenced by Indian (and especially Aztec) predecessors of the Spanish *conquistadores*.[32] It is supposed that Puerto Rican family structure, by contrast, is less influenced by Indian roots (because the Caribbean Indians were eliminated early) than by African elements from the slave population.[33] More important, however, is the general agreement that the family structure of Puerto Rican Island residents is profoundly influenced by almost a century of American occupation. *Machismo,* in particular, is changing. One Puerto Rican study, for example, centered on the late 1940s and the late 1950s in a rural community and concluded that migration had destroyed the patriarchal structure of the family in this relatively isolated community. Women and young people alike no longer were sustaining traditional roles.[34]

A somewhat different view of family patterns in both Puerto Rico and Mexico appears in the work of the anthropologist Oscar Lewis, who researched both societies.[35] Lewis became convinced early in his career that too many generalizations about family structure were based on what people said rather than on direct observations of behavior. After living with Mexican peasant families he noted that the patriarchal principles that informants claimed were "normal" were, in fact, violated routinely. After observing poor families in Mexico City and San Juan (and also Puerto Ricans in New York City), he argued that certain conditions of urban slum life produce a "culture of poverty" that transcends national cultures. These conditions include high unemployment, a cash economy, low wages, and the failure of the larger system to provide a stable political organization for the poor. In addition, Lewis argued, the society must have a kinship system that allows both men and women to have a voice in the family. Most important, there must be a class system that is believed to be based on personal superiority or inferiority. The cul-

---

[31] A. Lauria explores these related concepts, "'*Respeto,*' '*Relajo,*' and Interpersonal Relations in Puerto Rico," *Anthropological Quarterly,* Vol. 37 (1964), pp. 53–67; see also Alfredo Mirandé and Evangelina Enriquez in *La Chicana: The Mexican American Woman* (Chicago: University of Chicago Press, 1979), Ch. 4.

[32] Mirandé and Enriquez, *La Chicana.*

[33] Joseph P. Fitzpatrick, *Puerto Rican Americans* (Englewood Cliffs, N.J.: Prentice-Hall, 1971), Ch. 6; and R. Fernández Marina et al., "Three Basic Themes in Mexican and Puerto Rican Family Values," *Journal of Social Psychology,* Vol. 48 (1958), pp. 167–181.

[34] Edwin Seda Bonilla, "Interacción social y personalidad en una communidad de Puerto Rico," (San Juan, P.R.: Ediciones Juan Ponce de Leon, 1964). See, also, the discussion of the play *La Carreta* in Ch. 1.

[35] For Puerto Rico, see his *La Vida: A Puerto Rican Family in the Culture of Poverty—San Juan and New York* (New York: Random House, 1966). For Mexico, see his *Children of Sanchez* (New York: Vintage Press, 1961).

ture of poverty is "both an adaptation and a reaction of the poor to their marginal position in a class-stratified, highly individuated, capitalistic society."[36] Oscar Lewis found variations from one country to another. He noted that the poor in Mexico City were far more identified with symbols of the national culture and less marginal than were the Puerto Ricans—a possible result of American colonialism in Puerto Rico. Needless to say, the culture of poverty includes very negative elements:

> On the family level the major traits of the culture of poverty are . . . early initiation into sex, free unions or consensual marriages, a relatively high incidence of the abandonment of wives and children, a trend toward female- or mother-centered families and consequently a much greater knowledge of maternal relatives; a strong predisposition to authoritarianism; lack of privacy, verbal emphasis upon family solidarity, which is only rarely achieved because of sibling rivalry, and competition for limited goods and maternal affection.[37]

Moreover, according to Lewis, such a family produces a personality that is incapable of the kind of self-control that is necessary for upward mobility.

Lewis's hypothesis about "the culture of poverty" was interesting and seemed, at least for a time, adequate. It was applied almost immediately—and indiscriminately, perhaps because it was so convenient. It seemed to explain the continued poverty not only of Hispanics but of other minorities as well. It tends to ignore the importance of the limited opportunity structure and of discrimination. Rather, it focuses almost entirely on the culture of the poor themselves. It is now often used ideologically in political debates as an argument against programs for the poor. Thus it tends to limit the chances of the poor even more.[38]

Variations in the United States: national origin. Earlier (Chapter 4), we discussed some statistical differences among Chicano, Puerto Rican, and Cuban families. Although the plight of the poor is very similar, the variations in Hispanic subgroups are substantial and seem to demand an explanation. Unfortunately, there is very little comparative research. Yet it is striking to note that Puerto Ricans have the highest proportion of female-headed households and Chicanos the lowest. The most satisfactory explanation seems to hinge on the heavy concentration of Puerto Ricans in New York City—and the long-lasting economic depression in that city. Outside of New York, there are fewer broken families among Puerto Ricans.

In making comparisons, we must recall how very recently Puerto Ricans have entered American cities. Studies from the 1950s and the 1960s are emphatic about the conflict between parents and children in families of the first large waves of Puerto Rican migrants. As an example, the first substantial study of Puerto Ricans reported that "many women in the new situation revolt against the accepted island

---

[36] Oscar Lewis, *A Study of Slum Culture, Background for La Vida* (New York: Random House, 1968), p. 5.

[37] Ibid., p. 10.

[38] See William Ryan, *Blaming the Victim* (New York: Vintage Press, 1972), for a classic criticism of the culture of poverty idea and allied pseudoexplanations of the persistence of poverty. Ryan argues that they tend to blame the victims of oppression themselves for their plight and offer a convenient way for more prosperous people to justify their advantages.

pattern of male dominance. One woman made the point, as follows: "Whether I have a husband or not, I work. So I do what I want, and if my husband dare to complain, I throw him out. . . ." The male reaction is typified by these words: "Women get lost with the liberty they have up here, and many, not all, become bitches."[39]

Hispanic subgroups also show variations in size of families. Chicano families are the largest and Cubans, the smallest. Later when we discuss the changing role of women, we will find that a good explanation of the larger family size among Mexican Americans is their relatively low access to birth control measures rather than cultural differences. Further, Cuban women tend to work outside the home more than do Mexican-American women, and this alone importantly affects fertility.

In summarizing variations in the Hispanic family that might be traced to national origin, we can only say there is very little information to justify any clearcut conclusions, but the evidence does show that the image of *one* monolithic Hispanic family is flawed.

Variations in the Hispanic family—rural, small town, and urban. Although Puerto Ricans and Cubans live mostly in large cities, substantial numbers of Mexican Americans still live in rural and small-town areas. The family is far more traditional in such circumstances. Ethnographic studies of the 1950s done in small Texas towns, for example, indicate that the family is the most important facet of life for Mexican Americans, conforming closely to patterns described for Mexico itself.[40]

These patterns are well illustrated in a meticulous study of a family of Chicano Texas migrants in Illinois. In tracing one family (the "Sangres" and their children), Brett Williams, an anthropologist, found half the members of the family (20 of the 38) living in one migrant camp. Of the remaining Sangres, most had settled out of the migrant stream to live in a nearby town. The 20 family members in the camp were housed in five separate units. Williams terms this a "domestic convoy," and she argues that the extended family not only provides needed resources but also humanizes what might otherwise be a degrading work situation.[41] But it must also be said that only a comparatively few migrant families (only 7 percent of those studied in California) show this three-generational pattern.[42] The old Hispanic rural areas in northern New Mexico also showed strong traditional patriarchal families, often over three or four generations living in extended family households. The families were economically functional and also formed the political structure of the towns. But by the late 1960s, traditional family patterns were

---

[39] C. Wright Mills et al., *The Puerto Rican Journey* (New York: Harper, 1950), p. 97.

[40] The small towns of south Texas figure in two reports on Hidalgo County. One is a general treatment by William Madsen, *Mexican-Americans of South Texas* (New York: Holt, Rinehart and Winston, 1964), and the other is an analysis of one town by Arthur Rubel, *Across the Tracks* (Austin: University of Texas Press, 1966).

[41] Brett Williams, "Migrants on the Prairie: Untangling Everyday Life," in West and Macklin, eds., *The Chicano Experience,* pp. 83–108.

[42] G. Hawkes, et al., *Patterns of Living in California's Migrant Labor Families,* Research Monograph 12 (Davis: University of California, Department of Applied Behavioral Science, 1973). Michael Miller, "Variations in Mexican American Family Life; A Review Synthesis of Empirical Research," *Aztlán,* Vol. 9 (1978), pp. 209–231, argues that families might share if they could afford to do so.

broken in all except the most remote villages by the selective migration of younger people to the cities and by the loss of property.[43] In these small towns, middle-class Hispanic family life is equally traditional.

Does urbanism destroy familism and the patriarchal family structure? Obviously families must adapt to changing circumstances, but sociologist Maxine Baca Zinn argues that the familistic Chicano family has survival value in the industrial cities of the Midwest. First, the extended family helps in the process of migration and settlement. This has also been found to be the case for Puerto Rican and Dominican immigrants. Second, the extended family is a cushion for some time after migration to the city. It might also keep new families in a rather "clannish" mode of interaction with other people, a pattern seen as less appropriate to life in a large industrial city. On the other hand, the very high rates of marriage with Anglos in some midwestern cities reveals that such "clannishness" does not hold very long. Young Hispanics in the relatively small *barrios* of the Midwest tend to interact with a wide variety of people in the schools, even if their parents do not.

The other major issue is the patriarchy: Does the greater range of roles available in cities destroy the traditional patriarchal structure of the Hispanic family? We noted earlier that the options available in New York profoundly affected the position of women in the Puerto Rican families of the 1950s. Children also took on different roles and were more independent. Puerto Rican parents were particularly incensed about the freedom demanded by their female children. Particularly if children speak English and the immigrant parents do not, there is likely to be a role reversal.[44] Maxine Baca Zinn summarizes more than half a dozen studies of urban Chicanos, going back as far as the 1920s, which reiterate these findings. The primary factor is whether work is available for women. Employed wives "used their economic independence and extradomestic knowledge and skills to increase their power in family decisionmaking."[45]

Many other questions might be asked about the adjustment of the Hispanic families to life in the cities. But we must remember that the effects of "urbanism" are confounded by generation, by class, and by the effects of regionalism.

First, the confusion of generation. Some fraction of the Hispanics in any city will be newcomers from more traditional settings. There are always new Mexicans from Mexico, Mexicans from rural areas of the United States, or Puerto Ricans from the Island. Many of the conflicts between modern and traditional values will always be found, particularly since all subgroups of the Hispanics still have many new arrivals.

Second, the confusion of class. This will be discussed in a later section, but it is important to note that the new group of professional Hispanics appearing in large cities simply does not exist in small American towns.

Third, the confusion of region. "Urbanism" is very different in different regions of the United States. Substantially different life-styles are offered Hispanic families, sometimes even within the same city. As a single example, Puerto Rican

[43] Clark Knowlton, "Changing Spanish American Villages of Northern New Mexico," *Sociology and Social Research,* Vol. 53 (1969), pp. 455–474.

[44] Mills et al., *The Puerto Rican Journey,* p. 99.

[45] Maxine Baca Zinn, "Employment and Education of Mexican American Women," *Harvard Educational Review,* Vol. 50 (1980), pp. 47–62.

family life is different in New York from Puerto Rican family life in smaller cities. For Chicanos, "The Midwest experience is not simply an extension of the Southwest experience into the North."[46]

Variations in the United States: social class. Traditionalism is also a function of class status. It is not clear just how this relationship works, although we know that in small towns middle-class Hispanics are likely to be upholders of the traditional. Urban middle-class Hispanics in the 1980s are usually children from poor families, but there are also many Hispanics, like the Cubans, who were middle class in their country of origin and import middle-class versions of traditional Hispanic family values.

In one study done in the 1960s, however, an effort was made to test the well-established idea that an emphasis on family priorities rather than individual priorities is likely to be associated with a lack of progress in the class system. Testing this hypothesis, two questions were asked in San Antonio and Los Angeles. Is it important to live near the parents, even if it means losing a good job opportunity? Is it better to hire a relative rather than a stranger? The majority of all respondents disapproved of familism at the expense of efficiency.[47] Yet in both cities, poorer Chicanos were more likely than middle-income people to emphasize familism.[48] It appears that Mexican Americans doing reasonably well in the job market are indeed less likely to emphasize familism. But, then, the very fact of such achievement means that they do not need familism as much. Middle-income people are more likely to hold jobs in firms that promote competitive values—and much less likely to hold "dead-end" jobs or jobs where mobility is accomplished through a network of friends and relatives, which is typical of workers mired in the secondary labor market (see Chapter 5).[49] Actually, familism may be economically helpful in the poorer areas of large cities, just as in rural communities where people are bound to the land. Just to make it more complicated, familism is also functional for many business people, from small mom-and-pop storeowners, who do not have to pay their children, to the million-dollar family firm. This possible usefulness adds yet another difficulty in trying to describe and measure the process of urbanism.

Thus, it is very difficult to decide whether the familism supposed to characterize Hispanic families helps or hinders mobility in the American class system. Probably, the truth is that there is a complex interaction among family circumstances, family values, and individual job mobility, all occurring within a framework of explicit personal and community standards. (See Chapter 7 on culture and lan-

[46] Gilbert Cárdenas, "Los Desarraigados: Chicanos in the Midwest Region of the United States," *Aztlán,* Vol. 7 (1978), pp. 153–186, 158. See also June Macklin and Alvina Teniente de Costilla, "La Virgen de Guadalupe and the American Dream," in West and Macklin, eds., *The Chicano Experience,* pp. 111–143, for a discussion of Chicanos in Toldeo, Ohio, in which, for example there is a high rate of male outmarriage—an unusual pattern.

[47] Joan W. Moore, *Mexican Americans* (Englewood, N.J.: Prentice-Hall, 1976), p. 131.

[48] This finding is taken by some to reinforce negative stereotypes of the family. As an example, see Miguel Montiel, "The Chicano Family: A Review of Research," *Social Work,* (1973), pp. 22–31.

[49] See Paul Bullock, *Aspirations vs. Opportunity: "Careers" in the Inner City* (Ann Arbor, Mich.: Institute of Labor and Industrial Relations, 1973), for a description of the job-finding practices of the poor in Los Angeles.

guage change.) We do know that more affluent families are more able than the poor to provide resources—and several studies show that they do so.[50] In fact, wealthier families are generally more integrated with their kin than are the poor.[51] Research in Los Angeles among poor families suggests that family integration is often broken by the magnitude of the needs of members. A low-income family may simply be unable to provide the financial and support needs of a member. The resulting bad feelings on both sides may lead to estrangement. In the large cities, public and private welfare permits the survival of members who are in trouble, even if ties with their own kin are cut.[52] Such families suffer particular stress because they feel that other "normal" Hispanic families have supportive kin (although research shows that only about a quarter of Chicano families surveyed actually turn to their kin).[53]

The role of women: diversity and change. It is important to remember that the roles of Hispanic women are as diverse as is the population itself. Sheltered house-bound women live in male-dominated households, and there are independent, tough-minded women (middle-aged as well as young) who have achieved a living for themselves. There are lively, gossipy, grass-roots community leaders in poor *barrios,* and there are elegant wealthy women. There are prostitutes; there are women married to Anglo men; there are women who have children but no husband. To stereotype this diversity by describing a single role for Hispanic women would be a massive injustice.[54] Yet such stereotypical thinking is common.

Much of the discussion grouped around stereotypes is in terms of cultural imperatives and of culture conflicts for Hispanic women. But Hispanics have responded constantly to the need for change, in the past as well as in the present. Survival needs often stretch the limits of cultural prescriptions and imperatives. In discussing the roles of Hispanic women, we must bear these pressures in mind. Particularly we must be wary that the term "culture" may be reified, and we must watch for the pressures that life situations bring to transmitted values and beliefs. Women and men are reared with certain expectations about their proper roles, but women who are reared to believe that they are too feeble to do heavy physical labor cannot retain such ideas if heavy agricultural labor is the only means of survival. Nor can their husbands and fathers insist on the fragility of women. We will discuss two of these pivotal issues—work and child bearing—and then the changes and diversity in these roles.

In one important respect, there seems to be convincing evidence of the cultural expectations for working women. Hispanic women work at far lower rates than do Anglo or black women (see also Chapter 5). The traditional role prescribed

[50] Leo Grebler, Joan W. Moore, and Ralph Guzmán, *The Mexican American People* (New York: The Free Press, 1970).

[51] Keefe, "Urbanization, Acculturation, and Extended Family Ties."

[52] Unpublished research, Joan Moore.

[53] Susan Keefe et al., "The Mexican American Extended Family as an Emotional Support System," *Human Organization,* Vol. 38 (1979), pp. 144–152.

[54] Puerto Rican and Mexican-American women have played a strong role in many organizations. Vilma Martínez directed the Mexican American Legal Defense and Education Fund; Antonia Pantoja is considered the "godmother" of the Puerto Rican Forum; Dolores Huerta is one of the leading spirits of the UFW.

for Hispanic women rules out work outside the house. Some ethnographic studies in highly traditional towns in south Texas show that work "is simply not an option." But a study of early *Puertoriqueña* migrants in New York City shows that ideology can stretch:

> The role of Puerto Rican women in New York communities during the 1920s and 1930s was an extension of the role they played in their island society. During the early periods women were expected to stay at home caring for husband and children, but the term "housewife" was open to interpretation when applied to Puerto Rican women. While they basically thought of themselves as women of the home (*mujeres de la casa*), many engaged in activities designed to supplement family incomes, and various home-centered economic ventures emerged in response to their economic needs.[55]

Even under the earlier conditions of strong cultural imperatives, a full quarter of these Puerto Rican women worked outside their homes. In contemporary times, Cuban and Central and South American women tend to work even more frequently than do Anglo women; Mexican American women are tending to work more and more frequently during the 1970s. Puerto Rican women on the mainland work less than do Anglo or other Hispanic women—and Puerto Rican women living on the island work even less.[56] These differences are convincing evidence that something other than cultural expectations determines women's chances of staying at home or working. We note, for example, that Cuban American women are both more educated and have fewer children than do women of other Hispanic groups. The combination seems to help them to obtain better jobs and higher income than most Hispanic women.

Following these leads, Rosemary Santana Cooney and Alice Colón examined the labor force participation of Puerto Rican women. During the 20 years from 1950 to 1970, the women stopped working at an astonishing rate. (In 1950 Puerto Rican women were more likely to work than were women of any other ethnicity. By 1970 they were less likely to work than were women of any other ethnic group.) How could this be explained?

This decline occurred *only* for Puerto Rican women living in New York City. Elsewhere, there was an increase, just as there was an increase for women of other ethnic groups. Cooney and Colón argue that in New York "changes in demand for female labor by skill levels were dramatic and favored the more educated groups. . . . Even though the Puerto Rican female sample had improved their education in the past decade, these changes were slow compared to the dramatic shift in demand for highly-educated female labor."[57] But even this is not the end of the story. High unemployment for men as well as women led to an increase in female-headed households—and a greater dependency on welfare for Puerto Rican women. So this is not

---

[55] Virginia Sanchez-Korrol, "Survival of Puerto Rican Women in New York Before World War II," in Rodriguez, et al., eds., *The Puerto Rican Struggle*, p. 48.

[56] For 1970 census data, see Jaffe et al., *The Changing Demography of Spanish Americans*, pp. 156–58, 211, 258. For 1974, 1976, and 1978, National Commission for Employment Policy, *Hispanics and Jobs*, p. 33.

[57] Rosemary Santana Cooney and Alice Colón, "Work and Family: The Recent Struggle of Puerto Rican Females," in Rodriguez et al., eds., *The Puerto Rican Struggle*, p. 64.

a picture of contented female domesticity, but rather dire poverty and shrinking opportunity, in which cultural imperatives play a rather small role.

Child bearing is another area in which the weight of traditional norms can be tested. A predominantly Catholic population is not expected to practice birth control or to utilize abortion services. In addition, the cultural concept of *machismo* demands that the male control fertility in his household. Nonetheless, the available evidence shows both that increasing proportions of Hispanics (all the available research concerns Mexican-American women) approve of or utilize birth control—and also that they willingly utilize abortions when they are available. Surveys as early as 1964 show that Mexican-American men and women in Los Angeles were as likely as any others in the nation to favor birth control (64 percent of the Mexican Americans and 62 percent of a national sample). By 1974, easily used oral contraceptives were common. Study after study showed high proportions of Hispanic women using contraceptives.[58]

Even more significant is the willingness of Chicanas to use abortion services.[59] Again, this is a fairly recent development. Before a 1973 Supreme Court decision, abortions were legal in only a few states, and even in those states legalization has been very recent. After 1973, however, abortion clinics developed in many cities, and Hispanic women were very much in evidence among the clients. (In Puerto Rico abortions were legally available even when they were still illegal in the United States proper.) A full 46 percent of reported pregnancies among Mexican American clients of a family planning clinic in a medium-sized Texas city studied between 1973 and 1979 were terminated by abortion.[60] (This is a selected sample of women already trying to control their fertility, but the figures certainly gainsay abhorrence of abortion.)

This was a Texas city in which few doctors were willing to perform the oper-

[58] Review of the literature by Sally Andrade, "Family Planning Practices of Mexican Americans," in Margarita B. Melville, ed., *Twice a Minority* (St. Louis: C. V. Mosby, 1980). In 1979 a unique source of information became available in the form of a cooperative survey of several thousand Mexican, Mexican-American, and Anglo women in the border areas. Six large cities in Texas (including San Antonio) and 51 counties were surveyed. While differences exist among Anglo, Mexican-American, and Mexican women, the differences are not as great as one would expect from the stereotypes. Thus 75 percent of the Anglo women, 65 percent of the Anglo women, 65 percent of the Chicanas, and only 50 percent of the Mexican women were using some form of contraception. Also, see Charles Warren et al., "Contraceptive Use and Family Planning Services Along the U.S.–Mexico Border," *International Family Planning Perspectives,* Vol. 7 (1981), pp. 52–59. Anglos were more likely to be using sterilization (18 percent female and 23 percent male) than were Chicanos (19 percent female and 6 percent male) or Mexicans (20 percent female and 0 percent male). (Sterilization of women has been part of the Puerto Rican family planning programs and is encouraged in the island.) Among Chicanas, age differences appeared with respect to the proportion of women using the pill (46 percent of the women under 30 compared with 18 percent of those over 30) and rhythm (1 percent of those under 30 and 6 percent of those over 30).

[59] A large-scale Los Angeles survey in 1973 showed about as many Chicanas approving abortions as disapproving. Mexican-born respondents were far more disapproving. Sandra Rosenhouse-Person and G. Sabagh, "Attitudes Toward Abortion Among Catholic Mexican American Women: The Effects of Religiosity and Education," *Demography,* Vol. 20 (1983), pp. 87–89.

[60] Maria-Luisa Urdaneta, "Chicana Use of Abortion," in Melville, ed., *Twice a Minority,* pp. 33–51.

ations; many women had to make a special effort to obtain an abortion in another city. Urdaneta concludes that the use of abortion services (like birth control) is regulated less by culture than by the availability of services. Not only must such services be physically available, but they must also be socially accessible with a sympathetic staff that understands the language and the culture. Certainly the remarkable success of Mexico in its effort to regulate fertility during the 1970s is counter to traditional Mexican norms. The cultural prescriptions for women's roles in Cuba have changed even more drastically. No culture is static; every culture changes.

For Hispanics, the family has been a significant source of pride. For many, this pride has also involved the idea of women as docile and subordinate to men, with a sharp distinction between "good" girls and "bad" girls. That such stereotypes are still alive and well is shown by a study of Chicanas who had, indeed, strayed from the prescribed women's role. Many of these 85 women, interviewed in 1981, were active members of youth gangs during their adolescence, and all had become heroin addicts. When asked if they agreed with the statement, "Girls with a bad reputation as a teenager will have a hard time changing it," only 27 percent agreed. But when asked what they thought "most Chicanos" would think, 59 percent felt that other Chicanos would agree. Similar disparities were found with regard to their own and their notions of "most Chicanos" concerning work roles and the primacy of the family.[61]

This tendency to condemn "bad" women even extends to victims of rape. Comparing the attitudes of Anglo, Chicano, and black residents of San Antonio, Mexican-American women as well as men were found to be the most likely to blame the victims of rape as "inciters" and to follow other generally outmoded stereotypes. There is reason to believe that rape and other sexual assaults are seriously underreported among Hispanics because of the stigma that attaches to victimization.[62] Given the role of stereotypes of women among some Hispanics, it is no surprise that Hispanic feminists vehemently challenge what they conceive to be a false glorification of that aspect of Hispanic culture that degrades women. As Francesca Flores remarks, "Women who do not accept this philosophy are charged with betrayal to 'our culture and heritage.' Our culture, hell!"[63] In the mid-1970s, a number of Chicanas active in the Chicano movement began to make such a philosophy a point of issue within the movement. Even though the strong Hispanic emphasis on male dominance began to be defined as a reaction to minority status in American society rather than to cultural heritage, there were a series of strong statements against it.[64]

[61] Joan W. Moore and Alberto Mata, *Women and Heroin in Chicano Communities* (Los Angeles: Chicano Pinto Research Project, 1982).

[62] Joyce Williams and Karen Holmes, *The Second Assault: Rape and Public Attitudes* (Westport, Connecticut: Greenwood Press, 1981).

[63] In *Regeneración,* I (1971). For a fuller discussion of the problems of Hispanic feminists vis-à-vis Anglo feminists as well as internally, see Marta Cotera, "Feminism: The Chicana and Anglo Versions," in Melville, ed., *Twice a Minority,* and Chapter 7 of Mirandé and Enriquez, *La Chicana.* An interesting account of feminism in Mexico is given in Macias, *Against All Odds.* The title indicates the difficulties faced by feminists in Mexico.

[64] Maxine Baca Zinn, "Chicano Men and Masculinity," *Journal of Ethnic Studies,* Vol. 10 (1982), pp. 29–44. See, for example, the reaction of Mirta Vidal, *Chicanas Speak Out: Women: the New Voice of La Raza* (New York: Pathfinder Press, 1971).

Hispanic aged and the role of the family.   One of the most cherished stereotypes of the Hispanic family is the idea that Hispanic families care for their aged, in a manner sharply in contrast with the stereotype that Anglo families reject their aged. Before dealing with these concepts, it is essential to know that elderly people are a lower proportion of the Hispanic population than the general American population (see Chapter 4). There appear to be three reasons for this: first, some of the aged who were born outside the United States return to their birthplaces (most notably Puerto Ricans); second, the figures reflect a higher death rate in the early years; and third, the recent arrival of many working-aged Hispanics makes for a lower proportion of aged.

There is a mixture of evidence on whether the Hispanic elderly *want* to stay with their children and also on whether they can or do. Recently, David Maldonado has summarized a number of such studies by arguing that the modernization of the Chicano family may mean that "support" no longer extends to providing a home for older members in a multigenerational household in which the aged exert real authority. But these changes do not mean the demise of family respect, care, and attention to the aged member.[65] In Los Angeles, the Mexican Americans were far more likely than the black or white elderly to interact with children and grandchildren, and the same was found for Puerto Rican elderly in New York City.[66] Puerto Rican elderly also receive more—and more different kinds of—help from their children than did black or white elderly.

Economic support is critical to the elderly, and it is obvious that many older Hispanics worked in occupations covered neither by pensions nor Social Security. It is very likely that the economic base may be very frail—and indeed this has been found in many studies—and, in addition, most Hispanic elderly speak Spanish and services must cater to this special need.

There are some indications in the literature that the Hispanic elderly experience aging less positively than do either white or black. Thus, Puerto Rican elderly were twice as likely to be so severely impaired by ill health that they were bound to their homes, and Mexican Americans were found to be generally less positive toward aging and the aged than were whites or blacks. (They also perceived "old age" as beginning earlier: more than 30 percent say that "old age" begins at age 57, whereas blacks name 63 and whites 70.)[67] No matter what the relationship to the family, then, life for the Hispanic aged is not sheltered or easy.

Hispanic intermarriage with Anglos: the changing family.   A critical factor in the relationship between a minority and the larger society is, of course, the rate at

[65] D. Maldonado, "Aging in the Chicano Context," in D. Gelfand and A. Kutzik, eds., *Ethnicity and Aging* (New York: Springer, 1979). Other sources are cited in the review article by Frank Cota-Robles Newton, "Issues in Research and Service Delivery among Mexican American Elderly: A Concise Statement with Recommendations," *The Gerontologist,* Vol. 20 (1980), pp. 208-213.

[66] For Los Angeles, See V. Bengtson, "Ethnicity and Aging: Problems and Issues in Current Social Science Inquiry," and for New York, see M. Cantor, "The Informal Support System of New York's Inner-City Elderly: Is Ethnicity a Factor?" both in Gelfand and Kutzik, eds., *Ethnicity and Aging.*

[67] For Puerto Rican health, see R. Zambrana et al., "Health Services and the Puerto Rican Elderly," and for Mexican Americans, see Bengtson, "Ethnicity and Aging," both are in Gelfand and Kutzik eds., *Ethnicity and Aging.*

which the two groups marry each other. If there is a high rate of intermarriage, sociologists would generally argue that the Hispanic family and the Hispanic community are beginning to merge with other groups, to lose a separate Hispanic identity. Low intermarriage rates may mean great isolation or great antipathy. The data on Hispanic intermarriage once again emphasizes the importance of time and place in a highly diverse Hispanic population.

From Figure 6.1 it is evident that there has been a substantial increase in Hispanic intermarriage in the past generation. Before the 1940s in no place and at no time did more than a fifth of the marriages involve Anglo men or women. The rates of intermarriage began to climb in the 1960s. Here the importance of place becomes evident. The lowest rates of intermarriage were reported in south Texas, specifically in the border area of Hidalgo County where the proportion of exogamous marriages rose from a low 5 percent in 1961 to a high of 9 percent in 1971. This is an area around the city of Edinburg with substantial traditional prejudice and extreme poverty, probably very close to the traditional Southern caste system.

Other Texas intermarriage rates are also relatively low, but are higher in the Gulf Coast city of Corpus Christi and even higher in the tourist and military town of San Antonio. Here, by 1973, 27 percent of all marriages that involved Mexican Americans were exogamous. Intermarriage rates for Mexican Americans were highest in California, where state figures showed that in both 1962 and 1974 more than half the marriages involving Mexican Americans were exogamous. (Albuquerque and rural New Mexico locations tended to be more variable, with Albuquerque resembling the Los Angeles and California patterns. A "seven rural county" sample tended to approach the Texas pattern.)

Interestingly, the New York patterns for Hispanics diverge sharply from those in the Southwest. In 1975, Joseph Fitzpatrick found that 45.8 percent of Puerto Rican marriages, 55.0 percent of Dominican marriages, and 65.2 percent of South Americans (the three largest groups) were exogamous. These rates are quite high. But these are not Hispanic-Anglo intermarriages; largely they were between Hispanics of different national origins. Thus, most of the Puerto Ricans who married non-Puerto Ricans married Dominicans and South or Central Americans rather than Anglos, and this was even more true for the smaller Hispanic groups. Furthermore, the researchers found a decline in the rate of intermarriage for Puerto Ricans in New York between 1949 and 1975.[68] The decline may be because the Puerto Ricans most likely to intermarry (the more assimilated) are the most likely to leave New York City for surrounding towns. Outside of New York City, Puerto Ricans have higher intermarriage with Anglos.

Three patterns have been observed that support the notion that intermarriage is a good indicator of acculturation and assimilation. First, Hispanics born outside the continental United States (chiefly Mexico and Puerto Rico) are far less likely to marry outside their group. Second, persons of lower occupational status are less likely to marry outside their group. And third, men are less likely to intermarry than are women. Thus the most likely person to intermarry is an individual born in the United States and is a woman of higher occupational status. The factors of occupation and nativity are obvious. Education and other experiences characteristic of

[68] Joseph Fitzpatrick and Douglas Gurak, *Hispanic Intermarriage in New York City: 1975* (Bronx, N.Y.: Fordham University Hispanic Research Center, 1979).

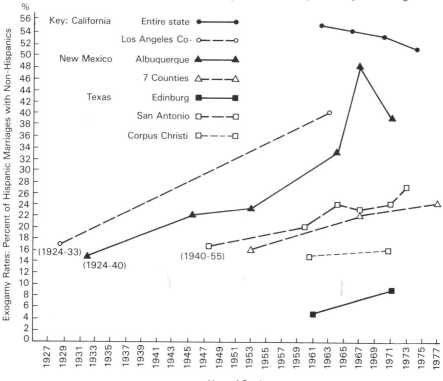

FIGURE 6.1   Percentage of Exogamous Marriages, Selected Years, 1927–1977

Sources: Albuquerque: 1924–1940, derived from Carolyn Zeleny, "Relations Between the Spanish-Americans and the Anglo-Americans in New Mexico," Ph.D. dissertation, Yale University, 1944; 1945–1946, "A Study of Certain Changes in the Spanish-American Family in Bernalillo County, 1915–1946," M.A. thesis, University of New Mexico, 1948; 1953, 1964, Nancie González, *The Spanish Americans of New Mexico* (Albuquerque: University of New Mexico Press, 1969); 1967, 1971, and *San Antonio,* 1964, 1967, 1971, 1973, E. Murguia and P. Frisbie, "Trends in Mexican American Intermarriage," *Social Science Quarterly,* Vol. 53 (1977), pp. 374–389.

New Mexico-Seven counties: 1953, 1967, 1977, L. Holscher et al., "Chicano Exogamous Marriages in New Mexico," unpublished paper cited in E. Murguia, *Chicano Intermarriage* (San Antonio, Tx.: Trinity University Press, 1982).

Los Angeles: 1924–1933, derived from Constantine Panunzio, "Intermarriage in Los Angeles, 1924–1933," *American Journal of Sociology,* Vol. 47 (1942), pp. 690–701; 1963, F. Mittelbach and J. Moore, "Ethnic Endogamy —The Case of Mexican Americans," *American Journal of Sociology,* Vol. 74 (1968), 50–62.

California (Entire State): 1962, 1966, 1970, 1974, R. Schoen et al., "Intermarriage Among Spanish Surnamed Californians, 1962–1974," *International Migration Review,* Vol. 12 (1978), pp. 359–369.

Edinburg, Texas, 1961, 1971; *Corpus Christi,* 1960–61, 1970–71: D. Alvirez and F. Bean, "The Mexican American Family," in C. Mindel and R. Habenstein, eds., *Ethnic Families in America* (New York: Elsevier, 1976).

San Antonio: 1940–1955, B. Bradshaw, "Some Demographic Aspects of Marriage," M. A. thesis, University of Texas at Austin, 1960; 1960, F. Bean and B. Bradshaw," Intermarriage Between Persons of Spanish and Non-Spanish Surname," *Social Science Quarterly,* Vol. 51 (1970), pp. 389–395.

upward mobility bring movement outside of the relatively restricted *barrio* existence. But why should it be women that tend to marry out?

Actually this pattern has been found in many populations at many times in history. Usually the group losing the women is of lower status than is the group they marry into. It is argued that this pattern (technically "hypergamy") provides men of higher status a wider choice in marriage partners than just the women immediately around them. And, of course, it offers women of lower-status groups a chance for upward mobility. This interpretation is strongly confirmed by some specific tests of the occupational levels of Chicano and Puerto Rican brides and non-Hispanic grooms.[69]

HISPANICS AND CHURCHES

Most Hispanics are at least nominally Roman Catholics. But this identification means something somewhat different for Hispanic Americans than it does for Catholics of other ethnic backgrounds.

To summarize these differences, first, Catholicism was introduced into Latin American nations as a religion of the *conquistadores*—and as a colonial institution. It has retained that atmosphere in most nations of Latin America until very recent years. Second, the first contacts of the Catholic church with Mexican and Puerto Rican congregations in the United States led to an emphasis on Americanization. This close marriage of religion and colonialism means that the Catholic church is not the same kind of institution for Hispanics as for European immigrant Catholics: it is not "their" church. As a consequence (which may be vital in the future), Protestantism has a somewhat different meaning for Hispanics than it did for other predominantly Roman Catholic populations. Protestant churches appear to be more vital *community* institutions than do Catholic churches. In this respect, Protestant sects (and particularly the growing fundamentalist and Pentecostalist churches) work for Hispanics in much the way the old Catholic "national" parishes worked for European immigrants.

The Catholic church in historical perspective. When the United States acquired the Southwest territories and their Spanish-American and Mexican populations, the Catholic church in the region was very near collapse. The magnificent mission properties had been expropriated by the Spanish and Mexican governments and their land transferred to large Mexican and Anglo ranchers. Residual fragments of the missions became ordinary parish churches, quite isolated from one another in a vast territory. They lacked either clergy or the means of supporting a clergy. Typically, the first American clergy to enter the Albuquerque region considered the resident Mexican Catholics to be not only unchurched (with many who had not been baptized or married by a priest) but even close to pagan (with at least one notable and influential priest who had been father to many children.)[70]

[69] Fitzpatrick and Gurak, *Hispanic Intermarriage,* pp. 52–54.

[70] For details of the troubles of the Roman Catholic church in its huge and remote Southwestern area, see Patrick H. McNamara, "Bishops, Priests and Prophecy: A Study in the Sociology of Religious Protest," (Ph.D. dissertation, University of California at Los Angeles, 1968), condensed in Grebler et al., *The Mexican American People.* Paul Horgan, *Lamy of Santa*

Thus the first problem of the Catholic church in the Southwest was survival. Missionary priests came from France and Spain and, with a few native priests, administered only the most essential religious services over a vast area. We can pick a single year in the late nineteenth century—1890—in the archdiocese of Tucson and find a lone parish priest trying to bring the basic sacraments of baptism, marriage, and burial to 1,052 Catholics spread over an average area of 7,000 square miles. In 1890 the combined dioceses of San Antonio, Corpus Christi (including Brownsville), El Paso, Santa Fe, Tucson, and Los Angeles (including Monterey and San Diego), there were only 193 parish priests and of this tiny number only 14 had Spanish surnames. There were few Anglo-American Catholics in this area, and, in fact, financial support came from Catholic sources in the East. Whatever its desires, the church could do very little to protect or to help its Mexican parishioners.

In Puerto Rico, survival was not the same overarching priority for the church at the time of the American conquest of the island, although there were comparatively few priests. Rather, the first effort to provide religious services for the Puerto Rican population coincided with Americanization. American priests began to work right after the occupation in 1898. Few could speak Spanish or had any interest in the local culture. As in the Southwest, much of the financial support came from the mainland. Joseph Fitzpatrick thinks that this effort had a negative impact, leaving "the majority of Puerto Ricans untouched. Lack of effective contact with the church and lack of formal instruction had remained a rather general condition of the people; the religion that characterizes the lives of many is still the folk religion."[71]

When Mexicans began to enter the United States in large numbers in the early twentieth century, the Catholic church gathered hundreds of thousands of new parishioners. But the new immigrants were as unused to American Catholicism (with its rather ascetic Irish influence) as was the average Protestant. Indeed, the immigrants appear to come from precisely that group in Mexico among whom Catholic influence was weakest. They were not accustomed to financial support of the church, to religious instruction or parochial schools for the children, or to regular attendance at mass, all of which are important to American Catholics. The American church, in sum, saw the new Mexican immigrants as likely "new converts" but not as true practicing Catholics.

> Contrary to the notion that immigrants would seek out the Church for support and comfort, the Church had to reach out for this newcomer if it was to perform its functions. This would have been difficult under the best of circumstances. The poor resources at the command of the Southwestern church made it an overwhelming task.[72]

In the 1920s, the fierce anticlericalism of the Mexican revolutionary period had interesting echoes in the United States. Refugees from the persecution of the

---

Fe (New York: Farrar, Straus and Giroux, 1975), presents a detailed and very readable account of the life of Juan Bautista Lamy, first American archbishop of Santa Fe. Bishop Lamy led the first major encounter of the American hierarchy with the very serious problems of Catholicism in New Mexico.

[71] Fitzpatrick, *Puerto Rican Americans,* pp. 118 ff.

[72] McNamara in Grebler et al., *The Mexican American People,* p. 450.

church (the *Cristeros*) found their way across the border and enlisted the sympathy of their fellow Catholics. There was a very real concern that the Mexican Revolution might spread to the United States and a deeper concern among the Catholic hierarchy that these new immigrants might turn to communism unless the church made extraordinary efforts.[73] The church began to interest itself in the building of parochial schools and in Americanization of the Mexican population. In this endeavor it was helped by substantial gifts from Catholic sources in the Midwest and East.

But neither in the American Southwest nor in the new colony of Puerto Rico were the resources enough. Even the efforts of the archdiocese of Los Angeles (the richest of the Southwestern religious divisions) were extremely limited. As an example, a drive to create a system of parochial schools met only very limited success. By 1930, the combined archdioceses of San Diego and Los Angeles had more than 300,000 Catholics but only 79 schools. (Baltimore contained approximately the same number of Catholics, served by 179 parochial schools.) Texas had even fewer schools in a state where nearly all Catholics were Mexican Americans.

This interest in Americanization was to have an exact counterpart in New York City a decade later with Puerto Ricans. This time, the reasons were different. New York had a large and powerful Catholic population with a wealthy church. Its immigrant roots were strongly associated with "national" parishes. Here Italian priests ministered to Italian immigrants and their children in a native language, following native traditions. Many other national parishes had their native priests. Often there was a parochial school attached. But in 1939 the few Puerto Rican national parishes that had been established in the 1920s were abandoned. (Unlike European immigrants, but like Mexicans, Puerto Ricans did not bring priests with them.)

The basis of this decision came from Cardinal Spellman. He felt that the Puerto Ricans probably would follow the assimilationist path of the European immigrants, and he wanted to avoid the problems posed by a national parish church whose only members were aging immigrants. Spellman's assumption was that the mainland-born Puerto Ricans would, in time, assimilate and cease to speak Spanish. Until that time, he felt the best solution was Americanization—to provide Spanish language services in "integrated" parishes. These special services were often held in a small chapel, and the main church was devoted to services in English for a predominantly Anglo population.[74]

Clearly, Spellman could not foresee the true nature of Hispanic migration. Fr. Antonio Stevens-Arroyo thinks the Americanization zeal is a form of "paternalism." Patrick McNamara regrets that although earlier groups were helped to link their

---

[73] F. E. Balderrama, "En defensa de la Raza . . . ," gives insight into this process. In the 1920s, a Mexico-based religious counterrevolutionary movement gained substantial support from Anglo as well as Mexican-American Catholics who wanted to ward off revolutionary influences among Mexicans in the United States. In the 1930s, this surfaced again, when Mexico's President Cardenas revived anticlerical measures.

[74] Fitzpatrick, *Puerto Rican Americans,* pp. 124–125. See also Antonio M. Stevens-Arroyo, "Puerto Rican Struggles in the Catholic church," in Rodriguez et al., eds., *The Puerto Rican Struggle.*

religion and nationality, neither Mexican Americans nor Puerto Ricans were helped
to produce a kind of ethnic Catholicism.[75]

Pastoral care and social action and the Catholic church. For its Hispanic
members until the 1970s, the Catholic church was a church of Anglo priests concerned primarily with the traditional pastoral goals with little interest in social action. As Mexican Americans in the Southwest became conspicuous "problems,"
particularly as in Los Angeles after the "zoot suit" riots of the 1940s, the church
wanted to show that it was an institution determined to instill American ideals. In
practice, this translated into objectives as diverse as citizenship instruction and
youth activities in the Catholic Youth Organization. Very often these socialization
efforts were combined with anticommunist preaching.[76]

In Los Angeles little effort was made to address the problems of Mexican-
American poverty. However, in San Antonio, as early as 1943, the pressure of great
poverty produced a different reaction. The leader at the time was Archbishop
Lucey, who complained that

> A very general lack of labor organizations, the absence of good legislation,
> and the greed of powerful employers have combined to create in Texas dread-
> ful and widespread misery. The evil men who are driving tens of thousands of
> our people into a slow starvation will be held to strict accountability by the
> God of eternal justice.[77]

Lucey's concern was not echoed elsewhere in the Southwest. McNamara points out
that the typical Southwestern Catholic parish is locked into association with the dis-
possessed Mexicans and is still very poor. Thus parishes are exceedingly vulnerable
to economic pressure, especially from Anglo Catholics. Typically, then, when direct
social action appears, it is nearly always initiated by a group from outside the area.
One of the first groups to appear in the Southwest was established in 1945 by the
American Board of Catholic Missions in Chicago, which set up a Bishop's Committee
for the Spanish speaking to serve Chicano migrant workers. The need for some sort
of social action in San Antonio was so obvious that when a chance to get federal
money appeared in 1964 through the Office of Economic Opportunity, it was the
San Antonio Catholic church whose projects became the single most important
channel for funneling federal money into poverty areas of San Antonio.

In New York, the sudden appearance of large numbers of Puerto Ricans after

[75] Antonio Stevens-Arroyo, "Puerto Rican Struggles," p. 130. June Macklin and Alvina
Teniente de Costilla detail the changing role of the church in a midwestern Chicano community
in "La Virgen de Guadalupe and the American Dream," in West and Macklin, eds., *The Chicano
Experience,* pp. 111–143.

[76] Immediately after World War II, the hierarchy in Los Angeles began an even more
massive program of parochial school construction. When completed by 1960, the system was
hailed by Catholic leaders as an important step in safeguarding the Catholic faith of Mexican
Americans.

[77] McNamara in Grebler et al., *The Mexican American People,* citing *The Spanish-speaking of the Southwest and West* (Washington, D.C.: National Catholic Welfare Conferences,
1943), pp. 3–4.

World War II rapidly overwhelmed the strategy of "integrated" parishes. Church officials were upset to discover that large numbers of Puerto Ricans were being married in Protestant ceremonies. The outcome was a renewed effort to provide more effective pastoral care. By the 1960s, it seemed that the church had turned the tide.[78] There was some settlement house activity in particularly poor areas of New York, but this form of social action was limited. In the 1950s the church began to sponsor a San Juan Fiesta, a day of cultural fiesta so attractive that it later needed a stadium. The archdiocese also began to send young priests to an Intercultural Institute, then directed by Ivan Illich, a man later to become well known for his strong emphasis on social action. But many traditional parishes in New York continued to resist the demands of their Hispanic parishioners.[79]

In the late 1960s, the latent pressure grew to the point where the church was forced into a more active stand, especially in the Southwest. A dramatic series of what McNamara terms "lay protests" involved Chicano and Anglo activists in Los Angeles (*Católicos por la Raza* and Concerned Catholics). Several jail terms resulted and considerable publicity, much of it centering on the negative reaction of the church itself.[80] In the agricultural fields of California, visiting priests were defying the local clergy to help César Chávez to organize Mexican farm workers. As Chávez remarked,

> We would ask, "Why do the Protestants come out here and help the people, demand nothing, and give all their time to serving farm workers, while our own parish priests stay in their churches?" . . . We could not get any help at all from the priests of Delano. But slowly the pressure of the people grew and grew until finally we have in Delano a priest sent by the new Bishop . . . When poor people get involved in a long conflict, such as a strike, or a civil rights drive and the pressure increases every day, there is a deep need for spiritual advice. . . . What do we want the Church to do? . . . We ask for its presence with us, beside us, as Christ among us. . . . We don't ask for paternalism. We ask for servanthood."[81]

In 1969 the priests who had worked with Chávez organized PADRES, an organization of Spanish-speaking priests, to press from within the church for more social action. At the same time in Latin America the Catholic bishops were committing the church to help the poor, following an ideology known generally as the "theology of liberation."[82] The priests in PADRES were aware of this movement and

---

[78] Fitzpatrick, *Puerto Rican Americans,* pp. 93, 125.

[79] Hendricks compares two churches serving Dominicans. In one, the Irish-American pastor strongly promoted assimilation: in the other the Spanish priest was far more attuned to his parishioners' expectations. See *The Dominican Diaspora* (New York: Teachers College Press, 1974), pp. 117–121.

[80] McNamara, "Catholicism and the Chicano." For a fictionalized but reasonably accurate account of the protests, see Oscar Acosta, *Revolt of the Cockroach People* (San Francisco, Calif.: Straight Arrow Press, 1973).

[81] César Chávez, "The Mexican American and the Church," *El Grito,* Vol. 1 (1968), pp. 9-12.

[82] See Isidro Lucas, *The Browning of America: The Hispanic Revolution in the American Church* (Chicago: Fides/Claretian, 1981), for a discussion of the Catholic church and Hispanics during the 1970s.

hoped to see its counterpart in the United States.[83] In 1972, the church seemed to be responding to the pressure from inside as well as from the lay protesters and organized the first National Hispanic Pastoral Encuentro, held in Washington, D.C. Predictably, the bishops were pressed for more social action. (There were, in fact, some Hispanic bishops: a dozen by 1980 with seats in major cities of the Southwest—Los Angeles, Santa Fe, and El Paso.)

By the mid-1980s, some of the activists began to feel that the church was becoming more responsive. As an example, they note that the churches have consistently welcomed undocumented Hispanics and that some parishes have sheltered Hispanic refugees. But the hierarchy in general has firmly resisted the theology of liberation because of its socialist implications.

There are only two church-organized Chicano social action efforts that remain during the 1980s. Both are very local. They are COPS (Community Organized for Public Service) in San Antonio and a sister organization in Los Angeles (UNO or United Neighborhood Organization). Both groups focus on local parishes and local problems, following the practices established by Saul Alinsky, a famed community organizer. The San Antonio COPS has worked on issues ranging from local sewage and drainage systems to statewide reforms on school financing.

Archbishop Flores supported the San Antonio group strongly and rallied the support of all the bishops in Texas. The California hierarchy was less supportive of UNO, but the group nonetheless managed to accomplish important changes in the institutions affecting local life. In 1983 they were working to persuade the local Safeway store to improve the quality of its products and services, to change insurance rates, to eliminate a toxic waste dump, and to force a local corporate office park to provide new jobs. Both COPS and UNO have added a significant new dimension to parish life and allow it to be a focus for the expression of community frustration and distress.

However, Hispanics continue to worry the Catholic church. In the early 1980s, for example, Hispanics were a third of all Catholics in the New York archdiocese. Very few—only 31 percent—went to church regularly, even though they were strong believers. The immigrants were still "folk Catholics," not attuned to the American church, and their children were even more secular. Repeatedly, Hispanics have tried to persuade the church that it must change to retain its Hispanic parishioners.[84]

Protestants and Hispanics. This background about the Catholic church is essential for understanding Hispanic Protestantism. Missionary efforts by the major Protestant denominations reach back into the nineteenth century, but it is only recently that any substantial efforts were made. In earlier times the Hispanic Protestants were segregated within the mainline Protestant denominations. Protestant settlement houses were always significant community institutions, particularly in Texas cities where there were few government-sponsored social services. Hispanic

---

[83] As late as 1981, there were very few Hispanic priests. The exact percentage is 2.4 percent—about a third from Latin America, another third from Spain, and about a third U.S.-born. Fewer than 500 native Hispanics were serving as priests in 1981; *ibid.*

[84] K. Briggs, "Among Hispanic Catholics, Another Pattern of Practice," *The New York Times,* January 9, 1983, p. 10. See also Rev. Frank Ponce, "The Enculturation of Hispanics in the Catholic Church," *Agenda,* Vol. 10 (November–December 1980), pp. 11–15.

ministers working in these houses took an early and significant lead in activist leadership.[85] Strong social action stances appeared during the 1960s. Typical of these is the Migrant Ministry, which worked with César Chávez in his farm worker organizing efforts. Even earlier than this, Protestant ministers had begun to work in the urban community organizing efforts during the late 1960s and early 1970s.

In the Protestant sects (contrasted to mainline denominations like the Methodists), there is even greater activism. There are important reasons for this activist leadership. It is very easy for lay leaders to become ministers. Thus, almost all of the Hispanic Pentecostal and evangelical churches have Hispanic ministers. Often they are former members of the congregation. Catholicism, of course, requires elaborate training, and there are still painfully few Hispanic priests. In other ways, the Pentecostal churches are very much part of the local community. Members meet every night and

> The pastor becomes a catalytic agent . . . by bringing together poor people in need of a broker between them and the complex urban ambiance, for comfort and meaning . . .. The Puerto Rican migrant, through his or her membership in the Pentecostal community, attempts to create and maintain strong bonds of *communitas* around a religious base which repeatedly reinforces the old way of life, by maintaining an identity as *puertorriqueño* through the constant flow of family and communication back and forth to Puerto Rico, through *testimónios* or stories about recent events which one or a close friend might have experienced on the Island; through the use of language and music and typical food in church or church related activities. . . . We see the Puerto Rican Pentecostals developing coping mechanisms in the city, since they do not have many other options. However, we did not experience the members rejecting the total society or its symbols of success. . . . When members turned their back on the "world," it is not on the society, but on specific behavior that pentecostals viewed as evil.[86]

The Pentecostal church is very pastor oriented, and while the pastor's main job is to provide meaning in the daily service, he also guides, helps, and brokers for individual parishioners in the course of their daily problems. The Pentecostal church is also an institution that (as Betances and Berry-Caban note) functions to preserve Puerto Rican culture and to keep alive the linkages to the island. In this sense, it serves much the same kind of function that the Catholic national parish served for the European immigrants of the past. The interpretation of the Pentecostal church as a "coping" device for Puerto Ricans adds depth to the findings of yet another substantial study. This research hints that the mental health of Puerto Ricans involved in Pentecostal communities is probably better than that of Catholics in the same community.[87] Betances and Berry-Caban observe that Pentecostalism does not represent a retreat from the world but, rather, a means of coping with its stresses,

[85] See Grebler et al., *Mexican American People,* for a discussion of mainline Protestantism and the Mexican Americans.

[86] Samuel Betances and Cristobal Berry-Caban, "The Puerto Rican Full Gospel Church of Milwaukee," unpublished manuscript 1979, pp. 27, 79, 85.

[87] V. Garrison, "Sectarianism and Psychosocial Adjustment: A Controlled Comparison of Puerto Rican Pentecostals and Catholics," in I. I. Zaretsky and M. Leone, eds., *Religious Movements in Contemporary America* (Princeton, N.J.: Princeton University Press, 1974).

Sectarian Protestants also are vigilant proselytizers, and homes within walking distance of such churches are routinely visited by evangelizing missionaries. Three-quarters of the Hispanics surveyed in a 1978 Gallup study reported that they had been approached by Protestant evangelists. Even though Protestantism still claims only a small minority of Hispanics (the exact proportion is unknown), its future with them may be important.

CHAPTER SEVEN
CULTURE AND LANGUAGE

American society is quick to recognize the cultures of the many ethnic groups in America and the value of their ethnic heritage. But we still expect most elements of this heritage and identity to disappear more or less quickly in the melting pot. Accordingly, the process of immigrant acculturation—the steady decay of immigrant culture and the acquisition of mainstream characteristics—was seen for many years as the most appropriate way to study ethnic culture. It assumed the decay of heritage, and alternative approaches did not seem very important.

In this context the Hispanic cultural "islands" in such areas as northern New Mexico were seen as survivals, somewhat similar to the survival of Elizabethan English customs in remote Appalachian villages.[1] However, when millions of Americans were inducted into military service in World War II, the Army trainers serving western states were astonished that virtually *all* "Mexican" recruits spoke Spanish, "no matter how many generations their ancestors may have lived in the United States."[2] This was the kind of discovery that began to lead social scientists into a concern with what factors account for such a remarkable persistence and to measure the actual extent of cultural retention and cultural change.

Much of this effort is concerned with language, both because the retention of

[1] John Burma, *Spanish Speaking Groups in the United States* (Durham, N.C.: Duke University Press, 1954).

[2] W. D. Altus, "The American Mexican: The Survival of a Culture," *Journal of Social Psychology,* Vol. 29 (1949), pp. 211–220.

Spanish is the most obvious and visible sign of retained Hispanic cultural character-istics and because of the continuous controversy about language and school achieve-ment. Thus, there are both important scientific issues and some important practical issues connected with language.

THE SPANISH LANGUAGE

Returns from the 1980 census tell us that the United States is now the sixth largest Spanish-speaking country in the world. In fact, testimony before the Congress noted there were 11½ million people who reported that they spoke Spanish at home in 1980.[3] Of course not all Hispanics speak Spanish at home, but over half of the people in this country who speak a language other than English did speak Spanish. Spanish speakers outnumber by seven times all other non-English speakers.

In Table 7.1 we see that people who speak Spanish at home are heavily con-centrated in just four states. Two-thirds of them live in California, Texas, New York, and Florida. A large proportion (30 percent) live in the state of New Mexico. Twen-ty percent of the residents of Texas and 15 percent of all Californians used Spanish in their home. Many of these people are bilingual, but a surprisingly large number had trouble with English. When asked in the census, they would reply that they spoke English "not well" or "not at all." Table 7.1 indicates that California had the highest number of Spanish-speaking individuals who functioned poorly in English—and New Mexico had the least number (although New Mexico's small population tends to conceal its position as the closest approximation to a truly Hispanic bi-lingual state).

Not all people with difficulties with the English language are noncitizens or recent immigrants. Nearly four out of five such people were U.S. citizens in 1980, a proportion that may have important implications in mustering the Hispanic vote. But language acquisition and retention is not a static process. Research on the use of Spanish in the United States seems to indicate that Spanish (just like other foreign languages in this country) is undergoing certain changes, but there is very little agreement about the nature and extent of these changes.

The most intriguing question for social scientists watching the merging of a new group of immigrants into American society is: How fast is the use of Spanish disappearing? Calvin Veitman takes one view when he suggests that first-generation immigrants speak their native language and learn some English. Their offspring learn some English first, and because the parents' native language is eroded, it will seldom be used by subsequent generations.[4] This view appears to be substantiated in the difference between native-born and foreign-born Hispanics in their use of English or

---

[3]Much of this material is based on a paper by Dorothy Waggoner, "Estimates from the 1980 Census on People in Homes in which Spanish is Spoken," presented before the Sub-committee on Census and Population, Committee on the Post Office and Civil Service, U.S. House of Representatives, September 13, 1983. See also Edith K. McArthur and Paul M. Seigel, "Developments in the Measurement of English Language Proficiency," unpublished paper, U.S. Bureau of the Census, 1984.

[4]Ronald Pedone, *The Retention of Minority Languages in the United States, a Seminar on the Catalytic Work of Calvin Veltman,* May 13, 1980 (Washington, D.C.: Government Print-ing Office, 1980).

TABLE 7.1   Estimated Numbers and Percentages of Home Speakers of Spanish, Aged 3 and
Older, by State: United States, 1980

STATE	NUMBER	% OF TOTAL POPULATION	% OF SPANISH SPEAKERS	
			BY STATE	CUMULATIVE
All States	11,559,000	5.3%	100.0%	100.0%
California	3,270,000	14.5	28.3	28.3
Texas	2,595,000	19.2	22.5	50.7
New York	1,453,000	8.6	12.6	63.3
Florida	807,000	8.6	7.0	70.3
Illinois	524,000	4.8	4.5	74.8
New Jersey	431,000	6.1	3.7	78.6
New Mexico	362,000	29.4	3.1	81.7
Arizona	343,000	13.3	3.0	84.7
Colorado	184,000	6.7	1.6	86.3
Pennsylvania	140,000	1.2	1.2	87.5
Massachusetts	114,000	2.1	1.0	89.4
Connecticut	108,000	3.6	0.9	89.4
Michigan	107,000	1.2	0.9	90.3
Ohio	101,000	1.0	0.9	91.2

Source: 1980 census, as presented in testimony by D. Waggoner (1983).

Spanish as the "usual" language.[5] (See Table 7.2, page 121.) Carlos Arce analyzed a large national sample of Mexican Americans and also found a movement from Spanish to English in different generations. Moreover, the direction of movement ran toward more English usage in each generation and toward English-dominant bilingual competence.[6] This normal and expected shift is further confirmed by Joshua Fishman, a leading expert on language, who believes that Spanish-speaking third-generation immigrants retain no more Spanish than any other similar group.[7] Fishman is suspicious of the accuracy of census data and observes that language retention is a subtle and complex process, not easily measured. In the United States, legal restrictions in the past tended to discourage Spanish, but language maintenance really depends a great deal on "closure"—that is, how isolated and self-sufficient is the immigrant population? He remarks further that Americans (and social scientists) tend to see native immigrant language as necessarily vanishing, to be found only "on the margins of society, among the dislocated, the retrogressive, the disad-

[5] One of the important difficulties in language measurement is the variation in terms in studying non-English language use. According to the terms used, the numbers may vary greatly. See Reynaldo Macias and Mary Spencer, *Estimating the Number of Language Minority and Limited English Proficient Persons in the United States: A Comparative Analysis of the Studies* (Los Alamitos, CA: National Center for Bilingual Research, 1983).

[6] Carlos Arce, "Language Shift Among Chicanos: Strategies for Measuring and Assessing Direction and Rate," *Social Science Journal*, Vol. 19 (April 1982), pp. 101–119.

[7] Joshua Fishman, "Language, Ethnic Identity and Political Loyalty: Mexican Americans in Sociolinguistic Perspective," a paper prepared for the Urban Institute, Los Angeles, California, March 14, 1984.

TABLE 7.2   Language Shift Patterns Among Spanish Speaking by Region, Native and Foreign Born, 1976

		ENGLISH USUAL LANGUAGE	SPANISH USUAL LANGUAGE
New York:	Foreign Born	30.4%	69.6%
	Native Born	62.5	37.5
Florida:	Foreign Born	25.4	74.6
	Native Born	62.7	37.3
Texas:	Foreign Born	15.4	84.6
	Native Born	39.9	60.1
California:	Foreign Born	29.6	70.5
	Native Born	78.7	21.3

Source: Ronald Pedone, *The Retention of Minority Languages in the United States, a Seminar on the Catalytic Work of Calvin Veltman,* May 13, 1980 (Washington, D.C.: Government Printing Office, 1980).

vantaged and the dissatisfied.[8] Fishman's idea is that a second language can be used to maintain intimate language and behavior networks without harming the nation or the individual. But Fishman may very well be underestimating the enormous Spanish-speaking immigration and the immediate handicaps faced by people dealing with complex bureaucracies and the public school system. Whatever the future of Spanish as a living language in the United States, certain important points should be kept in mind.[9] First, immigration is constantly refilling the *barrios* of large cities with new generations of monolingual Spanish speakers, creating an impression that the people in some areas never do learn to speak English. In reality, new residents constantly replace old residents, although the physical appearance of the *barrios* remains the same. (For details of the speed and importance of recent immigration, see Chapter 4.) Second, Spanish itself changes quite rapidly and in interesting fashion. These changes disturb Hispanic intellectuals considerably, but apparently the process of "degradation" began many years ago. Many of the immigrants speak one variety or another of rural Spanish. Mexican Spanish is heavily salted with Nahuatl words from the Indian background, but in northern Mexico, English is a major influence in new words and in changes in verbal conjugations.[10] Thus there are neologisms (*pochismos*) such as *el troque* (the truck) and *huáchale* (watch it!). Border cities in south Texas, bilingual for more than a century, have developed *pochismos* that exist nowhere else. Puerto Ricans living in New York rapidly developed "Spanglish." Third, some quite new and powerful forces are working to maintain the use of Spanish.

Unlike earlier immigrants, the Spanish-speaking are followed by a powerful complex of television and radio stations. The strongest of this group is Televisa, the

[8] Joshua Fishman, "Language Maintenance," in Stephen Thernstrom, ed., *Harvard Encyclopedia of American Ethnic Groups* (Cambridge, Mass.: Belknap Press, 1980).

[9] For an examination of general issues of Spanish in the United States, see Lucia Elias Olivares, ed., *Spanish in the U.S. Setting* (Rosslyn, Va.: InterAmerica Research Associates, 1983).

[10] Ignacio Bernal, "The Cultural Roots of the Border: An Archeologist's View," in Stanley R. Ross, ed., *Views Across the Border: The United States and Mexico* (Albuquerque, University of New Mexico Press, 1978), pp. 25–32.

dominant television broadcaster in Mexico, which owns SIN (Spanish International Network), a chain of Spanish language television stations and cable companies in the United States. Through SIN, the American-Spanish audience is fed an endless diet of television programming originating in Mexico, Latin America, and South America. The speed of this growth in media is so great that during the decade 1970 to 1980, the number of Spanish language radio stations grew to 200 from 60, newspapers to 65 from 40, magazines to 65 from 25, and markets served by Spanish television to 167 from 12.[11]

Beyond the questions of measurement and change, the American attitude about the use of Spanish is quite negative. (See Chapter 10 for its importance in Hispanic politics.) When Congress began to discuss bilingual schooling, it was always clear that bilingualism was the basic issue, not just schooling. The view that prevailed was that Spanish should be taught in the schools not as part of a culture, not as a step toward cultural pluralism, but as a device for learning English more efficiently and for more rapid integration into American life. But the prevalence of Spanish worries many Anglo Americans, perhaps a majority. "What does it mean when you walk the streets of your own country and you don't understand a word of the language?" asks Thomas Morgan in an article about Hispanics.[12] Morgan goes on to speculate about the possibility of a divided nation, one speaking English and another speaking Spanish. Others see the rise of Spanish as leading to separatism and point to the troubles of Quebec in Canada as an example of what can occur in a nation with a large language minority. Two cities (Miami and San Francisco, both with large Hispanic populations) passed referenda prohibiting the expenditure of public funds for services in languages other than English.

The Hispanic community has quite generally reacted to these emotional and xenophobic ideas with bewilderment. Very few Hispanics would argue that English is not the language of this nation. Furthermore, New Mexico has been bilingual since its entry into the Union, and Puerto Rico has used Spanish as its first language since its annexation. The reemergence of this nativism, dormant at least since the 1920s, brings up many issues that do not bode well for the future of the Hispanic minority.

HISPANIC CULTURE

What do we mean by culture? Even before beginning to discuss the touchy and value-laden subject of Hispanic-American culture we must recognize the major problem in defining what we are talking about. There is, for example, the highly visible surface of "Hispanic culture" to be seen by any visitor to a Chicano, Puerto Rican, or any other Hispanic community. There are "survivals" that even attract tourists, as in the case of the "islands" of northern New Mexico. But do either of these surfaces have anything to do with middle-class Hispanics? Are middle-class Hispanics "acculturated"? There are, for example, the increasingly visible signs of Hispanic theater, dance, music, and art. Is this what is meant by culture? In this section we will discuss some of these confusions and problems in definition.

[11] *The New York Times,* April 8, 1982.

[12] Thomas B. Morgan, "The Latinization of America," *Esquire,* Vol. 99 (July 1983), pp. 47–48, 50–56.

The visible surface includes a great range of odd and interesting variations. In Los Angeles, visitors are shown the shops of Olvera Street, the famous Plaza (a popular tourist center), and a huge baroque church in downtown Los Angeles that is much used by Mexican parishioners. In the Mexican-American communities, there may be distinctive modes of dress and hair style, especially among teenagers and Mexican immigrants. Such modes often identify specific types of Mexican-American life-style. On occasion, a visitor may see a sign advertising the services of a traditional folk healer or shops selling a variety of herbs used for medicine. There are many foods peculiar to Mexicans and, in fact, traditional Mexican dishes have become one of the most rapidly spreading food fads in the larger culture. Mexican music is played endlessly on Southwestern radio stations; Mexican and other Latin American soap operas are available on television channels and Spanish-dubbed versions of American movies are shown side by side with imported Mexican movies. Outside Los Angeles there are counterparts in other Hispanic communities throughout the nation. Primarily these areas serve the local Hispanic population, while restaurants and some specialty shops may also serve occasional Anglo-American tourists. Local newspapers and national magazines periodically feature illustrated and guided tours of such attractions. For example, the *botánicas* (herbal-religious supply shops) of New York's Puerto Rican neighborhoods were the subject for a photo-essay supplying not only the visible surface but an explanation of the artifacts and their use in spiritist healing rituals.[13] (See also Chapter 9 for a discussion of Hispanic folk medicine.) These are the interesting touches that a casual visitor can accept as "Mexican culture." Their quaintness and color is sometimes kept alive for commercial reasons in tourist centers (examples are Disneyland in Los Angeles and Balboa Park in San Diego) because they make money and please visitors. But these artifacts are simply facades of life in Hispanic communities. Many of them serve immigrants; others reflect specific life-styles. They can be only partly generalized to all Hispanics, and their exoticism is misleading.

Much the same is true of the survivors in the desperately poor villages of northern New Mexico (see Chapter 2). Until very recently, these isolated communities (composed largely of interacting relatives) sheltered the famous *Penitentes* or lay brotherhoods. These brotherhoods draw on the penitential traditions of Spain to produce spectacular processions of self-flagellation during Holy Week. Apart from the processions, the *penitente* chapters also provided a major basis of social and political organization for the villages, much as the neighboring Pueblo Indian religious societies provide the core for the organization of secular activities. Exotic as they are, these ceremonies reflect a specific life-style. Even as recently as the 1960s, these communities were changing; they were becoming less isolated and less self-sufficient as their range and farming land disappeared and young people moved to the cities. The result, according to some analysts, is a "poverty-stricken village population unable to live in the traditional manner."[14] Thus, beneath the visible surface lie many complexities in Hispanic ways of life. Under the visible surface in northern New Mexico is a disintegrating sociocultural system.

It should be clear that we cannot be satisfied with quaintness. Many students

---

[13] M. A. Borrello and E. Mathis, "Botánicas: Puerto Rican Folk Pharmacies," *Natural History* (August–September 1977), pp. 66–72.

[14] C. Knowlton, "Changing Spanish-American Villages of Northern New Mexico," *Sociology and Social Research,* Vol. 53 (1969), pp. 455–474.

of Mexican-American life complain that an equally important confusion is that which sees traits of the culture of poverty as equivalent to "Hispanic culture." Teachers may attempt to explain the failure of Hispanic children in school on the basis of Hispanic "culture." In reality, a better explanation may be pervasive poverty, overcrowding, financial insecurity, and other problems.[15] The distinction appears clearly in a case history of a Puerto Rican family that started in poverty. The husband spent considerable time away from home with men (and women) friends. In the later part of the marriage, the husband became convinced that he was middle class, in spite of continuing poverty. He developed a strong work ethic, a strong sense of family, and a home environment conducive to their children's school achievement.[16]

Perhaps the most important point is that Hispanics are culturally pluralistic. There are many Hispanic subcultures and ways of life, and there are variations within each national origin group that are very easy to overlook. The many new Hispanic immigrants bring variants of national cultures. The northern New Mexico villages clearly represent a distinctive Hispanic way of life, but it is invalid to generalize from them to the Hispanics living in New York City. The Texas-Mexican border areas are another distinctive culture with a substantial amount of real cultural interpenetration. Diaz-Guerrero and his colleagues studied these areas for many years and found that certain Mexican "core values" are held by Anglo Americans in the border communities as well as by Mexicans living in the United States. Certain "Texas-Anglo core values" are shared by Mexican Americans and also by Mexicans in a city not far from the border. Then there are certain values that show a "border effect." That is, they are expressed more by Anglos and Mexicans in border towns than in Mexico City or in central Texas.[17] Not only are there differences between national origins and regions in Hispanic cultures, there are differences *within* regions. New immigrant Mexicans live more according to Mexican values in some ways. Their neighbors, who are not new to the United States but who moved from a rural area, will live according to rural Texas values. A neighbor will live according to the values of the local *barrio,* which he has absorbed from older brothers. At least one author argues that the endless presence of mainland employers in San Juan and the endless traffic to and from the mainland has created a very special biculturalism in Puerto Rico's middle class.[18] There are also subcultures that vary by age or sex groups. The Chicano *palomilla,* as one example, is a recognized young male peer group.[19]

It is a tendency to overgeneralize that is the source of many stereotypes—

---

[15] See Y. A. Cabrera, "Schizophrenia in the Southwest: Mexican Americans in Angloland," in M. P. Douglass, ed., *Claremont Reading Conference 31st Yearbook* (Claremont, Calif.: Claremont Graduate School and University Center, 1967); and Edward Cassavantes, "Pride and Prejudice: A Mexican American Dilemma," *Civil Rights Digest,* Vol. 3 (1970), pp. 22–27.

[16] Lloyd Rogler, "A Better Life: Notes from Puerto Rico," *Trans-Action,* Vol. 2 (1965), pp. 34–36.

[17] R. J. Peck and R. Díaz-Guerrero, "Two Core-Culture Patterns and the Diffusion of Values Across Their Border," *International Journal of Psychology,* Vol. 2 (1967), pp. 275–282.

[18] E. Seda Bonilla, " Que Somos" *The Rican,* Vol. 2 (1975), pp. 81–107.

[19] A. J. Rubel, "The Mexican American *Palomilla,*" *Anthropological Linguistics,* Vol. 7 (1965), pp. 92–97.

along with the mistaken idea that there is no change. One study showed that when social science studies of the 1950s and 1960s were culled for images of the Chicano, they were found to be essentially the same as images held by Anglos in the middle of the nineteenth century. The author, understandably, decries the effort to describe Mexican Americans as uniform and unchanging. In particular, he finds the effort to understand all Mexican Americans in terms of traditional folk culture to be offensive.[20] Certainly, what Romano-V. criticizes about research on Chicanos is true also for research on other Hispanics. Thus many studies of the Puerto Ricans in New York were undertaken during the first decade of their settlement and stereotypes were established. Perhaps they may have been generally true of an immigrant generation, but they are not generally true today.

Why is culture important? There are many formal definitions of culture. Various authors refer to conceptions of culture that range from the most superficial visible surfaces (dress, diet, music, food) to the deepest possible assumptions that people make about their relationships with other people and their personal values and priorities. It is these deeper aspects that most interest social scientists and any others who are concerned about understanding Hispanics. Here we will touch on three issues that derive from that concern: first, culture and personality and cognitive style; second, research on values related to Hispanic behavior in major institutions; and, third, cultural conflict.

For many years Mexican scholars have been concerned with a concept of Mexican national character as distinctive. We need not be concerned with that idea here but, rather, with its possible effects in the study of Mexican Americans—and, by extension, to other Hispanics living in the United States.[21] The work of Diaz-Guerrero is concentrated on the contrast between Mexican and U.S. cultures and the related personality contrasts, employing a variety of objective measures. He summarizes his findings as follows:

> The historical traditional pattern of the United States will produce individuals who are *active.* . . . They will be independent, individualistic, autonomous, oriented toward achievement, competitive, somewhat impulsive and aggressive, and rather tense and nervous. The Mexican historical-socio-cultural pattern, on the other hand, will produce individuals who are obedient, affiliative, interdependent, orderly, cooperative, not oriented toward achievement, and not self-initiated.[22]

Similarly, Diaz-Guerrero concludes:

> Whenever members of the [U.S.] culture face stress, they seem to feel that the way to resolve the problem, diminishing the stress, is to modify the environment, whether physical, interpersonal, or social. . . . The Mexican socioculture, on the other hand, has chosen a different method of resolving the

[20] O. Romano-V., "The Anthropology and Sociology of the Mexican Americans," *El Grito,* Vol. II (1968), pp. 13–26.

[21] Rather romantic versions of this preoccupation with Mexican national character are found in Octavio Paz, *The Labyrinth of Solitude* (New York: Grove Press, 1961), and Samuel Ramos, *Profile of Man and Culture in Mexico* (Austin: University of Texas Press, 1967).

[22] R. Díaz-Guerrero, *Psychology of the Mexican* (Austin: University of Texas Press, 1967), p. xvii.

problems set by the environment . . . Mexicans seem to feel that the best way to resolve problems is to modify oneself.[23]

His other findings include the suggestion that "Americans tend to be more complex and differentiated in cognitive structure than Mexicans."[24]

Lately there has been an important development in this search for psychological differences. Differences in cognitive styles, of course, refer to particular ways of perceiving, organizing, being influenced by, and acting on reality. In effect, children are taught how to learn by their cultures. The technical terms for the differences are "field dependent" and "field independent." Researchers on this subject believe that field independence is more likely to occur among children who are "analytic and scientific." Field dependence is more characteristic of "nurturant, affiliative, socially sensitive, imitative individuals."[25] The importance of this research is that although the conclusions are far from proven, many educators not only believe this new and plausible explanation of Hispanics' difficulties in school but are busily using it to excuse themselves without really understanding the concept.[26]

But are Hispanics in the United States more field dependent than are Anglos? There is mixed evidence, at the best. Cuban Americans in New Jersey were found to be more field dependent than Anglo Americans (and females of both groups were more so than males).[27] But there is mixed evidence for Mexican Americans: some studies find more field dependence for Hispanic than for Anglo children. Some find that U.S.-born children (especially the third generation or more) are no different from Anglo children. One author finds that Chicanos in "traditional" communities are more likely to be field dependent than are Mexican Americans in nontraditional communities—and concludes with what should be the point of this discussion—a recognition of the heterogeneity among Mexican Americans and Hispanics in general.[28] The same researchers with Ramirez go on to argue that even if Hispanic children *are* more field dependent than Anglo children, this factor should not deny them education. Rather, they argue, educators should adapt classroom structure and curriculum to promote cognitive flexibility in children.[29] These views are careful and considered, and although they sound like an echo of the stereotypes of ear-

[23] Díaz-Guerrero, *Psychology,* p. xviii.

[24] R. Díaz-Guerrero, "Mexicans and Americans," in Stanley Ross, ed., *Views Across the Border* (Albuquerque: University of New Mexico Press, 1978), p. 294.

[25] W. Holtzman, "Personality Development and Mental Health," in ibid., p. 313.

[26] For applications and misapplications, see Thomas P. Carter and Roberto D. Segura, *Mexican Americans in School: A Decade of Change* (New York: College Entrance Examination Board, 1979), pp. 113–119.

[27] S. D. Britain and M. Abad, "Field Independence: A Function of Sex and Socialization in a Cuban and an American Group," *Personality and Social Psychology Bulletin,* Vol. 1 (1974), pp. 319–320.

[28] M. Ramirez, A. Casteñeda, and P. Herold, "The Relationship of Acculturation to Cognitive Style Among Mexican Americans," *Journal of Cross-Cultural Psychology,* 5 (1974), pp. 424–432; S. Kagan and G. L. Zahn find that field dependence does help to explain the lower school achievement of Mexican Americans, in "Field Dependence and the School Achievement Gap Between Anglo American and Mexican American Children," *Journal of Educational Psychology,* Vol. 67 (1975), pp. 643–650, but Kagan subsequently rejected the idea that it is an all-inclusive explanation.

[29] See the manuals by Manuel Ramirez et al., in P. Harper, ed., *New Approaches to Bilingual Bicultural Education* (Austin, Tex.: Dissemination and Assessment Center for Bilingual Education, 1978).

lier years, they must be taken seriously—if for no other reason than that many educators take them seriously.

In addition to cognitive style, there are other values that are supposed to affect Hispanic behavior in school and in contact with other major American social institutions as well. Most of these are discussed in Chapter 9 (health) and in Chapter 6 (family and religion). It is certainly true that enough cultural misunderstandings have arisen in institutions to provoke a special literature about Hispanic culture. In one notable area of public health practice, the apparent difficulty with Hispanic cooperation with medical personnel has prompted considerable research. Some such studies into Hispanic folk beliefs about the causes of illness are important to health professionals and interesting. Some (as we suggest in Chapter 9) are taken as causes for Hispanic underuse of health care facilities when, in fact, it is the nature of the facilities themselves that are at fault. Hispanic culture has for so long been taken as the first explanation for Hispanic exclusion that almost any discussion leads directly to controversy.

There are sound reasons for this controversy. "Hispanic culture" is blamed for a wide range of troubles that are just as likely to be problems of function in American institutions. Stereotypes are common and, unfortunately, they often are cast in scholarly fashion. "Culture" becomes a sophisticated substitute for the old genetic explanations. Thus the "innate propensity to violence" (inherited from Indian ancestors) is replaced by data on "differential values" that may accurately reflect the response of Hispanics to a questionnaire but that do not in any way reflect the realities of Hispanic life.[30]

But the idea of culture is too important to leave without further investigation. There may well be a complex of values that might be described as "traditional." This complex includes the ideas that Hispanics, and particularly Mexicans, emphasize the present rather than the future, intangible gratifications rather than material rewards and enjoyment rather than (as one Anglo respondent phrased it) the "run-run-run" of other Americans. The Hispanic is pictured as a serene, not an anxious, person, perhaps just a bit improvident in planning for the future, but his pleasure in life and living more than compensates.

At this point it is worth asking the source of this complex of values: Is it the "noble savage" of romantic myth? Is it possibly some kind of variation of the counterculture of the 1960s? Or is it an accurate statement of the archetypal value system of Mexico? Certainly neither at the level of empirical research (Oscar Lewis, Joseph Kahl, and Rogelio Díaz-Guerrero) nor at the level of philosophical analysis (Octavio Paz or Samuel Ramos) does any observer of Mexico develop such a version of Mexican culture. In fact, this version of "tradition" is found most clearly in the works of Florence Kluckhohn and her associate in their studies of a small village in New Mexico.[31]

---

[30] For critiques, see Miguel Montiel, "The Social Science Myth of the Mexican American Family," *El Grito,* Vol. 3 (Summer 1970), pp. 56–63; Amado Padilla, "Psychological Research and the Mexican American," in J. Burma, ed., *Mexican Americans in the United States* (Cambridge, Mass.: Schenkman, 1970); Octavio I. Romano-V., "The Anthropology and Sociology of the Mexican Americans," *El Grito,* Vol. 2 (1968), pp. 13–26; and Nick Vaca, "The Mexican American in the Social Sciences," *El Grito,* Vol. 3 (1970), pp. 17–52. Some of these critiques were reprinted in Octavio I. Romano-V., ed., *Voices* (Berkeley, Calif.: Quinto Sol, 1971).

[31] See Florence R. Kluckhohn and Fred L. Strodtbeck, *Variations in Value Orientations* (Evanston, Ill., and Elmsford, N.Y.: Row, Peterson, 1961).

The impact of this study has been phenomenal, despite the obvious limitations of such a milieu. Kluckhohn has been cited, quoted, and used as *the* authority on the traditional values of Mexican Americans to an extraordinary degree, despite both the unusual nature of the place she studied and her own comments that the culture of this small village was in the process of substantial change. It is unfortunate that not enough attention was given to her prediction that the culture of the village would undoubtedly change as it became more integrated into the institutions of the larger American society, particularly those concerned with economic life.

In fact, Kluckhohn's analysis of the culture of this village is an analysis of the adaptability of values to a local situation rather than an attempt to derive an archetype of Mexican culture. Her work has been badly distorted. The pace of change of society and technology is very slow in a remote village. The slow change of seasons and the natural risks of an agricultural society may mean that American urban values would be dysfunctional in a small New Mexican village.

Whatever these speculations, one can argue in retrospect that traditional values, at least at a time in the past, may very well have been of adaptive value to Mexican-American communities.[32]

But there is a certain amount of empirical data on the relationship of values to circumstance. Table 7.3 gives results from the three major cities of Los Angeles, San Antonio, and Albuquerque showing a strong relationship between the tenacity of traditional values and the income of the individual. The poor in all three cities were far more traditional. *Most* poor Mexican Americans saw comparatively little virtue in planning because "plans are hard to fulfill." *Most* poor Mexican Americans tried to "be content with what comes their way" rather than "expecting too much out of life." But, interestingly, comparatively few at any income level are wholeheartedly in favor of "thinking only about the present, without worrying about what is going to happen tomorrow." Apparently, even if you distrust planning for the future, it is wise at least to *worry* about the future. Differences between the three cities show (as with familism) that the middle-class Spanish Americans of Albuquerque are the most "acculturated" to these values.

A 1960 study of Chicano, black, and Anglo migrants to Racine, Wisconsin, using almost identical questions, reports a rather similar pattern. Most devastating for the notion that there is a unique Mexican value pattern is the Shannons' finding that Mexican-American and black migrants into this midwestern industrial city have a very similar world view, and it is dramatically different from the world view of Anglo Americans. This is true even when income is controlled. It suggests that the minority experience may be at least as significant in affecting values as is the particular cultural heritage.[33] In general the data suggest that cultural value patterns are highly responsive to the demands of a situation.

---

[32] A similar analysis of time perspective is made by Dorothy Nelkin, "Unpredictability and Life Style in a Migrant Labor Camp," *Social Problems,* Vol. 17 (Spring 1970), pp. 472–487. As concluded in research done by the Shannons, "the sense of causality, the relation between effort and return, is perceived in terms of an environment which may be neither predicted nor controlled." See Lyle and Magdaline Shannon, *Minority Migrants in the Urban Community: Mexican-American and Negro Adjustment to Industrial Society* (Beverly Hills, Calif.: Sage, 1973), p. 225.

[33] Shannon and Shannon, *Minority Migrants,* p. 230.

TABLE 7.3   Percentage of Mexican-American Survey Respondents Holding Familistic Values, by Income, Los Angeles, San Antonio, and Albuquerque, 1965–1967

VALUE	PERCENT AGREEING WITH ITEM					
1. Los Angeles	High Income		Medium Income		Low Income	
	Percent	Total N (= 100%)	Percent	Total N (= 100%)	Percent	Total N (= 100%)
A. Immobility[a]	7%	344	15%	292	26%	277
B. Nepotism[b]	22	353	36	292	41	272
2. San Antonio			Medium Income		Low Income	
			Percent	Total N (= 100%)	Percent	Total N (= 100%)
A. Immobility[a]			15%	317	35%	239
B. Nepotism[b]			29	291	58	228
3. Albuquerque	High Income		Medium Income		Low Income	
	Percent	Total N (= 100%)	Percent	Total N (= 100%)	Percent	Total N (= 100%)
A. Immobility[a]	4%	22	2%	50	28%	39
B. Nepotism[b]	4	22	6	50	28	39

[a]"When looking for a job, a person ought to find a position in a place located near his parents, even if that means losing a good opportunity elsewhere.

[b]"If you have the chance to hire an assistant in your work, it is always better to hire a relative than a stranger."

Sources: Data for Los Angeles and San Antonio were provided courtesy of the Mexican American Study Project, University of California at Los Angeles, and for Albuquerque by Operation SER, Los Angeles, California. All three surveys used probability samples of Mexican-American households. Income levels vary greatly among the three cities, and, accordingly, different definitions of "high," "medium," and "low" have been applied, though each refers to approximately comparable levels of living. The source for wording of items was Joseph A. Kahl, "Some Measures of Achievement Orientation," *American Journal of Sociology,* Vol. 70 (May 1965), pp. 680–681.

But there is yet another consideration. Certain Hispanic cultural assumptions and core values may, of course, affect the critical relationships with American institutions. There is also culture conflict—an overt conflict between cultures. Many Hispanic children may *not* be aware of the disjuncture between the home culture and the culture of the school, but in many parts of this nation Hispanics are indeed aware of conflict. This is particularly true in certain parts of the Southwest, a region with long-standing open conflict between Mexicans and Anglos—especially in such areas as south Texas and in parts of northern New Mexico. This conflict is an almost endless theme in novels, stories, and biographical accounts. A recent and good description appears in the novel *The Milagro Beanfield War* about New Mexico.

The folklorist Americo Paredes deals with a south Texas expression of conflict in popular culture.[34]

HISPANIC CULTURE CHANGE AND ACCULTURATION

It is true that Hispanic culture changes and that it persists. But, as Susan Keefe has observed, most American social scientists assume that "change primarily affects the minority ethnic group, whose culture is expected to become more and more like the Anglo majority's culture. This process has been called Americanization, Anglo-conformity, and assimilation."[35] Thus it is assumed that traits of Hispanic culture disappear and are replaced by traits of Anglo culture. As an example, an early study of Mexican immigrants to Detroit argued that "Those layers of . . . culture which are most immediately affected by contact are those most directly involved in getting a living and in protection from the elements. In these areas, utilitarian meaning competes with unutilitarian meaning, and, in the long run, the meaning having the greater utility supplants that which has the less." And, further, "Like the other immigrant groups in the northern United States, Mexican culture as a functional unity probably will be blotted out by the third generation in Detroit."[36]

But another model argues that there can be such a thing as biculturalism. That is, the traits of the "indigenous culture" need not be dropped—and there can be two modes of functioning.[37] (A comment on this model suggested wryly there might be such a thing as a 150 percent Indian.) Thus it is possible to gain Anglo culture traits without totally losing Hispanic culture traits. A third notion is that there is a new hybrid culture developing, possibly something close to the life-style of the borderlands of southern Texas, discussed earlier in this chapter, or of middle-class Puerto Ricans in San Juan.

In recent years there is increasing interest in developing measures of acculturation for Hispanics of various national backgrounds that could measure change in all three dimensions of the adoption of Anglo styles, loss of Hispanic styles, and biculturalism. There is now general agreement that the important dimensions for the individual are language familiarity and usage, interaction with fellow Hispanics, ethnic loyalty and identity, cultural awareness, and generational proximity.[38] Concentrating on just two of these (cultural awareness and ethnic loyalty), Padilla found that most of his sample of Mexican Americans in southern California showed moderate levels of ethnic loyalty and cultural awareness. Neither end of the range—

[34] John Nichols, *The Milagro Beanfield War* (New York: Ballantine, 1974), and Americo Paredes, "The Problem of Identity in a Changing Culture; Popular Expressions of Culture Conflict Along the Lower Rio Grande Border," in Ross, ed., *Views Across the Border.*

[35] Susan Keefe, "Acculturation and the Extended Family," in Amado Padilla, ed., *Acculturation* (Boulder, Colo.: Westview Press, 1980), p. 86.

[36] Norman Humphrey, "On Assimilation and Acculturation," *Psychiatry,* Vol. 6 (1943), pp. 343–345.

[37] J. Szapocnik and W. Kurstnes, "Acculturation, Biculturalism and Adjustment Among Cuban Americans," in Padilla, ed., *Acculturation.*

[38] See, for example, I. Cuellar et al., "An Acculturation Scale for Mexican American Normal and Clinical Populations," *Hispanic Journal of Behavioral Sciences,* Vol. 2 (1980), pp. 199–217, and E. Olmedo and A. Padilla, "Empirical and Construct Validation of Measures of Acculturation for Mexican Americans," *Journal of Social Psychology,* Vol. 105 (1978), pp. 179–187.

total loyalty and awareness nor total rejection of the culture and of Mexicans—is very common. The persons born in Mexico were, of course, the least acculturated. But there is a wide range of acculturation, even among third and fourth-generation Mexican Americans. Many are very loyal and very culturally aware.

These findings neatly fit earlier notions that Mexicans are unusually retentive of their culture. But Mexicans are more likely to be affected by schooling; the less schooling, the less likely the acculturation. Virtually no persons who attended college remained highly unacculturated even though comparatively few become fully acculturated. Padilla comments, "These individuals because of their schooling might best be labeled as bicultural. These individuals have acculturated to a sufficient extent to be able to function within the mainstream society, but at the same time they have not moved away from their culture of origin."[39]

But Cuban Americans are quite different. Both "behavioral and value acculturation were [found to be] linear functions of the amount of time a person was exposed to the host culture. The rate at which the behavioral acculturation process took place was a function of the age and sex of the individual," with younger family members acculturating more rapidly.[40]

Does acculturation produce stress for the individual? Diego Vigil suggests that it depends on the setting. In a *barrio* of the inner city, Mexican-oriented (or unacculturated) teenagers seem better adjusted, partly because of strong family support, than do either Anglo-oriented acculturated or Chicano-oriented (medium-acculturated) students. In nearby suburbs, the unacculturated students have a harder time and acculturated students show less stress. Chicano-oriented students still tend to display symptoms of stress.[41] In another study in the Mission District of San Francisco (a poor neighborhood, Hispanic but with mixed Mexicans, Central Americans, and some South Americans), the "least adjusted individuals were found to be either monocultural Latino or monocultural U.S. mainstream, and the best adjusted individuals were found to be bicultural/bilingual."[42] In appraising the value of these studies, it must be remembered that the most important factors associated with psychological well-being were income, education, age, and marital status. Thus the relationship of acculturation to psychological adjustment was not statistically significant. How acculturation affects stress or happiness still seems to depend on its relationship with other aspects of an individual's life, as shown in the Mission District study. Yet another study emphasizes the complexity of this issue. Christine Torres-Matrullo found in one study of Puerto Rican women in Pennsylvania that unacculturated women were more likely to be depressed and to have low self-esteem and a low sense of personal adequacy.[43] But a later study of Puerto Rican men failed to show any relationship between acculturation and notable stress or difficulty in personality adjustment.

[39] Amado Padilla, "Cultural Awareness and Ethnic Loyalty," in Padilla, ed., *Acculturation*, p. 75.

[40] J. Szapocanik et al., "Theory and Measurement of Acculturation," *Revista Interamericana de Psicologia*, Vol. 12 (1978), pp. 113–130.

[41] Diego Vigil, "Adaptation Stretegies and Cultural Life Styles of Mexican American Adolescents," *Hispanic Journal of Behavioral Sciences,* Vol. 1 (1979), pp. 375–392.

[42] J. G. Lang, et al., "Quality of Life and Psychological Well-being in a Bicultural Latino Community," *Hispanic Journal of Behavioral Sciences,* Vol. 4 (1982), pp. 433–450.

[43] Christine Torres-Matrullo, "Acculturation, Sex-Role Values and Mental Health Among Mainland Puerto Ricans," in Padilla, ed., *Acculturation.*

CHAPTER EIGHT
HISPANICS AND INSTITUTIONS OF THE MODERN STATE: I

Looking back over more than a century of Hispanic presence, it is important to remember that during this time, the receiving American society was changing dramatically. When Mexicans first had contact with Anglo Americans, it was a relationship between two separate societies, each with its own institutions. But American society of the 1840s was rather simple in terms of organization. There was almost none of the apparatus of government institutions that we now take for granted. There were virtually no public schools, no system of welfare, no system of federal taxes and no state-mandated protection for workers, such as unemployment compensation or Social Security. There were only the rudiments of a police and prison system.

When the revolutionary upheavals in Mexico brought the first large immigration in the early twentieth century, the structure of American society had changed. There was, for example, a public educational system well in place. But the United States was still a long way from a "welfare state"—and this was most particularly true in the American Southwest.

Then again, when the Puerto Ricans arrived in large numbers after World War II, most of today's familiar institutions were well established, particularly in New York. There was an expensive system of free public education, a large welfare system, and a complex criminal justice apparatus involving urban police, courts, and prisons. A substantial set of agencies cared for the health and mental health of the populace. And by the time the Cubans arrived in large numbers, an even more elaborate welfare state was in place and operating.[1]

Many of the classical sociological theories about the adjustment of ethnic and racial minorities ignore the role of these institutions. Typically, they focus on the extent to which the culture of the new group is compatible with the "core" American culture. (Some of these theories are discussed in Chapter 7.) But these older approaches have given way to a more careful examination of institutions and, in particular, their role in the collective lives of minorities. Thus if Hispanic children perform poorly in school, the traditional theories would look for failures in Hispanic culture. The new institutional approach is to ask what it is in the school system that leads to an incapacity to teach Hispanic children.[2]

One of the first scholars even to mention the institutional context and Puerto Ricans was the historian Oscar Handlin. He contrasted the experiences of these "newcomers" to those of the earlier European immigrants in New York City: "After 1933, the welfare state assumed many social obligations earlier immigrants had borne themselves; it seemed pointless then to duplicate its activities."[3] Handlin implies that the experiences of the "newcomer" groups cannot be easily compared with that of the older European stock immigrants: not only did the latter groups enter an entirely different economic opportunity structure, but they also entered an entirely different institutional context. Many Americans of European descent find it difficult to understand why newcomers do not adjust to American society as easily as did their ancestors at the turn of the century. They ignore these profound economic and social changes.

Some of the institutions of the state are supportive. The schools supplement the family's efforts to socialize young people to an ever-changing society. Government welfare, health, and mental health institutions provide an increasingly comprehensive insurance against catastrophe. But this enormous expansion of the welfare state is seen by some theorists as a mixed blessing for the newcomers and for minorities like the Hispanics as well. For one thing, state institutions may control and sanction people as well as support and help them. Thus, Hispanics are notably more likely than Anglos to be affected by the criminal justice system. Institutions of control include a bureaucracy (the Immigration and Naturalization Service) that is responsible for the admission or exclusion of many Hispanics in the first place. Some theorists argue that even the expanded welfare activities of the state function in a less than benevolent manner. Some Marxists suggest that tax-supported education, health care, Social Security for the aged, and the like are in reality subsidies for the private sector—for capitalism. According to this perspective, these services

[1] Some indication of the magnitude of the change can be shown by the fact that in 1850 the paid civilian employees of the federal government constituted less than one half of 1 percent of the total civilian labor force, while by 1980 government workers (federal, state, and local) comprised 15 percent. For 1850, see *Historical Statistics of the United States*, p. 72; for 1980, see *Statistical Abstract of the U.S., 1981*, p. 306.

[2] See Joan Moore and Burton Moore, *Social Problems* (Englewood Cliffs, N.J.: Prentice-Hall, 1982), for an analysis of the ways in which the schools, criminal justice system, welfare, and health and mental health institutions have come to be seen by sociologists as sources of social problems in American society.

[3] Oscar Handlin, *The Newcomers* (Garden City, N.Y.: Doubleday, 1959), p. 111.

increase the productivity of labor. But they also lower the cost to capitalists of socializing and caring for this increasingly productive labor, as the generations succeed one another. The "profits" of such investment go to the private sector, while the government is only minimally reimbursed through corporate and individual income taxes. This, they argue, invariably leads to budget crises at every level of government.[4]

It is also possible to see the welfare state as a mechanism of control for Hispanics just as British administrators once used the educational system as a means of controlling the populations in India. This concept of "internal colonialism" includes the idea that the welfare state places "agents" of the dominant system in every community. This is an "intermediary elite" who "interpret" or mediate between the minority community and the larger system. Because he is known to be reliable, because he may speak both Spanish and English, it is as if the *barrio* bureaucrat were "appointed to handle the Mexicans." This is seen by some historians and scholars as an usurpation of potential Hispanic community leadership right at the grass-roots level.[5] But other theorists argue that it is also possible to complain about the exclusion of minorities from the benefits of the welfare state as a form of oppression. A welfare bureaucracy creates dependence, to be sure. But much energy in the Chicano and Puerto Rican movement of the 1960s went into making governmental agencies responsive to their welfare needs.

The experiences of Cubans, Puerto Ricans, and Mexicans have converged in recent years. From the teeming slums of the South Bronx to the crumbling shacks of Albuquerque, Hispanics share experiences with the Anglo systems of education, health, mental health, welfare, and criminal justice. Of course, there are differences in the amount of service. But still, the similarities outweigh the differences. For this (and other reasons), political coalitions between the various Hispanic groups are more and more common. Only in the case of immigration, which we discuss first, does the experience of all groups of Hispanics differ dramatically. It is important to understand these differences, because they permeate the relationships of Hispanics with other institutions of the welfare state—the schools, health care and criminal justice systems.

IMMIGRATION AS AN INSTITUTION FOR HISPANICS

Most Americans have no direct experience with Immigration authorities. Even in the early part of this century, when many immigrants were arriving from Europe, the experience was comparatively brief. Many new arrivals had difficult experiences at a port of entry (possibly New York's Ellis Island), but they were either admitted

[4] "Fiscal crisis becomes the state budgetary expression of class struggle in monopoly capitalist society," according to Richard Child Hill, "Fiscal Collapse and Political Struggle in Decaying South Central Cities in the United States," in W. Tabb and L. Sawer, eds., *Marxism and the Metropolis* (New York: Oxford, 1978), p. 218.

[5] R. O. de la Garza, C. Cottrell, and G. Korbel, "Internal Colonialism and Chicanos: A Reconceptualization," paper presented in 1976. T. Almaguer, "Historical Notes on Chicano Oppression," *Aztlán,* Vol. 5 (1974), pp. 27–56; F. Cervantes, "Chicano Politics as Internal Colonialism and American Pluralism: A Conceptual Paradox," paper, 1976. See also Joan Moore, "American Minorities and 'New Nation' Perspectives," *Pacific Sociological Review,* Vol. 19, (1976), pp. 447–468, for a review of some of these controversies.

or not admitted. No such clarity prevails in the experiences of Hispanics. Even the Puerto Ricans have had their share of ambiguity, although as American citizens they are exempt from the worst abuses.

About a quarter of the Hispanics in the United States are immigrants, and comparatively few have become naturalized citizens. In 1980, more than three-quarters of the Mexicans, South Americans, and Central Americans remained citizens of their native lands, even though many had been in the United States for decades. Only the Cubans have naturalized at rates approximating those of other immigrants. While there are many explanations for this, it is clear that these individuals do not feel that they are fully part of the United States.[6]

Immigration as an institution for Hispanics has been most important for those of Mexican origin. The long and shared land border between Mexico and the United States has been more or less continuously patrolled since 1917. The border and its ambiguities have concerned Mexican immigrants most of all, but lately these problems have been extended to Dominicans, Colombians, Salvadorans, and Guatemalans. As a consequence, the U.S. Immigration and Naturalization Service is an institution that greatly affects the Mexican community and also some other Latin American communities. Only the Cubans (as refugees) and Puerto Ricans (as citizens) are generally relieved from the continuing need to deal with *la migra*.

Immigration policy: Mexicans as "exceptions."   Over the past hundred years, American immigration policy has been more and more exclusionary. Until very recently, the laws excluded people largely on pseudoracial grounds, but Western hemisphere residents have been special. Thus Mexicans and other Latin Americans were admitted, and deported, and admitted again in a bewildering series of changes. Immigration policy in the Western hemisphere is an endless struggle between racial and culture prejudice—and economic opportunism. This tug of war is a basic theme. As a consequence, to manage this unmanageable situation, Mexican immigrants (and, later, other Hispanics) always were "exceptions to the rule." Entry was increased or decreased by changes in law enforcement rather than by changing a policy. The rules changed very little; enforcement of those rules changed speedily. Now for some details.

Before 1875 there were no federal statutes regulating immigration.[7] At that

---

[6]Explanations for the low naturalization rate include proximity (and the belief among many that they will return home), marginal attachment to the labor force, a sense of discrimination and feeling that the home country provides protection, and the undocumented status of some. For a study of changing attitudes toward the United States among Cubans, see the results of A. Portes' panel study of 1973 immigrants in "The Rise of Ethnicity, Determinants of Ethnic Perceptions among Cuban Exiles in Miami," *American Sociological Review,* Vol. 49 (1984), pp. 375-384. For an overview of citizenship and Hispanics, see *Proceedings of the First National Conference on Citizenship in the Hispanic Community* (Washington, D.C.: NALEO Education Fund, 1984).

[7]See Maldwyn Jones, *American Immigration* (Chicago: University of Chicago Press, 1960), for a standard history of immigration. For Mexican immigration, see Manuel Gamio, *Mexican Immigration to the United States* (Chicago: University of Chicago Press, 1930); Leo Grebler, *Mexican Immigration to the United States: The Record and Its Implications,* Advance Report 2 (Los Angeles: University of California, Mexican-American Study Project, 1966); and Julian Samora, *Los Mojados: The Wetback Story* (Notre Dame, Ind.: University of Notre Dame Press, 1971). For other Hispanic Immigration, see W. Cornelius, *Mexican and Caribbean Migration to the United States* (La Jolla: University of California, Program in U.S.-Mexican Studies, 1979).

early date, Congress was concerned only with qualitative considerations applying to individual immigrants, not whole national categories. Later, Chinese and Japanese began to be refused on racial grounds. But economic concerns were always important, especially in the developing West. Thus during World War I both the prices and the demand for products of Southwestern mines and agriculture greatly increased the need for labor. Special exemptions from such immigration requirements as literacy and the head tax were issued every year between 1917 and 1920 to admit 50,000 "temporary" Mexican miners, farm workers, and railroad laborers. (The "temporary" provisions were not enforced, and in June, 1919, one report showed that two-thirds of an initial group of 30,000 Mexican workers admitted after 1917 simply remained in the United States.)

Elsewhere in the United States there was growing demand to limit the admission of new immigrants. After more than a decade of legislative hearings and investigations, Congress passed a national origins quota law. This 1924 version (implemented in 1929) became the basis for all future immigration policy. Much of the debate in Congress centered on racial questions—of the desirability of admitting immigrants from Southern and Eastern Europe. There was little question about the open bias that pervaded these superficially "scientific" hearings.[8] Although there was intense racial bias against Mexicans in the hearings of the early 1920s, immigration from the Western hemisphere was exempted from the national origins quota system.[9] There were basic reasons for this exemption: first, strong pressure from border state ranchers and employers who made a powerful case for this continuing need for Mexican labor and, second, the ideology of pan-Americanism as an overriding and traditional policy. There were as yet comparatively few immigrants from either Mexico or Canada, and it was easy for Congress to be a "good neighbor." By 1926, however, a great increase in immigration from Mexico once again encouraged the congressional restrictionists to make a strong drive to "close the back door." The racial bias emerged again. The chairman of the House Committee on Immigration and Naturalization, Representative John Box of Texas, talked about the Mexicans as "illiterate, unclean, peonized masses."[10] But it was still impossible to begin new, permanent restrictions. Rather than offending the many powerful interests, a series of "administrative controls" were developed. Thus, in the late 1920s, just as the Great Depression began to dry up the demand for labor, U.S. consular officials in Mexico began to turn down wouldbe immigrants on the grounds that they would become "public charges"—or that they were illiterate.[11] Congress was not forced into passing laws specifically excluding immigrants from a friendly Western hemisphere power, but they were excluded just as effectively.

As the depression deepened during the 1930s, state and local governments joined the federal government in reversing the flow of immigrants from Mexico. The reasons for this sudden interest were economic. When the pinch of the depression increased, large numbers of Anglo urban workers sought employment in farm work. As Mexicans were pushed out of their traditional jobs, the relief burden on

---

[8] For a good account of how the American "open door" was closed, see John Higham, *Strangers in the Land* (New York: Atheneum, 1966).

[9] Jones, *American Immigration*, p. 289.

[10] Grebler, *Mexican Immigration*, p. D-10.

[11] Abraham Hoffman, *Unwanted Mexicans in the Great Depression* (Tucson: University of Arizona Press, 1974), p. 32.

states and localities increased—and it seemed to become disproportionately Mexican. An effort to send Mexicans "home" occurred at every level of government. Federal immigration officers stepped up their search and deportation procedures for undocumented or "illegal" aliens. Local agencies used a variety of devices, including the stoppage of welfare payments, to encourage legal residents to undergo "voluntary" repatriation. In some cities of the West and Midwest, Mexicans who applied for relief were referred to variously named "Mexican bureaus," designed solely to get Mexicans off the relief rolls by repatriation. The possibility that a "Mexican" might be an American citizen was seldom considered. These moves were organized by local authorities with small regard for the niceties of immigration law or, for that matter, constitutional rights. Mexican authorities cooperated, although in the end the backlash of anti-American sentiment was bitter. Carey McWilliams witnessed one of these county-sponsored "repatriations" in Los Angeles.

> It was discovered that, in wholesale lots, they could be shipped to Mexico City for $14.70 per capita. The sum represented less than the cost of a week's board and lodging. And so, about February 1931, the first trainload was dispatched, and shipments at the rate of about one a month have continued ever since. [1933] A shipment consisting of three special trains left Los Angeles on December 8. The loading commenced at about six o'clock in the morning and continued for hours. More than twenty-five such special trains had left the Southern Pacific Station before last April. The repatriation programme is regarded locally as a piece of consummate statecraft. The average per family cost of executing it is $71.14, including food and transportation. It cost Los Angeles county $77,249.29 to repatriate one shipment of 6,024. It would have cost $424,933.70 to provide this number with such charitable assistance as they would have been *entitled* to had they remained—a saving of $347,468.41.[12] [Emphasis added]

The Mexican government made a number of efforts to cope with the flood of repatriates—estimated at more than 400,000 between 1929 and 1934, all without formal U.S. deportation proceedings. Each repatriate meant enormous community dislocation in both the United States and in Mexico—and this was a direct result of the action of government institutions.

But a few years later the process was again reversed. Work force emergencies of the early years of World War II made Mexicans and other Western hemisphere immigrants welcome again. In the border states workers were recruited with the cooperation of the Mexican government in the famous *bracero* (contract labor) program of 1942. For a time after the end of the war in 1945, the admissions stopped. But agricultural employers were able to build such a strong case for resuming the *bracero* program that in 1951 Congress enacted Public Law 78, replacing the earlier executive agreements. In the years between 1951 and 1960, an annual average of 356,000 Mexicans entered the United States.[13] The opposition and counterarguments offered by labor unions and public welfare organizations did not have much effect.

In the East, there was a parallel temporary contract labor program (H-2) that

---

[12] Carey McWilliams, "Getting Rid of the Mexicans," *The American Mercury*, Vol. 28 (March 1933), pp. 322–324.

[13] Cornelius, *Mexican and Caribbean Immigration*, p. 37.

involved Caribbean migrants. About 100,000 laborers from the British West Indies also entered. Beginning in 1947, a special program also recruited Puerto Rican workers. Previous experiences of Puerto Ricans in farm work made it necessary for their government to guard them from a variety of abuses. Employers were required to recruit through the Department of Labor of Puerto Rico and to sign a contract providing substantial guarantees.[14] (It is an interesting counterpart to the efforts of the Mexican consuls to protect Mexican *bracero* workers.) A total of more than 350,000 Puerto Ricans came to the mainland over a 30-year period, with many of them "settling out" in the United States to form the nucleus of communities in New Jersey, Massachusetts, and Michigan. (By the 1970s, Puerto Rican contract labor had lost its appeal for agricultural employers. The island farmers had gone to island cities and city-bred workers from Puerto Rico had difficulty adjusting to the demands of U.S. farm labor.)[15]

By 1960 many changes had occurred in the border states, and Congress was more willing to listen to labor interests, religious groups, and others demanding the termination of the *bracero* program. Agricultural needs no longer dominated legislative thinking, most likely because of the rise of urban influence. Moreover, there was a steady and large-scale immigration of Mexican workers without papers—the so-called "illegals" who were even more easily exploited than contract laborers.[16] The *bracero* program was halted (with some minor exceptions) at the end of 1964.

The next legal step was predictable, given the fierce interplay between economic needs and racial prejudice in American immigration policy. Around this deadlock, the American ideal of open immigration heedless of race, creed, or color gained some support. The very next year after the *bracero* program ended, Congress passed legislation that for the first time imposed a ceiling of 120,000 immigrants a year from Western hemisphere countries—to become effective in 1968. This was a critical change in immigration for Hispanics, and particularly for Mexicans. For the first time, Hispanics were accepted into a close parallel to the same national origins quota system that had been used since the 1920s for Europeans. Soon the first per-country quotas were actually established for Western hemisphere nations at the rate of 20,000 per nation per year. Immediate family members of U.S. citizens were exempt from these limits. This meant that the limit of 20,000 would actually be exceeded, and indeed, the limit for Mexico was greatly exceeded.

It is important to realize that although the restrictions sound firm and inviolate, they are not at all firm. All the basic laws on immigration leave loopholes to allow the importation of workers even when it may appear the main purpose of the laws is to restrict such importation. Whatever the intent of Congress, the loopholes can always be opened or closed administratively. An excellent example is the con-

---

[14] Fitzpatrick, *Puerto Ricans*, pp. 17–18.

[15] Cornelius, *Mexican and Caribbean Immigration*, p. 59.

[16] Cornelius believes that the H-2 visas (which replaced the *bracero* program) were issued only very marginally to Mexicans—only 1,000 per year as compared with 12,000 Jamaicans. "Given the restrictive way in which the Labor Department [U.S.] has chosen to administer the labor certification process, most U.S. employers in the Southwest and Mid-West find it considerably easier to recruit illegal migrants from Mexico than to obtain legal "H-2" contract workers; and illegals are readily available." Ibid., p. 60. On July 1, 1963, the U.S. Department of Labor announced that any job offer would have to be certified by the Department as well as state employment agencies. No Mexican could take a job that would adversely affect domestic wages and working conditions or one that had domestic applicants.

tinuous admission of Mexican citizens as "commuter" workers. These are people employed almost entirely in border cities of the United States, most often in cities with a large "twin" across the border. (For example, El Paso, Texas, has its "twin" just across the Rio Grande River–Ciudad Juarez.) These workers obtain legal immigration status (that is, qualify for immigration) and are then issued a green card that shows that they are permitted to live in Mexico and to commute daily to work in the United States. In some areas, commuters or "green carders" may form a major portion of the local work force. Even in the large city of El Paso commuters are 20 percent of all workers.[17]

American immigration laws have been administratively juggled in the case of Mexicans. But it is American refugee policy that affects another major portion of the Hispanic immigrants—the Cubans. Although the United States prides itself on its tradition of asylum for religious and political refugees, the architects of the 1924 immigration laws overlooked this tradition. This went unnoticed until the 1930s, when the persecution of Jews and other anti-Nazis led to a demand that the national quotas be expanded. But there was no provision in the law to do so. (Congress refused to liberalize the immigration laws, and as a consequence, only about 250,000 refugees, all entering under existing national quotas, escaped the fate of 6 million Holocaust victims.) European refugees were admitted, in a set of short-term arrangements following World War II, but not until 1965 was legislation passed that would provide for refugees.

American thinking concentrated on European refugees from communism. When Fidel Castro came to power in Cuba in 1959, pressure began to build to allow Cubans to be "paroled into" the United States. This "parole" provision authorizes the U.S. attorney general to admit any alien temporarily "in emergencies or for reasons in the public interest." Once admitted, the immigrant must apply for adjustment of his or her status and apply for an immigrant visa under the normal national quota systems. This, then, became the basic legal mechanism for the Cuban exiles. Between Castro's takeover in 1959 and the Cuban missile crisis of 1962 about a quarter of a million Cubans were "paroled in." In the time of President Lyndon Johnson, a Cuban airlift program began to bring in refugees at the rate of two flights daily, eventually delivering 297,000 Cubans. By April 1973, Cuba stopped the airlift, concerned about the flight of the more educated people. Ultimately all the Cuban immigrants were required to regularize their status in the United States, and special laws were passed to allow this to happen. (They became "aliens admitted for permanent residence.") Amendments to the Immigration and Nationality Act in 1976 allowed the first group of immigrants from the 1960s not to be charged against the new Western hemisphere ceilings.

Then, quite suddenly in April 1980, the Cuban government allowed the flight of 123,000 new Cubans from the port of Mariel. But the new refugees had no legal status beyond that of illegal aliens. However, the Immigration service once again bowed to the winds of public sentiment and found a way to give them visas and authorize them to work[18] (see Chapter 2).

[17]Ibid., pp. 36, 40.

[18]For the curious and difficult legal status of these most recent Cubans, see Robert L. Bach, "The New Cuban Immigrants: Their Background and Prospects," *Monthly Labor Review*, Vol. 103, no. 10 (October 1980), pp. 39–46. Other sources are Cornelius, *Mexican and Caribbean Immigration*, pp. 71–73, and Catherine McHugh, *Refugees in the United States: Laws, Programs and Proposals*, Issue Brief Number IB77120, Library of Congress, November 16, 1978.

Hispanic immigration: enforcement a surrogate for policy change. This complex of laws and administrative rulings does not disguise the fact that the most important aspect of immigration as an institution for Hispanics is that it is also a law enforcement apparatus.

Enforcement and formal control over the traffic across the U.S. and Mexican border did not begin until 1886. Not until 1907 was a definite control pattern established. As late as 1919, the entire border, a rough 2,000 miles, was patrolled by only 151 inspectors, most of them serving at 12 ports of entry. Thus the border was an informal arrangement. The Border Patrol of the INS was set up in 1924, at the time of the first national origin laws, and entry into the United States without a visa became a punishable offense in 1929. It is estimated that while many Mexicans obtained papers for entry, at least an equal number of new arrivals did not.[19] Mexicans were deported only if they got into trouble with local police, and this served as an informal method of law enforcement. Ernesto Galarza, among others, suggests that border state legislators deliberately keep appropriations for the Border Patrol so low that it is impossible to do much more than the most rudimentary control. Thus the flow of cheap labor deemed so essential for the Southwestern economy was kept secure.

It is immediately after World War II that the number of "illegals" caught by the Border Patrol began its almost explosive rise (Table 4–1, page 54). In 1947 a total of 183,000 were apprehended; five years later, in 1952, a total of 543,000 undocumented workers were caught, although all these figures include many "repeaters." American agribusiness continued to offer employment to all arrivals because it was not against the law to hire undocumented workers. In fact, during the 1940s and 1950s, legal *braceros* and illegal "wetbacks" often worked on the same crews. At one point, administrative processes reached the ultimate in absurdity. Because they were needed so much, "illegals" could be caught, transported back across the border, and then readmitted as "legally contracted" workers. The process was aptly called "drying out the wetbacks." American agriculture needed workers: the federal government and the Mexican government found themselves cooperating to fill that demand.

But the real drama of the decade of the 1950s was "Operation Wetback," a repeat of the large-scale repatriation of the Depression era, 20 years earlier. This time the roundups were based on illegality rather than indigence. Operation Wetback was carefully planned and conducted with military precision. It began in June 1954 with California the first target and then Texas, but the campaign was widened to include cities as far from the border as Chicago, Kansas City, and Spokane. It was very successful. Apprehensions reached a huge 1,075,168 in 1954. In five years, an astonishing 3.8 million "illegal" Mexican immigrants were apprehended and expelled. Only 63,515 were deported in formal proceedings, while the others were simply removed under threat of deportation. Most of those returned were sent not to the border, but (with the cooperation of the Mexican government) to points in Mexico near their original homes. However, many still contrived to return.

But just as with the earlier repatriations of the 1930s, the resulting shock waves in the Mexican-American communities greatly deepened the prevailing dis-

[19] Ernesto Galarza, *Merchants of Labor: The Mexican Bracero Story* (San Jose, Calif.: Rosicrucian Press, 1964); Cornelius, *Mexican and Caribbean Immigration.*

trust and alienation. There were important violations of civil rights. Hundreds of thousands of American citizens were stopped and interrogated because they "looked Mexican." If, in fact, a person who "looked Mexican" could not immediately produce documentary evidence of legal status when questioned in the street or any other public place, he or she ran the risk of arrest and detention. (This quick and rude form of "enforcement" is still standard INS procedure, despite a series of court cases questioning its legality.)

While immigration officials believed that the huge volume of repatriations had solved, at least for the present, their problem, one consequence of Operation Wetback was more pressure for the importation of legal contract workers. Thus in 1956, the number of apprehensions shrank to 72,442, but the number of *braceros* admitted rose to 445,197. It is easy to see how one form of unofficial immigration replaces another, regardless of the Immigration Act, if there is enough economic demand.

It is important to realize that most of the traffic across the U.S.-Mexico border is organized. It is possible to purchase forged documents. It is possible to find a *coyote* (professional smuggler) who will smuggle you in. Most important, it is possible to use legal short-term entry papers and simply "disappear" into the American landscape. This short-term legality is found, for example, in the use of so-called "shopping cards" that allow the holder to cross the border for up to three days within 25 miles of the border. But the holder of this card is not allowed to work. Of course, many do. As Cornelius remarks:

> The cards have been easy to obtain: U.S. immigration officials in the border cities issued over 2.2 million of them in the 1960–69 period and several thousand cards are still being issued each month.[20]

Many businesses and tourist attractions (the famed San Diego Zoo is an example) depend heavily on tourists and shoppers from Mexico. The "shopping card" fills an important legitimate function. Its use to evade the need for legal papers, just to get across the border, is also echoed in the most common forms by which non-Mexican undocumented Hispanic immigrants enter—that is, by tourist visas.

Fewer than 5 percent of the Mexican undocumented workers enter with tourist or student temporary visas, but the vast majority of Dominicans, Colombians, and Guatemalans who become "undocumented" first entered either on tourist or student visas—and usually by airplane. Cornelius notes that 124,528 Dominicans entered the United States as tourists in 1973. Most Dominican entrants obtain tourist visas to go to nearby Puerto Rico (which is counted as entry into the United States) and from there simply fly (as Puerto Ricans) to New York.[21]

Mexican undocumented differ from other Latin American undocumented in a curious way, directly related to Immigration enforcement practices. Again quoting Cornelius:

> The enforcement practices of the Immigration and Naturalization Service are primarily responsible for the overwhelming dominance of Mexicans among

[20] Cornelius, *Mexican and Caribbean Immigration,* p. 57.

[21] D. Hendricks, *Dominican Diaspora* (New York: Teachers College Press, 1974).

those actually apprehended (more than 90 percent in recent years). The Agency's enforcement personnel are concentrated along the Mexican border, where the majority of apprehended Mexicans are caught (mostly within 72 hours of crossing the border). By contrast, the vast majority of migrants from the Caribbean enter the U.S. legally, on tourist or other temporary visas, and have ample time to seek housing, jobs, and even legal assistance before becoming "illegals" (by overstaying their visas).[22]

Questions about undocumented workers are important in debates about modifications of the immigration laws, especially in times of economic downturn. Mexican (and other Hispanic) labor may be a "necessary" pool in times of labor shortage (e.g., in the 1920s and 1940s), but in the 1980s, they are seen as a "threatening" labor surplus. In the first period defined as a time of labor surplus (the Great Depression), the solution was "repatriation." In the 1950s a surplus of labor defined as "wetback invasion" was met by Operation Wetback. In the late 1970s it seemed that a new crisis of labor surplus was brewing. In 1974 the commissioner of the Immigration and Naturalization Service estimated in a provocative manner that there were between 5 and 12 million "illegal aliens" in the United States, and media attention turned to this new "threat." On August 8, 1977, a front page headline in the *Los Angeles Herald-Examiner* announced "State Threatened by Alien Horde." The article claimed that a quarter of a million Mexicans were poised in the nearby border town of Tijuana, ready to enter if certain proposed immigration changes were made. Subsequent articles toned down the news considerably, tracing the estimates of alien invaders to a statement by a single police official in the city of Tijuana. Three days of follow-up stories revealed that the official apparently had left the city on vacation and his estimate could never be confirmed. But the shock of the original headline remained.

Other newspapers were no more careful. The *Los Angeles Times* estimated that an old, well-established Chicano community in the city was "70 percent illegal." True or not, these statements fell on the Los Angeles community with great force, offering images of rampant disease and hungry children. In Los Angeles an emergency ad hoc Mexican-American coalition was driven to buy a large newspaper advertisement, noting the fact that most Hispanics in the city are native-born Americans and contribute substantially to the life of the city. Nonetheless, for the first time, the media uproar in Los Angeles and elsewhere did *not* result in massive expulsions, because it had been determined that such expulsions would seriously undermine the validity of data collected in the 1980 census. Yet the damage is always extensive. Agency officials often react to these frights by making efforts to "clear the rolls" of undocumented aliens. Aliens in varying statuses are quite vulnerable to such pressure. (See Chapter 9 for the Texas denial of public education for undocumented children.[23])

Throughout these controversies, it became more and more apparent that the immigration bureaucracy is something of an administrative nightmare. It is an

---

[22] Cornelius, *Mexican and Caribbean Immigration,* p. 57.

[23] For a list of restrictions and recent decisions on many public benefits and services affecting aliens, see David Carliner, *The Rights of Aliens* (New York: Avon Books, 1977). A number of efforts have been made to estimate the extent to which documented aliens represent a drain on tax-supported services. Generally, it is conceded that the undocumented more or less pay their way with sales tax, withholding, and other tax contributions.

enforcement approach to a complex social problem, complicated by a heavy dependence on judicial solutions.[24] But not even the enforcement efforts of the Border Patrol work very well—now or in the past. Juan Ramon Garcia tells the story of the Border Patrol up to 1954, noting that it could scarcely do very well working against the "contradictory laws, low appropriations, poor organizational structure, ineffective leadership and direct and indirect pressures."[25] On the other hand, the ability of the INS to enforce regulations when it wishes may actually work very well in minimizing the competition between new undocumented workers and native workers.[26]

Perhaps the final effort at massive enforcement occurred in 1982 when the Reagan administration tried to flush out undocumented workers holding jobs that paid more than the minimum wage. But "Operation Jobs" was not successful. Public debate shifted to proposals for changing the immigration laws.

The new immigration proposals. It may be a sign of changing times that the immigration legislation proposed during the Carter and the Reagan years deals almost entirely with Western hemisphere immigration. Two basic issues dominate the debate on these new laws, and both issues try to deal with the critical matter of undocumented workers.

First, should employers who hire undocumented workers be penalized? At one time or another 11 states passed such laws, but the legislation was found unconstitutional in some states and ineffective in all. Nothing more serious happened to the employers than a single fine of $250. Attempts since 1970 to pass federal legislation have been unsuccessful. The opposition from Hispanics rests on a well-founded fear that such a policy would lead employers to discriminate against perfectly "legal" Hispanic workers who "look" and "sound" like Mexicans or Dominicans.

The second issue concerns temporary workers. In recent years many nations of northern and western Europe began to import "guest workers" from southern Europe and Turkey. These experiences suggest that the United States might mitigate some of the problems of Hispanic undocumented workers by a supervised version of the "guest worker" program.

Some of these ideas and solutions were built into the Simpson-Mazzoli bill which was debated in Congress in the spring of 1984. This most sweeping change in immigration law since 1965 would (1) prohibit most employers from hiring undocumented workers, (2) grant the chance to obtain legalized status to many persons now illegally resident, and (3) allow the temporary importation of seasonal farm workers.

The debate and political maneuvering around this bill is important. First, it is the first immigration bill in which the ideas and political muscle of Hispanics were seriously weighed, particularly in terms of the presidential election of 1984. Second,

[24] Gilberto Cárdenas, "Policy Paper on the Legal Immigration Approach to Undocumented Migration from Mexico," in Mauricio Mazon, ed., *Mexico-United States Relations* (Los Angeles: University of California, Chicano Studies Research Center, 1982).

[25] Juan Ramon Garcia, *Operation Wetback* (Westport, Conn.: Greenwood Press, 1980), p. 113.

[26] Michael Piore, *Birds of Passage: Migrant Labor and Industrial Societies* (Cambridge: Cambridge University Press, 1979), Ch. 7.

the idea of an "amnesty" for the submerged and invisible undocumented Hispanics was an essential part of the legislation. Predictably, Hispanics generally favored the amnesty provision, even if limited to certain categories of people. But the sanctions for employers stirred much opposition: it was feared that employers would discriminate against legal workers with accents just because it is easier than checking. The proposal for allowing more seasonal farm workers was of course anathema to a Hispanic community familiar with the *bracero* programs of the past.[27]

More direct evidence on the attitudes of Hispanic leaders is available not only from congressional action and testimony over the past two decades but also in a survey of some 225 Chicano leaders, elected and appointed. Interestingly, none of them mentioned immigration or the presence of undocumented immigrants as a major issue facing Mexican Americans in general—or their constituents, in particular. (Inflation, jobs, education, and housing were the critical issues.) When asked a very broad question about their views on undocumented workers, only 22 percent responded with the negative stereotype that "undocumented workers displace Chicano workers." A full 42 percent felt undocumented persons were "an asset."[28] These attitudes are in sharp contrast to the ambivalent or negative views often attributed to Mexican Americans.

[27]Estevan Flores, "1982 Simpson Mazzoli Immigration Reform and the Hispanic Community," *LaRed/The Net,* Vol. 65 (1983), p. 15. See also Joaquin G. Avila, "Immigrant Non-Bill," *The New York Times,* December 19, 1982. Avila was the president and general counsel of the Mexican American Legal Defense and Education Fund.

[28]Rodolfo O. de la Garza and Gilberto Cárdenas, "Chicano Elite Views of the Undocumented Worker Issue," unpublished manuscript 1982.

CHAPTER NINE
HISPANICS AND INSTITUTIONS
OF THE MODERN STATE: II

While American immigration controls greatly shaped Mexican life in this country, this remained primarily a Mexican experience until recently, when they also touched many other new Latin American immigrants. But the other institutions—education, health and mental health care, and criminal justice—are impartially a common Hispanic experience. As we shall see, the Hispanic contact with these institutions of the modern state is quite uniform.

SCHOOLS AND THE CHILDREN

There is no possible doubt about the failure of the American school system to serve Hispanics. The magnitude of this failure is obvious from earliest times to the present day—from the most neglected *barrios* of south Texas to the slums of New York City. The modern failure (and some slow gains) are easily visible in the tables of Chapter 5.

Thus, quality education is a concern, almost an obsessive concern, in all Hispanic communities. Even recently, Mexican Americans have had to contend with overt segregation and inferior schools in most parts of the Southwest, even after more than a century of contact with Anglo-American institutions. Even though there were comparatively few blatant Jim Crow laws in the Southwest to exclude Chicanos from Anglo schools, there is still a strong history of exclusion based on local actions. In Texas throughout the nineteenth century, most Mexican Americans could only attend "Mexican" schools and even during the early part of the twentieth century many districts barred Mexicans from their high schools. In California, a number of communities used a state law that permitted the segregation of Indian students so Mexican children could be denied admittance to Anglo schools. The practices were attacked by Mexican consular authorities with some success. But because these actions were usually local decisions (or were not given wide publicity), they were overlooked by researchers who were looking for a "southern" pattern of school segregation.[1] In general, the Southwestern feeling about the education of Hispanic children is well summarized in a 1930s report:

> Mexican [children] are diligently enrolled on the census, while the revenues are applied principally to the education of the American children. The practice is justified by the fact that the Americans are the principal taxpayers. The prevailing opinion is that "educating the Mexican is educating him from his job . . .. He learns English and wants to be a boss. He doesn't want to grub. . . . Someone has to transplant onions . . .. What would we do if 50 percent of the Mexican pupils showed up? It would take more teachers and school houses. We would not have enough lumber for school houses nor enough teachers in Texas . . .." The dominant view of the local Americans is that it is undesirable to educate the Mexicans.[2]

A more formal and yet damning summary appeared in 1981 when a U.S. district court found that the evidence in a case against the Texas state education system contained proof of "pervasive, invidious discrimination against Mexican Americans throughout the state of Texas. The extent of the discrimination is comparable in magnitude to the overwhelming evidence of state supported racial segregation that was found more than ten years ago."[3]

Although it is difficult for most Americans to imagine racial segregation outside the black-white context, separate Mexican schools were established in the Rio Grande Valley by the turn of the century and spread throughout Texas. By 1942 segregated schools were in operation in at least 122 Texas school districts in 59 counties.[4] The same pattern appeared in California, most notably in small- and medium-sized cities where Mexicans traditionally were segregated. So pervasive is this segregation, in fact, that a noted Mexican-American educator could remark in the early 1950s that "In all parts of the Southwest, at one time or another, some Spanish named children have had to attend segregated public schools or classes."[5]

The rationale for segregation followed the idea of the "unassimilable" Mexicans and carried a strong air of patronization. Separate schools were built and maintained, in theory, simply because of residential segregation or to benefit the Mexican child. The Mexican child had a "language handicap" and needed to be "Americanized" before mixing with Anglo children. As Thomas Carter notes, Anglo

[1] Oscar Uribe, "Measuring the Degree of Discrimination," *Agenda,* Vol. 9 (1979), pp. 14–15.

[2] B. Schrieke, *Alien Americans* (New York: Viking, 1936), p. 50.

[3] *U.S. v. State of Texas,* 1981.

[4] Ibid.

[5] George Sánchez, *Concerning Segregation of Spanish Speaking Children in the Public Schools* (Austin: The University of Texas, 1951), p. 1.

educators felt that Mexican American children could better overcome their deficiencies by separation from Anglos and would not suffer from excessive competition.[6]

This patronizing approach was used to justify many inequalities and rigid segregation. "Mexican schools" generally were inferior in physical plant and in teachers, and usually there were larger classes. Black children were sometimes assigned to these schools, implying a low social status. There was a notable lack of effort in enforcing the weak school attendance laws. Secondary level school students often were discouraged from attending school. Migrancy was an additional handicap: many of the children of migrant farm workers did not go to school at all.

It is important to understand that only the Mexican community felt the deprivation. For their part, Anglo school officials (as in El Paso) found that they were expending a great deal of money and effort in civilizing a ragged and extremely transient community of laborers, refugees, and paupers. "It is impossible to estimate the general good that this school is doing and has done among these benighted Mexican people," said an official school report in 1904. Cleanliness, discipline, habits of punctuality, the acquisition of English, and various manual skills were the objectives.[7] Retiring principals and superintendants thought of the Mexican schools in El Paso as their greatest career accomplishment. But Garcia's backward look at the educational accomplishments shows us that the 5 "Mexican schools" of the 16 schools in El Paso enrolled nearly half of the children during the 1919–1920 school year. Not until 1927 was a Mexican high school available. Between 1898 and 1920 only 22 Spanish-surnamed students graduated from El Paso High School compared with 812 Anglo Americans.[8]

Once the education of Mexican children was recognized and defined as a "problem," there were attempts to cope with it by explanation. In the process, many shallow and overgeneralized stereotypes were developed as "reasons" for the enormous failure rates. Many Mexican children are, of course, bilingual, but educators often saw this bilingualism as the primary cause of failure, assuming that it is detrimental to intellect and thus to the teachability of the child. The second generalization concerned "lack of motivation." This second explanation was (and is) extremely popular and is used to explain the behavior of Mexican Americans in cities as diverse as Los Angeles and the most remote villages of northern New Mexico.

For their part, Puerto Ricans were not exposed to the explicit and covert segregationism of the Southwest. By contrast, there are two separate stories behind Puerto Rican education. The first is the public education system of Puerto Rico, which is largely responsible for the education of many Puerto Ricans before World War II. The second aspect is the experience of Puerto Ricans in the schools of the mainland Northeast. As it happens, education on the Island prior to 1900 was ex-

---

[6]Two editions summarizing the important work of Thomas Carter are available. They are Carter, *Mexican Americans in School: A History of Educational Neglect* (New York: College Entrance Examination Board, 1970), and Carter and Roberto D. Segura, *Mexican Americans in School: A Decade of Change* (New York: College Entrance Examination Board, 1979).

[7]See the careful description of Mexican life in El Paso by Mario T. Garcia, *Desert Immigrants: The Mexicans of El Paso 1880-1920* (New Haven, Conn.: Yale University Press, 1981), Ch. 6.

[8]Ibid., pp. 124–125.

tremely poor, with only 14 percent of the school-age population in school. Most failed to reach the third grade. By 1940 there was progress, but it was very slow: only 50 percent were attending school. Not until 1954 were all children in Puerto Rico enrolled in the first grade. Thus by the 1980s, the Puerto Rican educational system lagged seriously behind its counterparts on the mainland. Puerto Rican public education was further complicated by arguments about which language to use in the classroom. English became the "official" language of the island immediately after American occupation, but this was never fully accepted. In 1948 "pedagogy prevailed over politics," and Spanish became the language of the classroom.[9]

In the urban schools of the Northeast, the Puerto Ricans repeated the experience of earlier immigrants—that is, an encounter with a school system that wanted quick Americanization and was not able to deal with non–English-speaking children.

A young age of leaving school meant, in practical terms, that children who could not learn English left school early and were much less obvious. But, by 1948, the education of Puerto Ricans in New York, the area of greatest concentration, was an obvious and a serious problem.

Facing up to failure.   Recognition of a problem common to Hispanic children was at least a beginning step. Handicaps based on motivation and on language and culture could be approached seriously, if one is willing to overlook how neatly the diagnosis pictures an excluded child. The solution in far too many schools was simply to "track" or to group students "according to ability." In 1969 the U.S. Civil Rights Commission found that about two-thirds of the public schools in the Southwest used some form of "ability grouping" and, not surprisingly, that Chicano students tended to be grouped into the less able groups.[10] In its most pernicious form, it was the overrepresentation of Hispanic children in classes for the mentally retarded. Thus in California there were about twice as many Chicano students in "special education" classes as would be expected from school population ratios.[11] In New York City almost 30 percent of the "educable mentally retarded" were Hispanic, in figures from the early 1970s.

Other forms of adjustment to language and culture include the lowering of standards inside the school to the point where much less work is demanded of the students. This pattern is obvious in heavily Mexican-American schools in the Southwest: in Los Angeles it appears as early as the third and fourth grades and continues until graduation from high school. Eventually, in college and in the job market, the Hispanic graduate may be seriously undereducated.

Grade retention is a popular technique for dealing with the ethnic child. It is widespread in the Southwest and in Eastern schools, most notably in Philadelphia. In New England, generally, it has been found that in an ordinary year in the 1970s about 25 percent of the Hispanic children were held back at least three grades and 50 percent, two grades. A witness before the U.S. Commission on Civil Rights told of the inevitable consequences:

[9] Kal Wagenheim, *Puerto Rico: A Profile* (New York: Praeger, 1970), p. 203; and see also Erwin H. Epstein, *Politics and Education in Puerto Rico* (Metuchen, N.J.: Scarecrow, 1970).

[10] U.S. Commission on Civil Rights, *Toward Quality Education for Mexican Americans,* Mexican-American Study Report No. 4 (Washington, D.C.: USCCR, February 1974).

[11] See Jane Mercer, *Labeling the Mentally Retarded* (Los Angeles and Berkeley: University of California Press, 1973), for an analysis of this process.

They came from Puerto Rico, they're in the 10th, 11th, or senior year of high school, and they're 17, 18, 19 years old. . . . They came to Boston and they placed them in the 6th and 7th grades. You're wondering why they dropped out?[12]

A major technique for dealing with the language and culture of the "ethnic deviant" or Spanish-speaking child has been the simple suppression of Spanish. This is usually masked as a positive approach by stressing conformity to the "normal" means of instruction. Outright prohibition of the speaking of Spanish in the classroom is probably the most extreme example. The arguments for this practice are a mixture of the moral and the pedagogical. The moral arguments include such axioms as "English is the national language and must be used at all times." The pedagogical argument is that such an unsupported idea as bilingualism is mentally confusing. As late as 1972 the U.S. Commission on Civil Rights found that a third of the elementary and secondary schools discouraged the use of Spanish in the classroom. Most of these schools are in Texas. It is rare in California.[13] Other cultural differences are often severely suppressed as well.

The most negative reaction was that of Texas, which found a "legal" way of simply not educating Mexican children at all. In the late 1970s, the legislature passed a law allowing local school districts to charge tuition for the children of undocumented aliens. Without tuition they were not allowed to attend school.

A long court battle ended in 1982 with a decision from the U.S. Supreme Court that such exclusion violated the constitutional rights of the children. Undocumented children were actually excluded in a few districts. If enforced throughout the state of Texas, it would have deprived some 30,000 children of all schooling.[14]

Changing the system. At least since the time of the great civil rights movements of the 1960s, educational change has been a dominating interest in the Hispanic communities of this nation. But schools are not easy to change. As Thomas Carter and Roberto Sequra explain, educators are willing enough to attach certain programs to existing arrangements (particularly if federal or state money is provided). But they strongly resist fundamental change. Demands for such change came inevitably, with the growth of Hispanic militancy in the 1960s and in the sweeping gains made among young people by *Chicanismo* (see Chapter 10).

These cumulative effects of Hispanic militancy and the slow, but effective, integration of the *barrios* into American social and political life are very great. There are five major efforts (or directions) that are important enough to trace in some detail. The first is a series of court decisions. The second and third are community factors: political changes in a small Texas town, and the relative strength of Puerto Ricans in cities. The fourth was developed by educators, not activists,

[12] U.S. Commission on Civil Rights, *Puerto Ricans in the Continental United States: An Uncertain Future* (Washington, D.C.: USCCR, 1976).

[13] U.S. Commission on Civil Rights, *The Excluded Student: Educational Practices Affecting Mexican Americans in the Southwest,* Mexican American Education Study Report No. 3 (Washington, D.C.: USCCR, May 1972), pp. 15–16.

[14] See *The New York Times,* December 2, 1981, for arguments in the case. Estimates are from *The New York Times Summer Survey of Education,* August 21, 1983.

and is a careful experiment engineered to untangle some factors in Mexican-American underachievement in the large Texas City of San Antonio—the Edgewood experiment. The fifth was a national effort to make *all* schools more responsible to Hispanic children through federal legislation. Only the court decisions and the federal rules greatly affected the Puerto Ricans or *Cubanos* and other Hispanics.

The court decisions. A subtle but important form of discrimination is that of school financing. Poor neighborhoods cannot tax themselves heavily enough to match wealthy neighborhoods in the quality of schools. Consequently, disadvantaged groups have begun to bring lawsuits that might even out or equalize the money available to local schools. This litigation began seriously with a suit brought by an East Los Angeles Chicano: the important *Serrano* v. *Priest* case (487 P.2d 1241 [Cal. 1971]) decided that tax monies for education be "fiscally neutral," that is, not drain into richer schools. A parallel case, stemming from a Texas suit that reached the U.S. Supreme Court two years later, established that "fiscal neutrality" was *not* a right under the U.S. Constitution, even though it might be a right under separate state constitutions. Accordingly, each state must decide separately whether its state-supported program is constitutional (*San Antonio Indep. School Dist.* v. *Rodriguez,* 411 U.S. 1 [1973]). Once legislatures and school districts had established whether their arrangements satisfied these questions of equity of resources, they began to rule on adequacy of public education; increasingly the courts are interested in outputs, as for example whether graduates can perform certain tasks. Thus we see the importance of the U.S. Supreme Court decision (*Lau* v. *Nichols,* 414 U.S. 563 1974). This decision ruled that a group of San Francisco Chinese-speaking children were not receiving equal educational benefits with an all-English curriculum. Hispanics immediately saw its relevancy to their situation. This notion of adequacy fits neatly into a growing public interest in improving the quality of its educational products, offering realistic and concrete goals.[15]

Crystal City—experiment in power. The rebellion of Mexican citizens in Crystal City was one of the pivotal events in Hispanic political life of the past few decades. Typically, it was precipitated by a demand for educational reform. Up until the early 1960s, Crystal City was a very typical Southwestern agricultural town, differing only in its unusually large Mexican-American population. A relatively powerless Mexican agricultural labor population was dominated by an Anglo establishment.

The high school, typically, maintained a delicate balance of rewards and honors between Chicano and Anglo students. This precarious balance was upset in a dispute over cheerleaders, followed by a boycott of the school supported by Mexican parents and the Mexican community. Then Anglo control of the town crumbled rapidly, beginning with the school system. A Chicano superintendent was hired and funds from foundations and federal sources were acquired to implement a variety

[15]For a full discussion, see M. McCarthy and P. Deignan, *What Legally Constitutes an Adequate Public Education?* (Bloomington, Ind.: Phi Delta Kappa Educational Foundation, n.d.). We appreciate the advice of James Cibulka and Delbert Clear of the School of Education, University of Wisconsin-Milwaukee, on these topics.

of innovative programs. The thrust of the programs was to motivate students to finish high school and go on to college and also to bring adults (often parents of the students) to complete high school. Texas officials were extraordinarily repressive, placing obstacles at every juncture. But the events in Crystal City were attracting national attention. When Texas institutions refused to provide training, the school officials turned to San Francisco State College and Chicago State College. Texas discouraged its teachers from working in Crystal City; national recruiting not only gained enthusiastic teachers but established a base for national dissemination of their experience among Hispanic educators. Repression continued throughout the 1970s with continual efforts to discredit the people and their activities—including litigation against a Mexican former superintendent of schools. Thus Crystal City not only became an important Mexican-American source of inspiration but also a model for educational efforts with migrant workers and with students with limited proficiency in English. State legislation may well have been affected by the events in Crystal City.[16]

Community factors for Puerto Ricans. The Crystal City episode aptly reveals the interlocking nature of a small Texas city, its Hispanic community, and the school system. It seems evident that to change one factor implies change in all the factors, although it is a difficult topic to study because the data are nearly impossible to assemble. Nonetheless the Puerto Rican researchers of Aspira of America (an organization formed in the early 1960s to promote higher education for Puerto Ricans) made an effort to study such factors. The authors were particularly concerned with explaining variations from one community to another in the proportion of Puerto Ricans who were over age in their school careers. The 1970 census data showed that about 47 percent of Puerto Rican students from 14 to 17 years of age were still in elementary grades. "Delayed education" is almost certain to result in dropping out. Puerto Ricans were dropping out at a rate about twice that of the general population.

Were there some factors in the community that made this rate so high? Beyond family factors (the usual explanation for student failure), the researchers interested themselves in the nature of the Puerto Rican community (number of recent migrants and persons in poverty) and the Hispanic community generally (number of Spanish origin persons in the city). Certain other features of the system were considered, specifically, the expenditure per student. The strongest explanatory factor turned out to be the "disadvantaged position of Puerto Ricans" in the community—in short, the proportion of poor and recent migrants in the city. Adding up the factors, the researchers found that the most unfavorable circumstance would be a recently migrant community with a fair degree of poverty, few well-educated parents in white collar jobs, located in a city having below average financing for its school system." (Interestingly, "delay and dropout rates were significantly reduced" in cities with large Hispanic communities.) The interpretation of this research stresses the idea that in "early . . . or very limited community development, Puerto Ricans must struggle for recognition and eventually minor concessions, and

---

[16]Interview with Angel Noel Gonzáles, assistant superintendent of Dallas Independent School District, 1983. We thank Salomón Flores of the University of Wisconsin-Milwaukee for this reference.

will most likely continue facing a basic posture of avoidance by school authorities."[17]

Edgewood—direct change in the schools. A professional effort to make changes in the school system itself appeared in San Antonio when the federal government established a program in 1972 that would allow five years of "experimental schools" funding. There were four other programs in the nation, but the experiment in the Edgewood school district involved only Hispanics. It was directed to a poverty-stricken and conservative, predominantly Mexican-American, community.

The Edgewood experiment (ESP) was built on a "theory of incompatibilities," arguing that poor school performance by Mexicans was based on a basic incompatibility between the home culture and social expectations and the behaviors and expectations of the classroom. In practical terms, this translated into changes in both personnel and curriculum. More Chicano teachers and administrators were hired. Spanish was used more frequently in instruction and in the school environment. Culturally relevant topics were introduced. This design was established in one high school (and one "feeder" middle school and four elementary schools). Another set of schools was used as controls.

The results disappointed the experimenters. Edgewood students performed no better than did students in the control schools, either in achievement or self-concept and motivation. There are questions that can be raised about the special circumstances of the experiment, but Carter and Segura conclude, "Despite these omissions, the findings are based on a large sample of Mexican Americans, corroborated by many similar studies in southern Texas, and supported by research elsewhere. The results seriously weaken both the deprivation and incompatibility arguments."[18] Ironically, this experiment ran its course only a few miles from Crystal City where both motivation and achievement appear to have been reached. Perhaps, as Carter and Segura suggest, the missing element in the Edgewood experiment was the enthusiasm of Crystal City:

> It is possible that the principal justification for the five-year experiment was nothing more than the need for federal funds to augment the budget of an incredibly poor school district. The information gained from interviews leads us to suggest: (1) the administration did not accept or understand ESP and gave it only perfunctory attention because they considered it a terminal program; (2) the ESP staff perceived the experiment as an opportunity to improve their own socioeconomic positions and professional opportunities; . . . (3) The instructional staff saw the experiment as an imposition from which they would get no socioeconomic and little professional reward from participation. . . . They were given more work without concomitant improvements in professional, economic or personal status.[19]

As the authors remark elsewhere, "schools strongly resist fundamental changes." But despite the "failure" of the experiment, change was to come to Edgewood,

---

[17]José Hernández et al., *Social Factors in Educational Attainment Among Puerto Ricans in U.S. Metropolitan Areas* (New York: Aspira of America, 1977).

[18]Carter and Segura, *Mexican Americans in School*, pp. 313–322.

[19]Ibid., p. 321.

again in a way that strikingly demonstrates the interdependence of social system and school. The director of the experimental program was appointed superintendent of the district. Others associated with ESP moved into administrative programs, and the district changed dramatically. It would no longer be possible to describe it as a "conservative" district; Edgewood has rapidly grown open to innovation and community involvement. In fact, it was in the Edgewood district of San Antonio that an important Mexican American grass-roots community organization (COPS) was organized. Later COPS pushed strongly for state legislation to equalize school financing from one district to another. Such legislation was introduced in Texas in 1983 with strong backing from the governor. Educational improvement is integrally tied to nascent political power.[20]

But there is yet a third approach in changing the school system, and that is bilingual education.

Bilingual education. "Bilingual education" began as a serious approach to teaching bilingual-bicultural children among Cuban students in Miami.[21] It is a concept that almost immediately caught the fancy of Hispanics generally and was built into the many "Great Society" reforms sponsored by President Lyndon Johnson. President Johnson once taught in a Mexican school in south Texas, and it is quite possible that he could well identify with the educational problems of youngsters who do not speak English and "who gradually lost their will to learn in a school environment characterized by what to them, was a foreign language."[22]

The legal basis for federal help is Title VII of the Elementary and Secondary Education Act of 1965. Under Title VII, federal help for bilingual education was $7.5 million in fiscal year 1969 to a high point in 1980 of $166.9 million.[23] Since 1980, the federal allocations have declined steadily, although much of the money and effort needed for bilingual education is supplied by state and local governments. A long series of legal cases required bilingual education help from the states, and this was supplied (1981) by 20 states, at least for the elementary school level.[24]

Some states moved quickly to help; others were slow. Eastern and Midwestern school districts were notably unresponsive, even among some smaller cities with large proportions of Puerto Ricans. Aspira brought suit against the New York City Board of Education charging unequal treatment. Aspira's victory in 1974 greatly stimulated bilingual programs in the East.

But bilingual education has become a controversial program at the federal level and often in the states. There are many reasons for this—some are based on ideology, and some are based on misconceptions. Adding to the confusion is the

[20] Interview with Jose Cárdenas, March 1983.

[21] Alan Pifer, *Bilingual Education and the Hispanic Challenge* (New York: The Carnegie Corporation, 1979).

[22] Interview with Congressman Edward R. Roybal, December 1983.

[23] For further information about the appearance of bilingual education and its acceptance, see Herman LaFontaine, Barry Persky, and Leonard Golubschick, eds., *Bilingual Education* (Wayne, N.J.: Avery Publishing Group, 1978), and Raymond Padilla, ed., *Bilingual Education and Public Policy in the United States* (Ypsilanti: Eastern Michigan University, 1979).

[24] Much of this material is based on background papers prepared by Lori S. Orum of the National Council of La Raza, Washington, D.C. (May 1982).

very hesitant agreement among educational researchers and educators about its usefulness.

First, "bilingual education" means different things to different people.
Although a "bilingual person" can speak two languages, it is not the object of
"bilingual education" to make school children fluent in two languages, certainly as
intended by the U.S. Congress. It is intended to permit a limited English-speaking
child to develop enough proficiency in English to learn in English. Nor is it the only
program serving Hispanic children; more Hispanic children were served by Title I of
the Elementary and Secondary Education Act. There are a wide variety of approaches, including English as a Second Language, "immersion" in all-English class-
rooms, and special tutoring. In fact, bilingual education covers such a wide range of
programs from school to school and district to district that Carter and Segura remark that there is very little true bilingual education indeed because they assume
that an effective program must include an institutional bicultural-bilingual approach.
This, they say, is rarely understood by school practitioners. Ironically, then, Hispanics and others who favor bilingual education are placed in a difficult situation—
favoring the federal action in principle but often not its application.[25] From a
stance of ideology, bilingual education irritates many conservatives (even in the Hispanic community) who see teaching fluency in English as a major objective of the
schools, not realizing the importance of other skills and attitudes. The fact is that
many Americans are extremely reluctant to sanction the use of any language in this
country except English. For legislators and many ordinary people, bilingual education seems an expensive dilution of American ideals.

Second, it is hard for some critics to understand why other immigrant groups
managed without bilingual instruction. Actually, earlier arrivals did not manage.
Young children left school in such large numbers and at such an early age that
failure was scarcely noticed. Furthermore, the dropouts survived by fitting themselves into a much less demanding economy. A high school diploma is now a bare
minimum for many jobs. A wider range of children are now expected to remain in
school—not just a chosen few from upper-income groups.

Third, many people think that schools should teach only mainstream American culture. Hispanics argue that other values and beliefs help us to achieve a more
balanced and democratic acceptance of our collective heritage. At its best, bilingual-
bicultural education is an additive rather than a detraction.

Fourth, there is some fear that bilingual education programs will accelerate
segregation of Spanish-speaking students. This is carefully forbidden in Title VII
legislation, even accidentally. Language skill segregation is done quite carefully because such separation would undermine the whole purpose of bilingual education.

Solid evidence that bilingual education is effective is still lacking. This is
a complex question and is intertwined with some thorny questions of educational
evaluation. Lori Orum defends the lack of convincing research by (1) asking
for more time and (2) describing the poor state of educational research and (3) not-

---

[25] For a complex but interesting analysis of the practical effects of bilingual education in
Southwestern schools, see Carter and Segura, *Mexican Americans in School,* pp. 328–371.
Another critical view is available from Keith Baker and Adriana de Kanter *Bilingual Education:
A Reappraisal of Federal Policy* (Toronto: Lexington Books, 1983). Also, Diego Castellanos,
The Best of Two Worlds: Bilingual-Bicultural Education in the U.S. (Trenton, N.J.: New
Jersey State Department of Education, 1983).

ing the complex sociopolitical climate in which bilingual education must be established. Meanwhile the question of effectiveness is not met—and there are other serious problems, not the least among them being the general decay in money and resources available, the endless difficulties in finding the right people to teach, the right materials, and hostile reactions at all levels of government and Anglo community.

Bilingual education is now a major objective of Hispanic political and social organizations (see Chapter 10). This support—a series of favorable legal decisions, a growing constituency in the Hispanic population, and some friendly liberal politicians—succeeded in establishing bilingual education. Major efforts were made by Senator Joseph Montoya, Senator Edward Kennedy, Representative Edward R. Roybal, and Commissioner Baltasar Corrada. Yet several factors endanger its future. Perhaps most important is that the program was established by legislative fiat with a very weak constituency. The parents of children who do not speak English (often themselves people who do not speak English) are a group that is the least likely to be influential in the policy process. Contrary to popular opinion, the "powerful forces" supporting bilingual education at the national level were a handful of Hispanic legislators (none of them ever directly involved in bilingual education), the national Hispanic organizations, and a few individuals. Not until the late 1970s did any bilingual educators begin to appear at the national level.

These educators found themselves venturing into a battlefield. Federal policies, grants, and administrative rulings are the targets of a wide range of powerful advocacy groups, including the American Federation of Teachers. These groups utilize skilled lobbyists in the legislature and in the executive branch; they are adept at strategy and information sharing. On the other hand, policymakers both in Congress and in the administration had very little information about actual classroom practice.

When the reaction against Great Society programs began (after the presidency of Lyndon Johnson, in the 1970s), it was only a matter of time before bilingual education also came under critical questioning. Lacking information about the programs, policymakers were susceptible to exaggerated stories. There were also strong nativist sentiments, perhaps best expressed by the late Secretary of Education in California, Max Rafferty:

> When you move into a foreign country with a different language from yours, you expect to have trouble communicating at first. But you can't expect that country to spend itself into bankruptcy teaching you to speak its language. . . . Immigrating was YOUR idea. So the burden of learning the new language falls upon you—or should.[26]

HISPANIC EDUCATION AND NATIONAL POLICY

Given this background, it is not surprising that bilingual education is so controversial. The current policy debate has two aspects—first, a question of civil rights concerning the rights of all non-English speaking children to bilingual education and, second, a question about its effectiveness.

[26] Max Rafferty, "Bilingual Education: Hoax of the 80s," *The American Legion Magazine*, Vol. 110 (March, 1981), pp. 14, 38-40.

The civil rights issue grows from a response of the Department of Education to a series of federal court cases and Title VI of the Civil Rights Act of 1964. In *Lau v. Nichols,* the U.S. Supreme Court ruled that certain San Francisco students must receive instruction in their own language. Not to do so would violate the Civil Rights Act of 1964. The Department of Education responded by issuing a policy paper known as the *Lau Remedies.* School districts must provide instruction in a child's strongest language until the child is able to participate in an English-speaking classroom. The *Remedies* were confusing to local school districts and did not specify what procedural steps schools should take. After another federal court order, the U.S. Department of Education issued regulations in August 1980. The result in public reaction was a firestorm of controversy. Newspapers were heavily opposed, school districts threatened bankruptcy, and Americans generally discovered that there were non-English-speaking children in many languages. (Eventually 15 different languages would be a concern of bilingual education.)[27]

With hindsight, one could argue that the Department of Education issued these regulations too soon. It appeared that a federal department was telling local school districts how to run their affairs. Hispanic groups felt that these regulations were protecting equal educational opportunity for all children. If black children, the handicapped, and women were enjoying equal educational opportunity, why not the children who did not speak English? Yet school regulations, customs, and tradition are a jealously guarded area of local control in most American cities. The issue of equal opportunity very quickly became lost in a controversy over the effectiveness of bilingual education, an area, as noted earlier, where its supporters were unable to make a strong case. As a result, one of the first actions of the new Reagan administration in educational policy was to withdraw these regulations. So bilingual education began the 1980s under heavy attack. The new administration hoped to trim costs wherever possible; Department of Education funds were early targets. Local school districts and school boards were concerned about the costs of trained bilingual teachers and special programs, especially if no funds were coming from the state or federal government. Some of the powerful professional groups of educators were doubtful or opposed to the programs. And deep, almost visceral, reactions came from some segments of American society.

Hispanic activists are still firmly supporting bilingual education. Meanwhile, even the existing programs fall very short. In 1978 no state was serving more than 60 percent of the children with limited English-speaking skills with any kind of second language or bilingual education.[28] This gap is probably increasing as federal funds diminish and as the number of Hispanics of school age increases.

Carter and Segura are pessimistic about compensatory education in all its forms, predicting that it will disappear and that the nation's schools will be little changed by the experience. Perhaps despairingly, they believe that the future of Hispanic schooling depends on political and economic trends:

[27]See "Defining Bilingual Education," *The Chicago Tribune,* August 8, 1980, Section 1, p. 12, and "Debating the New Bilingual Rules," *Christian Science Monitor,* August 7, 1980, p. 24.

[28]Department of Health, Education and Welfare, Office of Civil Rights, "State and National Summaries of Data Collected by the 1976 Elementary and Secondary School Civil Rights Survey, 1978," cited in background papers, Lori Orum.

Compensatory education does not work, and the conditions that contribute to their academic failure have not significantly changed. The aggregate of low teacher expectations, defeatism, irrelevance, rigid instruction, tracking, and the many other unjust practices described engenders a negative school social environment. This plays a crucial part in the poor school record of Mexican Americans.[29]

The meaning of the Carter and Segura forecast is straightforward: the structure of society determines educational practices. Substantial changes in the schools must wait for changes in the community.

Hispanic powerlessness in the American political system is the source of their powerlessness in articulating their problems with the schools. In the years immediately after World War II, change was brought about by legal decision. Then during the 1960s and 1970s, change came about through street riots and confrontation, aided to some extent by a responsive federal government. None of these changes began in the schools nor were they easily accepted by the schools. Educational policy in public schools will continue to be a controversial issue for the Hispanic community. Because elementary and secondary schools are failing so badly, few Hispanics survive to enter higher education. Michael Olivas points out that the public perception is that Hispanic enrollments have greatly increased, but in reality, neither affirmative action programs nor governmental efforts have met this perception. Three problems continue to be critical: discriminatory employment practices toward Hispanic faculty members, high student attrition rates, and limited access. Only a small number of higher education institutions are actively enrolling Hispanic students.[30]

Hispanic children and parochial schools. Private and parochial schools were never important factors in the education of Hispanic children. At present 90.3 percent are enrolled in public schools—a figure smaller than Anglos, although Hispanics are overwhelmingly Catholic. Yet poor Hispanics are more likely to use the system, even though they incur tuition costs. Recent figures show 41.8 percent of Hispanics who send their children to private schools have family incomes of under $15,000, as compared with 19.5 percent of Anglo-Americans with similar incomes.[31]

The reasons for this small Catholic influence are given in Chapter 6. Yet the larger areas of Hispanic settlement always had some educational facilities. In El Paso small schools appeared as early as 1892, but as in the public schools, an Italian, Irish, and American clergy tended to stress Americanization and gave only basic instruction in the lower grades. El Paso was also a significant area of effort for

[29] Carter and Segura, *Mexican Americans in School,* p. 391.

[30] Michael A. Olivas, "Federal Education Policy: The Case of Hispanics," *Educational Evaluation and Policy Analysis,* Vol. IV (Fall, 1982), p. 305.

[31] Data are from a *Current Population Survey* conducted in October 1979 and reported in "Testimony on Private, Elementary, and Secondary Education" submitted to the Subcommittee on Elementary, Secondary and Vocational Education of the Committee on Education and Labor of the House of Representatives on May 13, 1981, by the administrator of the National Center on Educational Statistics.

Protestant missionaries, working through a variety of part-time schools and the El Paso YMCA.[32] In time the Catholic parochial system would expand greatly, but it was never enough, not even in southern California.

HEALTH AND MENTAL HEALTH CARE SYSTEMS

Illness and early death are the recognized companions of the poor, and America's Hispanics share this fate. The extent to which this is true and the fashion of its truth is touched on in another chapter (Chapter 5). Here we are concerned with the delivery systems of the American institutions for health and mental health. Is adequate care available for the Hispanics in this country? The basic problem to be addressed is the finding that Hispanics generally underutilize these systems. What are the special problems in the delivery of these services?

There have been two streams of research on health systems closely resembling the research on education. These seek to find, first, what is different in the culture and society of Hispanics that affects their use of the systems? And, second, what features of the system affect its use by Hispanics?

Hispanic culture and health. Hispanics brought with them an indigenous system of health and mental health personnel. Further, some researchers argue that the Hispanic social structure provides its people with support and protection that seems to diminish the frequency of certain types of mental illness. It is a reasonable conclusion that the standard health system of the United States is not always superior and that Hispanics can—and do—choose between two systems or use both simultaneously. Thus underutilization does not—in this view—mean that Hispanics are underserved.

The Mexican-American segment of the Hispanics has been the most thoroughly studied. Among Mexicans, an elaborate system of health and health care was in place well before modern times. Not only has this system endured, but it is continually refreshed by new immigrants from Mexico. Early observers were fascinated by the survival of medieval Spanish and Arab practices, and the occasional intermingling of practices from Indian sources and herbal remedies.

Home remedies emphasize herb teas grown in the garden or purchased at local *botánicas* and the use of massage. Local experts (usually particularly skilled older women) may be called upon for advice and help, sometimes for pay but more often as a favor. Such practices were common in Chicano communities in earlier years and are found among other Hispanics as well. Recent studies find that this theory is fading among urbanized Hispanics. Still, a distinctive disease classification survives in Mexican-American *barrios* and home remedies persist.[33]

There is even more interest in the *curanderas* or faith healers. In traditional communities, certain symptoms of mental illness are defined differently from Anglo psychiatry, and local *curanderas* (often paid practitioners) are used. Sometimes there is strong religious imagery.[34]

[32] Garcia, *Desert Immigrants,* Ch. 10.

[33] For an excellent overview, see Beatrice Roeder, "Health Care Beliefs and Practices Among Mexican Americans: A Review of the Literature," *Aztlán,* Vol. 13 (1982), pp. 223 ff.

[34] Ari Kiev, *Curanderismo: Mexican American Folk Psychiatry* (New York: The Free Press, 1969).

For Hispanics of Caribbean origin, folk medicine shares some elements with Mexican herbalism and *curanderismo*. Basic to both types of treatment lies an ancient Spanish theory of the causes of disease and remedies. But the Caribbean versions of faith healers are far more influenced by the special mix of populations in the area. African slaves transmitted some of their beliefs and practices, and these rarely crept into either Mexico or the Mexican-occupied Southwest. Health and mental health workers began to confront these beliefs in the early years of Puerto Rican settlement in New York when patients began to display symptoms of a mental health problem known as *ataque de nervios* (nervous attack). It turned out that *ataque* could be managed with the help of *espiritismo*, that is, with the assistance of a spiritualist.[35] Further exploration in Puerto Rico showed that the spiritualist was not simply acting like a medical practitioner to whom an afflicted patient went with a specific set of symptoms. Rather, the patient was usually a member of a spiritualist church, led by a leader who became a therapist when the need arose.[36] Similar patterns were found among Dominican immigrants in New York and also among Cubans in Miami.[37] By the mid-1970s, mental health clinics in Puerto Rican and Dominican communities in New York City were beginning to work closely with spiritualists in a team approach, although there were still skeptics about the use of such nontraditional therapists.[38]

The combination of the two approaches does demonstrate the ability of Western-trained mental health practitioners to use available resources within the Hispanic communities—and thus to do a highly innovative form of community mental health.

Recent research in traditional settings in Texas still finds *curanderismo* to be in operation and "working"; but other research in Los Angeles found from a sample of 500 Mexican respondents that the preferred treatment resource for mental illness is the general practitioner, not the *curandero*.[39] The Los Angeles study was done before mental health centers were established in Hispanic communities.

Until very recently, mental health services were scarce in any low-income areas, and Hispanic communities are no exception. Now that they are available, will Hispanics use them? A recent study shows that Hispanics are more likely to name a trained therapist as the preferred resource (and almost never a *curandero*), but

[35] W. J. Grace, "Ataque," *New York Medicine,* Vol. 15, no. 1 (1959), pp. 12-13.

[36] Lloyd Rogler and August Hollingshead, "The Puerto Rican Spiritualist as a Psychiatrist," *American Journal of Sociology,* Vol. 67 (1961), pp. 17-21. J. D. Koss, "Terapeútica del sistema de una secta en Puerto Rico," *Revista de Ciencias Sociales,* Vol. 14 (1970), pp. 259-278.

[37] C. S. Thomas and V. Garrison, "A Case of the Dominican Migrant," in Roy Bryce-Laporte and C. S. Thomas, eds., *Alienation in Contemporary Society* (New York: Praeger, 1976), pp. 216-260; and M. C. Sandoval, "Santeria: Afrocuban Concepts of Disease and Its Treatment in Miami," *Journal of Operational Psychiatry,* Vol. 8 (1977), pp. 52-63.

[38] P. Ruiz and J. Langrod, "The Role of Folk Healers in Community Mental Health Services," *Community Mental Health Journal,* Vol. 12 (1976), pp. 392-398; and N. Galli, "The Influence of Cultural Heritage on the Health Status of Puerto Ricans," *Journal of School Health,* Vol. 45 (1975), pp. 10-16. For a balanced view of the medical role of *espiritismo,* see V. Garrison, "Doctor, Espiritista or Psychiatrist? Health-Seeking Behavior in a Puerto Rican Neighborhood of New York City," *Medical Anthropology,* Vol. 1 (1977), pp. 65-191.

[39] Robert Edgerton et al., "Curanderismo in the Metropolis: The Diminished Role of Folk Psychiatry Among Los Angeles Mexican Americans," *American Journal of Psychotherapy,* Vol. 24 (1970), pp. 124-134.

when asked who is actually used, they overwhelmingly turn to friends and relatives.[40] Two kinds of answers suggest themselves. First, that some features of the Hispanic social structure protect or insulate Hispanics. This was the major theme of earlier studies trying to account for the lower presence of Hispanics in mental health facilities.[41] But many more recent studies suggest a second explanation—that it is not only geographic availability but "functional" availability that is important. Are they affordable—and are they culturally accessible? In one Hispanic community two mental health centers differed in only one respect: one was predominantly staffed by Hispanics, the other, by Anglos. In the first center, 90 percent of the patients were Hispanics. In the latter, less than a fifth were Hispanics.[42] As Alfredo Gonzalez remarks, "The language factor, of course, is a crude indicator of the more pervasive problem of cultural differences between client and professional."[43] Such cultural differences are absolutely critical in mental health care, where misunderstandings can lead to atrocious misdiagnoses. Researchers were shocked to find that Puerto Ricans were admitted to mental health facilities at twice the rate of Anglos, but when the data were closely examined, they found strong implications of diagnostic distortion and possible bias. This was especially true in admissions for mental retardation.[44]

Apart from the obvious difficulties of language, it is easy to assume that cultural differences are not important in the care of physical ailments. This is not the case. The role of cultural factors extends throughout a wide range of medical beliefs and practices and has been extensively explored.[45] This is a complex subject around which a substantial literature is available. The bottom line in terms of policy is essentially community pressure to staff public health facilities (county hospitals and local clinics) with enough Hispanic personnel to avoid problems in communication and cultural insensitivity. This is difficult in itself. There are few Hispanics working at a professional level in health services. In New York City, to cite only one example, only 2 percent of the professionals working in municipal hospitals in 1979 were Puerto Rican.[46]

[40] E. S. Levine and A. Padilla, *Cultural and Mental Health* (New York: Macmillan, 1959).

[41] See, for example, E. Gartly Jaco, *Culture and Mental Health* (New York: Macmillan, 1959).

[42] Armando Morales, "Institutional Racism in Mental Health and Criminal Justice," *Social Casework,* Vol. (1978), pp. 387–395.

[43] Alfredo Gonzalez, "Resource Utilization by the Families of Chicano Prisoners," in Joan Moore and John Long, eds., *Barrio Impact of High Incarceration Rates* (Los Angeles: Chicano Pinto Research Project, 1981), a useful analytic overview of resource utilization, especially the availability of extended kin networks.

[44] Jose Oscar Alers, *Puerto Ricans and Health: Findings from New York City* (Bronx, N.Y.: Fordham University, Puerto Rican Hispanic Research Center, 1978). Similar very high rates of admission for mental illness were found by researchers as far back as the 1940s. (See Chapter 4.)

[45] For example, see Lyle Saunders, *Cultural Differences and Medical Care* (New York: Russell Sage, 1954), for New Mexico. Clark, *Health in the Mexican American Culture* (Berkeley, Calif.: University of California Press, 1959), deals with California Mexican Americans, and Arthur Rubel, *Across the Tracks* (Austin: University of Texas Press, 1966), deals with Texas communities. Central and South Americans living in Washington, D.C., are the subject of Lucy Cohen, *Culture, Disease and Stress Among Latino Immigrants* (Washington, D.C.: Smithsonian Institution, Research Institute on Immigration and Ethnic Studies, 1979).

[46] Alers, *Puerto Ricans and Health,* p. 72.

Hispanics and the structure of health delivery. The most serious criticism of the Anglo health and mental health delivery system is very simple—they have not been available. Mental health clinics have appeared in urban Hispanic communities only in recent years. Public health services are available in larger metropolitan areas, but some areas of the nation are seriously underserved. The consequences of any change in this situation can be dramatic. In rural and small-town areas of south Texas, shortly after the appearance of federally funded health care programs, there was a dramatic decline in birth-related deaths. In the ten-year period from 1969 to 1979, the decrease was 65 percent.[47] This decrease was so striking that several analysts termed the idea that Hispanic patients "do not really need" modern medicine (because of their indigenous care system and insulating social system) to be simply institutional racism—or simply an excuse not to provide medical care. The figures on prenatal care in south Texas prompt Antonio Zavaleta, an anthropologist, to remark, "In spite of the tremendous strides made during the decade, thousands of women [in South Texas] still receive no, or inadequate, prenatal health care. . . . The incidence of birth-related defects and mental retardation resulting from complications in unattended births are very high along the border."[48]

Not only are health resources less available in poor Hispanic communities, but there is a special problem for the undocumented. A series of legal decisions forced hospital emergency rooms to give services, and, in California especially, undocumented women make heavy use of the maternity services of public hospitals. The result is a heavy public cost and much controversy in the Southwest. But in Chicago and New York, public health administrators argue that public health care (particularly the control of dangerous diseases) affects the entire public, not just individual recipients, and accordingly asks no questions about the legality of sick people.[49] The attitudes of service providers is another important part of accessibility.

Mental health care is especially sensitive to nuances of interaction. In fact, the attitudes and values of professionals are probably more important than are those of clients. Like teachers, mental health professionals have preferences about clients. Generally, those found most desirable among psychotherapists are young, attractive, verbal, intelligent, and successful. By contrast, low-income patients are often seen as hostile, suspicious, and crude.[50] It is logical to expect that therapists treating low-income Hispanics will behave differently than when faced with middle-class Anglos, and indeed "diagnostic stereotypes" and treatment both vary. A number of studies show that Hispanics are less likely to receive extensive psychotherapy than are other groups. Therapists also tend to treat Hispanic patients with drugs more

[47] Antonio Zavaleta, "Federal Assistance and Mexican American Health Status in Texas," *Agenda,* Vol. 11 (1981), pp. 19–25. These deaths have begun to rise again nationally as federal funding for maternal and infant care declined.

[48] Ibid., p. 24.

[49] U.S. Department of Health, Education and Welfare, *Unpaid Medical Costs and Undocumented Aliens* (Washington, D.C.: U.S. Department of Health, Education and Welfare, Office of Special Concerns, 1979).

[50] W. Shofield, *Psychotherapy: The Purchase of Friendship* (Englewood Cliffs, N.J.: Prentice-Hall, 1964); and R. P. Lorian, "Patient and Therapist Variables in the Treatment of Low-Income Patients," *Psychological Bulletin,* Vol. 81 (1974), pp. 244–354, cited in Gonzales, "Resource Utilization."

frequently than with psychotherapy. Even when there are social class differences among minority patients, they are treated more like one another than are Anglos.[51]

In public mental health services, Hispanic usage is much lower than is either that of blacks or Anglos. Several nationwide surveys in 1975 covered the use of private and public inpatient and outpatient psychiatric services. In most services, Hispanics were admitted at lower rates (per 100,000 population) than either blacks or Anglos. Outpatient services were most frequently used, but still, the Hispanic use rate was only 528 per 100,000 as against 814 for blacks and 639 for Anglos. Both Hispanics and blacks were more likely to be diagnosed as schizophrenic. In state and county mental hospital inpatient services, drug and alcohol problems were important, accounting for 40 percent of Hispanic admissions).[52]

HISPANICS AND WELFARE SERVICES

From the point of view of the American public, no interaction of the Hispanic population with public institutions is more critical than is "welfare dependency." Such an alleged dependency is a persistent stereotype in Los Angeles for Mexican Americans and in New York for Puerto Ricans. And, in fact, 1970 figures show that almost a quarter of Puerto Rican families in this country depended on welfare payments, compared with only 5 percent of other U.S. families.[53] Furthermore, the use of public social services by undocumented immigrants is very controversial.

First, we must examine the data on welfare as a source of income for all groups. "Welfare dependency" became a policy issue in the late 1960s with most focus on the aid to families with dependent children. In the 1930s when the program began, most recipients were Anglo and widowed mothers. In time, the mothers began to include minority people, many of whom were bearing children out of wedlock. This produced a mixture of racism and morality that is a potent combination for stigmatizing a "welfare" population. There began to be research on whether Aid to Families with Dependent Children was an "aid in transition" through a short-term financial crisis or, as critics charged, a permanent way of life. Two groups were most likely to need public help for longer periods of time: first, black families headed by women and, second, Hispanic families headed by women, especially in big cities. Thus in 1977, 31 percent of all AFDC recipients were long term, and 38 percent of the Hispanic female-headed households in large cities were long term.[54] This, of course, is a small percentage of all families, but it seemed to indicate the existence of problems that were no longer being managed by the family system alone.

But there are many public benefits in addition to cash payments to families. They are food stamps, medical benefits (Medicare for the aged, Medicaid for the

[51] Gonzales, "Resource Utilization."

[52] National Institute of Mental Health, Series CN No. 3, "Hispanic Americans and Mental Health Services: A Comparison of Hispanic, Black and White Admissions to Selected Mental Health Facilities, 1975," DHHS Publication No. (ADM) 80-1006 (Washington, D.C.: Government Printing Office, 1980).

[53] U.S. Commission on Civil Rights, *Puerto Ricans on the Continental U.S.,* p. 47.

[54] S. Erie, G. Fisher, and E. Dayan, "Preliminary Findings of the AFDC Population Study," unpublished (December 1980).

TABLE 9.1   Percent of Poverty-Level Households Receiving or Covered by Various Noncash
Benefits, 1979.

PUBLIC SECTOR	TOTAL ALL POVERTY-LEVEL HOUSEHOLDS	WHITE	BLACK	HISPANIC
Food Stamps	37.4%	30.5%	56.7%	53.5%
Medicare	34.8	37.5	29.2	18.0
Medicaid	39.8	32.7	59.2	52.3
School Lunches	60.7	52.5	75.8	70.4
Public Housing	22.3	17.1	33.2	17.6

Source: U.S. Department of Commerce, Bureau of the Census, "Characteristics of Household and Persons Receiving Noncash Benefits, 1979," Current Population Reports, Series P-23, No. 110.

indigent), school lunches, and public housing. These are given in Table 9.1, from a sample survey, without distinguishing between types of Hispanics. About a third of all poverty-level households[55] but slightly more than half the poverty-level black and Hispanic households received food stamps. Much the same pattern appears in the use of Medicaid (health care for the poor). Similarly, Hispanic poverty-level households were somewhat more likely than their white counterparts to receive free or reduced-price school lunches, reflecting the greater number of children in the population. But Hispanics were less likely to use public (or subsidized) housing. (There is much less public housing in the Sunbelt than in northeastern states.)

They were less likely than Anglo families to receive Medicare, probably because the Hispanics include fewer aged people who are eligible for this special health care subsidy.

It is difficult to conclude that Hispanics use these benefits disproportionately. In general, the patterns seem to be those that would be expected from a poverty population that has large numbers of children and comparatively few old people— whose age dependency ratio diverges from that of the Anglo population. But it is tempting to probe further into stereotypes. For example, do undocumented immigrants utilize such benefits? This is a question that has led to frantic efforts to "get the illegals off the welfare rolls" in many localities. Much resentment is generated by the widespread belief that the undocumented Hispanics utilize tax-supported welfare services. However, most studies indicated that the taxes collected from such persons (through sales taxes, Social Security, and income withholding taxes) substantially outweigh the costs of providing services, with the exception of schooling.[56] Puerto Ricans, even if they are not immigrants, are also stigmatized. It is suggested, for example, that Puerto Ricans accept public aid routinely because public

---

[55] "Poverty level" is defined very specifically by federal agencies: in this survey, for example, a four-person nonfarm household was considered "poor" if the family income was $7,412 or less. A two-person nonfarm household was "poor" if the income was $4,725 or less.

[56] Wayne Cornelius et al., *Mexican Immigrants and Southern California: A Summary of Current Knowledge* (La Jolla: Center for U.S. Mexican Studies, University of California, San Diego, 1982), summarize these studies. See also Thomas Muller, *The Fourth Wave, California's Newest Immigrants: A Summary* (Washington, D.C.: Urban Institute Press, 1984).

aid is routine on the Island. (Although it *is* true that 56 percent of the islanders were receiving food stamps in 1982, other forms of federal and state aid are smaller on the island.[57]) However, with Puerto Ricans as with other immigrants, there are strong indications that "during the first few years after the Puerto Ricans come to the city, they do not have too many problems because relatives and friends help them." It is only in the second stage, when some are successful but some are not, that immigrants turn to public sources of help.[58]

HISPANICS AND THE CRIMINAL JUSTICE SYSTEM

Perhaps more than any other institution except immigration, the criminal justice system reflects a great diversity of experience between groups of Hispanics. Mexicans endured a long period of conflict with Anglo law enforcement under post-conquest colonial control and later.[59] There has always been a special relationship with the Border Patrol, the enforcement arm of the Immigration and Naturalization Service. It is shared to a minor extent with some of the more recent arrivals from Latin America—the Dominicans, for example. But such conflict is not part of the experience of the other two large Hispanic populations. Puerto Ricans are citizens, and the Cubans are refugees; neither group gets deported. Mexican concentration in rural areas and in small towns tended to obscure the problem until the appearance of large urban concentrations after World War II. But more recently the negative experiences of Mexicans with urban police and courts and with the federal and state prison systems are being shared.

Officers of the Border Patrol not only stop entry of aliens but have wide authority to apprehend deportable aliens *anywhere* in the United States and to enforce all pertinent federal laws that affect the heavy traffic across the border. Thus a single patrol officer represents the laws and regulations of some 20 federal agencies. He can stop a car carrying members of a Mexican family anywhere on a California highway. His wide authority allows him to demand documentation of the right of every member of this family to live in the United States. Local law enforcement agencies have never hesitated to put pressure on Mexican-Americans merely by summoning the patrol. Thus a California Highway Patrolman reported his contact as follows:

[57]Barry Levine, "Puerto Rico—Cashing out Food Stamps," *The Journal of the Institute for Socioeconomic Studies,* Vol. 7 (1982), pp. 47–56.

[58]Carmen Garcia, *Study of the Initial Involvement in the Social Services by Puerto Rican Migrants in Philadelphia* (New York: Vantage Press, 1968). See also G. Sternlieb and B. Indik, *The Ecology of Welfare* (New Brunswick, N.J.: Transaction Books, 1973), pp. 63 ff., for a description of living conditions of Puerto Rican and other welfare recipients.

[59]See Larry Trujillo, "La Evolución del 'bandido' al 'pachucho,'" *Issues in Criminology,* Vol. 9 (1974), pp. 43–67, for an analysis of the continuity in the history of Mexicans of their relationship with the criminal justice system; and Rodolfo Acuña, *Occupied America: A History of Chicanos* (New York: Harper & Row, 1981), especially Chs. 4 and 8. The Texas Rangers, the Arizona Rangers, and vigilante and private "goon" squads in mines were extremely violent toward Mexicans. See Carey McWilliams, *North from Mexico* (Philadelphia: J. B. Lippincott), 1949.

4-28, male, age 27. Packing house worker (Mexican national) cited for weaving in roadway. Subject was apprehensive but aware of violation. Negative toward questions, asserted ignorance, unable to understand or speak English. Subject was then asked to show passport, but still showed negative compliance. He was then informed that the Border Patrol would be contacted for assistance. Subject became more open, a little English spoken. He then presented a California driver's license.[60]

Mexicans call the Border Patrol *la migra* (not a term of affection), and since many Chicanos who cross the border as tourists, for example, can be hassled by *la migra* as strenuously as can Mexican aliens without papers, they tend to feel that the patrol is rude, dangerous, and arbitrary. Periodic raids in Chicano communities and workplaces have been frequent, with great disruption of family and economic life. In recent years, more than three-quarters of a million "deportables" were being apprehended each year. In the normal pursuit of its duties, the Border Patrol swoops down on garment factories in East Los Angeles and the Lower East Side of New York City, packing sheds in Sacramento, neighborhood bars and bus stops in Chicago—virtually anyplace where undocumented workers might be found. Buses northbound from the border are routinely stopped and checked. In 1973 the patrol reported questioning more than 5 million passengers in automobiles, more than 1 million bus riders, and more than 2 million pedestrians (including those at border entry points).

The new convergence. Mexican experience with law enforcement on the federal, state, and local level is longer than that of any other Hispanic group, and in some respects it is unique. The experience continues with considerable friction on the local level, and there it is not unique. There is a steady flow of complaints about police malpractice. In Los Angeles, to name only one urban area, the complaints are unremitting. Between 1975 and 1980, Los Angeles County law enforcement agencies accounted for about seven Mexican-American deaths per year. Most concerned people who were clearly unarmed. As one researcher reported:

> The leaders interviewed were probably among the best educated and socio-economically and professionally successful members of Los Angeles' Mexican-American community. Yet the majority pointed to personal experiences with police harassment and violence. Two reported that they had personally been beaten or violently attacked and maced. Three others said that they had been threatened or intimidated either verbally or by the systematic destruction of their office or home. Two others said they had been harassed apparently simply because their appearance identified them as Mexican Americans. Three others said they had been present when friends were severely beaten by police for no apparent justifiable reason; two others had witnessed strangers being beaten or choked for no apparent reason . . . . Six leaders described incidents in which Mexican American social occasions—parties, weddings, and the like—were violently disrupted by police.[61]

[60] Henry T. Levesque, "Ethnic Groups and the Police Officers," unpublished.

[61] Jerry Mandel, *Police Use of Deadly Force: Los Angeles* (Washington, D.C.: National Council of La Raza, 1981). See also Rodolfo Acuña, *Occupied America,* Ch. 12, and Armando Morales, *Ando Sangrando (I Am Bleeding)* (La Puente: Perspective, 1972).

Chicano leaders suggest that police misinterpretation and misunderstanding create the problems:

> Given the distance and lack of understanding, leaders believe that police enter Mexican American communities with an exaggerated sense of fear. . . . A lawyer agreed that the fear emanates from top administrative levels: "I see it as a management problem. If they set the tone as 'It's OK to use force because in a sense you're a paramilitary unit occupying dangerous and violent neighborhoods of savage people,' then it's condoned."[62]

It is certainly true that older generations of police officers were taught to think of Mexican Americans as a "savage people." A famous Los Angeles Police Department report "analyzed" Mexican youth of the 1940s as inherently bloodthirsty because of their Aztec blood. Twenty years later, the Los Angeles chief of police remarked that local Hispanics were "not too far removed from the tribes and mountains of Chihauhua." Even into the 1970s and the 1980s, spokespersons for the Los Angeles police still ignored the possibility of genuine grievances and blamed the protests of Chicanos on the influence of "swimming pool communists" upon unsophisticated local Mexican Americans.[63]

This acute tension between Hispanics and law enforcement occurs in many cities. In 1975 in Los Angeles 24 percent of the people killed by police officers were Hispanic. In the same period, two studies show that more than a fifth of the people killed in New York were Hispanics. A third study revealed that Chicago Hispanics were killed by police 13 times more often than were whites.[64] Houston has suffered a series of major confrontations. In smaller towns, excessive violence against Hispanics can be routinely vicious. So routine, in fact, that in an effort to demonstrate that they were *not* discriminatory, the police of a small Texas town let television cameras record a series of severe beatings of Texas Chicanos. The video tapes shocked the nation when they were shown on national television in 1981.

It would be encouraging if there were some progress on this issue, and there are occasional efforts. The Texas Police Association (Texas chiefs of police) recently considered the problem and in Los Angeles a successful effort was made to reduce the police use of deadly force. Still, police insensitivity and, perhaps, anxiety, remain high.

Inevitably the end result of many of the processes of criminal justice is a period of time in prison. Here, Hispanics are notably more likely to be incarcerated than are Anglos, although less likely than blacks.[65] This reflects both the fact that the Hispanic population is much younger than other groups and also something about the processes of the criminal justice system. In dealing with the fact that 50

---

[62] Mandel, *Police Use of Deadly Force,* p. 53.

[63] Ibid., p. 52.

[64] Larry Trujillo, "Police Use of Excessive Force, Police Crime in the Barrio," paper prepared for the National Urban League, 1980, p. 6.

[65] U.S. Department of Justice, Bureau of Justice Statistics, *Prisoners in State and Federal Institutions on December 31, 1980* (Washington, D.C.: Government Printing Office, 1982). Data on Hispanic inmates were available for about 70 percent of all prisoners. Of the 52 jurisdictions, 12 did not report data on Hispanic origin, including Florida with the fourth largest Hispanic population at the time of the survey.

percent of the arrests in one Chicano community were for drunk driving, a ratio much higher than in the rest of the area, one researcher found that at least one reason for the disparity is the much larger number of police officers who are on patrol in Mexican-American areas. The difference was considerable: 13.5 officers per square mile in the *barrios* as against 3.5 per square mile in the Anglo neighborhoods.[66] Thus any Hispanic drunk driver has a far greater chance of being arrested than does any Anglo drunk driver. It may well be that other high arrest rates may be explained in the same way. Higher incarceration rates might also be due to differential treatment in the courts. Inadequate counsel, high bail, and fewer releases on recognizance might tend to result in longer prison sentences. Data from both California and New York do indeed show longer sentences in prison, on the average for Hispanics.[67] A recent Rand Corporation study blames the longer sentences on the belief of probation officers and judges that Hispanics are high risks to repeat crime.[68] Both federal and state Hispanic prisoners are heavily overrepresented among narcotics offenders, a group who tends to get mandatory prison sentences in many instances and longer sentences. (It is noteworthy that Puerto Rican and Mexican drug offenders tend also to be narcotics addicts. Other Hispanics, especially in New York, tend to be unaddicted Colombians or Dominicans who illegally import drugs.[69])

Once inside prison, Hispanic inmates tend to perpetuate the social ties and some of the values of the free world. Much attention has been paid to inmate culture and even more to the sensationalism of prison riots.[70] But the basic fact is that most Hispanic prisoners, like most others, return to the streets in a fairly short time. The important question concerns the impact of prison experience on that later life. Not only do Hispanic prisoners tend to heed the networks and values of the free world inside prison, but this retention has both negative and positive consequences for their postprison behavior.[71]

On the positive side, Hispanic prisoners are more likely to believe in the continuing reality of the world outside prison and somewhat less likely to become "prisonized" than are many Anglos. Hispanic friends and acquaintances also tend to go to prison, and their prisonmates reappear on the streets. The circulation of inmates from the same communities tends to reinforce their belief in the continuity of life outside. In turn, this helps to keep them facing the necessity of relating effectively to the world of family and work (neither of these is much of a reality in prison).

[66] Armando Morales, "Police Deployment Theories and the Mexican American Community," *El Grito*, Vol. 4 (1970), pp. 52–64.

[67] Federal data from Peter Sissons, *Hispanic Experience of Criminal Justice* (Bronx, N.Y.: Fordham University Hispanic Research Center, 1979). Data from California were supplied by California Department of Corrections, *California Prisoners* (Sacramento, 1969).

[68] Summarized in the *Los Angeles Times*, June 30, 1983.

[69] Sissons, *Hispanic Experience of Criminal Justice*, p. 59.

[70] See, for example, Lee Bowker, *Prisoner Subcultures* (Lexington, Mass.: Lexington Books, 1977), and John Irwin, *Prisons in Turmoil* (Boston: Little, Brown, 1980). Although Hispanics are 6 percent of national prisoner populations and up to 56 percent in at least one state, both these general books offer little information.

[71] See Joan Moore et al., *Homeboys* (Philadelphia: Temple University Press, 1978), and Francis Ianni, *Black Mafia* (New York: Simon & Schuster, 1974).

This sense of continuity was best expressed in the development of Chicano self-help organizations in most federal and state prisons during the 1970s. Self-help groups provided an organizational base for motivating prisoners to think through their lives and their relationship to Chicano communities and Chicano issues. These organizations eroded in the social climate of the 1980s with its diminished emphasis on grass-roots Hispanic community participation in civic affairs. They also diminished in the face of Hispanic prison "gangs" that tend to form about Hispanic "state-raised youth," who have been incarcerated so frequently during youth that the world of prisons is the only reality. Prison gangs have been very much sensationalized, and there is little doubt that they are a product of the prisons themselves. There is no strong evidence that these gangs are the basis for organized crime in Hispanic communities outside of prison.

A final negative effect of the criminal justice system is the impact on families and communities. Wives and children undergo economic hardship and, often, social stigmatization. This is particularly difficult for children. Parents and brothers and sisters often are traumatized by the failure of the system to help their troubled relative. (Family and community reactions to a case of police and judicial mistreatment in the 1940s in Los Angeles is dramatized in the play and movie *Zoot Suit*.) Recent research shows that family members of a prisoner (usually not involved in criminal behavior) are notably more alienated from the larger social system, particularly younger male respondents.[72] The major sources of this alienation are family experiences with the police and courts—and also fear for the incarcerated relative. Because these experiences are more widespread in Hispanic communities with their youthful age structure, the overall impact of the criminal justice system is much more important than the impact on the offenders alone.

[72] Joan Moore and John Long, *Barrio Impact of High Incarceration Rates.*

CHAPTER TEN
POLITICS AND THE HISPANIC COMMUNITY

Hispanic political power in the United States carries two contradictory images. One is that of a community with growing political force and a huge potential. The second grows from a long history in the United States and holds that Hispanics do not participate politically as other groups do in American society. Politicians, journalists, and academic researchers all have speculated on why Hispanics do not participate to their full potential and why "Hispanics don't vote."

In this chapter we first consider an overview of factors affecting Hispanic political participation in the electoral process and why two such contradictory images have developed. We then examine the political developments of each of the major Hispanic subgroups in the continental United States. Finally, we explore the growing national Hispanic political presence that coalesces Cuban Americans, Mexican Americans, Puerto Ricans, and other Hispanics and that is having an ever-increasing impact on national domestic policy.

HISPANICS AND POLITICS: AN OVERVIEW

With the doubling in size of the congressional Hispanic Caucus in the 1982 elections, with over 100 Hispanic state legislators holding office, and with the election of Hispanics to mayorships in such key cities as Miami, San Antonio, and Denver, many analysts are now examining the political potential of the Hispanics. These political gains occurred in spite of several factors that limit the electoral impact of the Hispanic community commensurate with its numbers.

TABLE 10.1 Hispanic Congressional Representation and District Composition, 1982

STATE AND DISTRICT	NUMBER OF HISPANICS IN CONGRESSIONAL DISTRICT	PERCENTAGE OF DISTRICT RESIDENTS WHO ARE HISPANICS	PERCENTAGE OF STATE HISPANIC POPULATION IN CONGRESSIONAL DISTRICT[a]	REPRESENTATIVE IN 1982
Arizona				
2	192,632	35.5%	43.7%	(D) Udall
5	92,979	17.1	21.1	(D) McNulty
California				
25	334,168	63.6	7.4	(D) Roybal*
30	284,532	54.2	6.3	(D) Martinez*
34	250,298	47.6	5.5	(D) Torres*
29	169,739	32.3	3.7	(D) Hawkins
28	155,368	29.6	3.4	(D) Dixon
17	148,423	28.3	3.3	(R) Pashavan
10	147,394	28.0	3.2	(D) Edwards
15	141,042	26.8	3.1	(D) Coehlo
24	138,687	26.4	3.1	(D) Waxman
38	137,499	26.2	3.0	(D) Patterson
44	137,023	26.1	3.0	(D) Bates
26	132,876	25.3	2.9	(D) Berman
19	132,689	25.2	2.9	(R) Lagomarsino
Colorado				
1	91,194	18.9	26.8	(D) Schroeder
3	82,499	17.1	24.3	(D) Kogovsek
Florida				
18	260,289	50.7	30.3	(D) Pepper
17	126,485	24.7	14.7	(D) Lehman
19	111,934	21.3	13.0	(D) Fascell

State / District				
Illinois				
8	31.6	25.8	164,164	(D) Rostenkowski
5	26.0	21.2	135,062	(D) Lipinski
9	9.5	7.8	49,558	(D) Yates
New Jersey				
14	26.6	28.5	140,013	(D) Gvarini
10	13.8	14.7	72,519	(D) Rodino
8	12.9	13.8	67,849	(D) Roe
New Mexico				
3	39.0	35.3	168,577	(D) Richardson*
1	37.4	34.0	162,171	(D) Lujan*
New York				
18	51.3	16.0	265,963	(D) Garcia*
11	38.0	11.9	196,706	(D) Towns
16	37.9	11.8	195,920	(D) Rangel
7	19.7	6.2	102,073	(D) Ackerman
9	16.6	5.2	85,780	(D) Ferraro
Texas				
15	71.7	12.7	378,195	(D) De La Garza*
20	61.7	10.9	324,926	(D) Gonzales*
27	61.5	10.9	324,120	(D) Ortiz*
16	60.2	10.6	317,592	(D) Coleman
23	53.1	9.4	279,390	(D) Kazen

*Members of Congressional Hispanic Caucus.

[a]These districts cumulatively include at least half of each state's Hispanic population. Thus, half or more of Arizona's Hispanics live in the two districts listed.

Source: Derived from U.S. Census, *Congressional District Profiles: 98th Congress*, PC80-S1-11.

The first of these factors is that Hispanic population growth (while generally spectacular) is still regional and confined to a few key states (see Chapter 4). Furthermore, even within these states, the growth is concentrated geographically. Table 10.1 shows how Hispanics concentrate in certain congressional districts. In California, 50 percent of the state's Hispanic population is found in 13 congressional districts in southern California (out of a total of 45). In Texas, five congressional districts in the southern part of the state contain 50 percent of the Mexican-American population. In New York five congressional districts in the New York City area contain 51 percent of the Hispanic population. This concentration has certain implications. Many elected representatives at the local, state, and federal levels have few Hispanic voters in their district.

This has affected the national political visibility of Hispanics. Hispanics seeking political office face a relatively small number of districts where the majority of the population is Hispanic. Data from the congressional districts show that only 10 congressional districts have more than 50 percent Hispanics (see Table 10.2). Seven out of the 10 Hispanic members of Congress in 1982 come from these same districts. The importance of ethnic populations in electing ethnic candidates may be demonstrated by the fact that 14 out of 17 black representatives in the U.S. House of Representatives came from congressional districts with more than 40 percent black population.

Not only is the bulk of the Hispanic population geographically concentrated, but the demographic characteristics of the community have political significance. As noted in Chapter 4, the Hispanic population is younger than the American population as a whole. Nearly 40 percent of the Hispanic community was below voting age in 1980. Although a substantial group of potential new voters will be coming of age every two years in the 1980s, large numbers of Hispanics are still in the age groups that participate less in the electoral process. Furthermore, as the population ages, it will tend to participate more in the electoral process.

There is yet another factor that influences Hispanic voting participation.

TABLE 10.2   Congressional Districts with 50 Percent Hispanic Population in 1980 and Their Congressional Representatives

STATE	DISTRICT	PERCENTAGE OF HISPANIC POPULATION	CONGRESSIONAL REPRESENTATIVE
California	25	63.6%	Edward Roybal[a]
	30	54.2	Matthew Martinez[a]
	34	47.6	Esteban Torres[a]
Florida	18	50.7	Claude Pepper
New York	18	51.3	Robert Garcia[a]
Texas	15	71.7	Kika de la Garza[a]
	20	61.7	Henry P. Gonzales[a]
	27	61.5	Solomon Ortiz
	16	60.2	Ronald D. Coleman

[a]Person of Hispanic origin

Source: U.S. Census, Congressional District Profiles, 98th Congress PC80-S1-11.

TABLE 10.3   Voter Participation Rates—White, Black, and Hispanic—With and Without
Ineligible Voters, 1974-1980

			HISPANIC	
YEAR	WHITE	BLACK	TOTAL	WITHOUT INELIGIBLES[a]
1974	46.3%	33.8%	22.9%	31.0%
1976	60.9	48.7	31.8	42.6
1978	47.3	37.2	23.5	34.3
1980	60.9	50.5	29.9	44.1

[a]Not eligible due to citizenship.

Source: U.S. Bureau of the Census, *"Voting and Registration in the Elections of November 1974, 1976, 1978, 1980, 1982"* (Series P-20) *Current Population Reports,* April 1982.

Many Hispanics are foreign-born or recent immigrants. The presence of this large noncitizen population is a factor that is often overlooked in most studies of Hispanic political participation. At first glance, it appears that Hispanic political participation is much lower than is either Anglo or black electoral participation. But if one controls for citizenship, then Hispanic political participation is comparable to that of the black population (see Table 10.3). Every in-depth study of the Hispanic community, however, confirms the high percentage of Hispanics who cannot participate because they are not citizens.[1]

Surprisingly, this problem of noncitizenship also affects most localities where Puerto Ricans are concentrated because they are also areas of South or Central American concentration. As an example, in New York City's two congressional districts with the most Hispanics, (the 18th and 11th districts), non–Puerto Rican Hispanics form 21 percent and 16 percent of the total population, respectively. In some cases in the Northeast (as in New Jersey's 14th district), Puerto Ricans are actually less than a third of the Hispanics in the district. (These figures reflect the heterogeneity of the Hispanic communities in this region.) The second image of Hispanic politics, as a population that "doesn't vote" or as a "sleeping giant," grew from a number of factors. We have seen that such inactivity is related to demographic factors. But some analysts blame "Latino political culture," and class characteristics. We know now that many of the characteristics of political nonparticipation are really class linked. Poor people lack the opportunities and resources (such as money and prestige) necessary for successful political activity. Moreover, class biases inherent in our political system (e.g., residency requirements)

[1]Thus, a study among Mexican Americans in Houston, Texas, found that "the population figures used in districting, which include noncitizens, overstate the real electoral potential of this ethnic group. See Susan McManus and Carol Cassek, "Representing America's Mexican Americans: The Districting Difficulties," a paper presented at the 1980 Annual Meeting of the American Political Science Association, Washington, D.C., August 1980. In Chicago, a study of Chicano, Puerto Rican, and Cuban political behavior found that "about 70 percent of Mexican Americans and Cubans in Chicago are foreign citizens": see Luis Salces and Peter Colby, "Mañana Will Be Better: Spanish American Politics in Chicago," a paper prepared for publication in *Illinois Issues,* 1980. The 1970 census showed that 33 percent of the residents in East Los Angeles census tracts were foreign-born Mexican citizens; see Harry Pachon, "Politics in the Mexican American Community," in *Mexican Americans,* 2nd ed., by Joan Moore with Harry Pachon (Englewood Cliffs, N.J.: Prentice-Hall, 1976).

also inhibit participation. Given the incidence of poverty among Hispanics (see Chapter 4) and the certainty that it was greater in the past, there is good reason to accept the statement that researchers on Hispanics overlooked the question of class.

A final factor lowering Hispanic political participation is the continued influx of immigrants. Most new immigrants do not become integrated into their new environment until some time has passed. Puerto Ricans encounter a great difference between Election Day in New York City and Election Day in Puerto Rico. In Puerto Rico, elections are held on weekends, and Election Day is considered a national holiday. In contrast, in New York elections are held on weekdays, come at frequent intervals, and are held for a variety of offices.

Yet another aspect of the immigrant experience is the phenomenon of relative deprivation. Newly arrived immigrants may not feel deprived. Living conditions may be better than in the immediate past of the individual. Cuban Americans who escaped a repressive regime in Cuba may view the political world of the United States quite differently from a Mexican-American political activist born and reared in the *barrio* who can trace generations of his family caught in the same environment.

These factors are all present in the community. But there are other external factors that are equally relevant—and that were already present in the institutions of Anglo society. The first of these is the nature of Hispanic interaction with the larger society after the Anglo-American conquest, a factor overlooked by a previous generation of scholars. It is said that "history is written by the victors." In this case the victors have written out violence and domination. This is particularly true in Chicano and Puerto Rican history. Social banditry and rebellions swept the native Mexican population in the 1850s and later. Puerto Ricans developed a nationalist movement. Political unrest was widespread in the island of Puerto Rico in the 1930s and resulted in *La Masacre de Ponce* of 1936.[2] Most analysts tend to dismiss these incidents as simply acts by terrorists or deranged individuals, refusing to see their political nature.

But there are yet other institutionalized obstacles to Hispanic political activity. Devices such as the discriminatory poll tax, the White Man's Union in Texas (which existed until 1944), gerrymandering to dilute Hispanic political power, and overt suppression by threats, economic sanctions, subterfuge, and violence hampered Hispanic participation. English literacy tests disenfranchised Hispanics after the 1890s in nearly all the states and New York. (New Mexico was the only exception.) Voter residency requirements still disenfranchise significant segments of the Mexican and Puerto Rican migrant laborers.

The nature and extent of political domination demonstrates the great gaps in our knowledge of Hispanic participation in traditional politics. Actually, political and proto-political organizations appeared very early for both Mexican Americans and Puerto Ricans. In New Mexico, for example, the Fraternal Order of Penitent Brothers (*Los Penitentes*) made substantial contributions to the state constitutional convention and to the insertion of a bilingual provision in the state constitution.[3]

Mexican Americans were very active in the trade union movements of the Southwest during the 1920s and 1930s. The earliest attempts to unionize agricultur-

---

[2] Kal Wagenheim, *Puerto Rico: A Profile* (New York: Praeger, 1970), p. 72.

[3] Jose Amaro Hernandez, *Mutual Aid for Survival* (Malabar, Fla.: Robert E. Krieger, 1983), p. 22.

al workers in California came through the *Confederation de Uniones Obreras Mexicanas* and the *mutualista* societies, such as the *Sociedad Benito Juarez* of El Centro (established in 1919) and the *Sociedad Mutualista Hidalgo* of Brawley (established in 1921).[4] Puerto Rican mutual aid societies, trade unions, political clubs, and special interest organizations appeared in New York after the turn of the century. The Puerto Rican Brotherhood of America (*Hermanidad Puertoriquena*) was established in 1923—the same year as the *Club Democrata Puertoriqueno*. There was a Puerto Rican Committee of the Socialist Party. All are examples of early social and political groups developed to cope with a new environment. Yet these efforts appear to be overlooked by scholars who could say, "The relative absence of organizations is only an indication of their apolitical history."[5]

A possible reason for these oversights is the tendency to use models of Anglo-American political organizations. In Hispanic communities, these may not be applicable. It is possible that in Chicano and Puerto Rican communities political organizations were not found because observers could not see that many such groups were multifunctional and undifferentiated. Michael de Tirado notes that the Mexican American during the early part of this century would "establish undifferentiated multipurpose organizations which not only served his political needs but also his economic, social and cultural ones as well."[6] This multifunction is illustrated by the *Alianza Hispano Americana* with functions that ranged over a 60-year period from providing insurance benefits for burial to civil rights advocacy in the 1950s. The goals of the Puerto Rican Brotherhood included the normal activities of a mutual assistance society as well as a call for the involvement of mainland Puerto Ricans on behalf of Puerto Rico. Another oversight is involved when Hispanic political activity is constantly compared with that of black Americans and European immigrants of the late nineteenth and early twentieth centuries. The comparison is usually negative. Yet both analogies are misleading. Hispanics arrived at a different time and in a different place. The differences are important. Because Europeans tended to settle in the East, they immediately met institutions favoring political participation—the political machines of urban America in the 1800s and early 1900s, which actually depended upon successive waves of new Europeans. It was a type of political organization that gave the new immigrants both material and psychic rewards. The machine politicized the immigrants and established avenues for upward political movement—from precinct worker to precinct captain and eventually to elected office. It fought rural-dominated state legislatures and defended immigrant life-styles against the nativists. But urban political machines were either missing or very weak in most of the Southwest.

There were few exceptions. Machine-type politics were important in some parts of Texas and New Mexico. In four counties of south Texas during the late 1890s and early 1900s, a type of Democratic machine appeared. It was, in brief, a network of county organizations giving basic social and economic services to a

[4]Charles Wollenberg, "Huelga, 1928 Style: The Imperial Valley Cantaloupe Strike," *Pacific Historical Review,* Vol. 38 (1969), pp. 45-58.

[5]James Jennings, *Puerto Rican Politics in New York City* (Washington, D.C.: University Press, 1977).

[6]Michael de Tirado, "The Mexican American Minority's Participation in Voluntary Political Associations," unpublished dissertation (Claremont, Calif.: Claremont Graduate School, 1970), p. 11.

small elite of farmers and merchants and a mass of Mexican-American laborers, farmers, and ranch hands. Political control depended on control of Hispanic votes and access to patronage.[7] This corrupt control of the Mexican vote survived political changes and the enormous economic shock of the shift from cattle ranching to intensive irrigation. In fact, it has survived to some extent to the present time and was a critical factor in the political career of Lyndon Johnson.[8] Perhaps unfortunately for Puerto Ricans, there were very few Hispanic immigrants when New York's famed Tammany Hall organization held most of its power. Puerto Ricans began to appear in significant numbers during the 1930s, a time when the established Democratic machine was losing power.[9]

Nor is it reasonable to compare Hispanic political activity with that of black Americans. Both groups are racially distinctive, of course, but Hispanics are much less so.[10] As a result, Hispanic communities experience upward mobility and assimilation much more than do blacks. The relative lack of racial bias, the fact that some Hispanics can "pass" or "escape" from Anglo-American color consciousness has affected the development of political solidarity. Hispanics are not inextricably bound to being Hispanic.

Yet another difference in experience between blacks and Hispanics is their relative concentration. Until very recently Hispanics lived almost entirely in the Southwest and in New York City. This low national visibility, especially in the East, helps to explain why such groups as the Democratic party, labor unions, various liberal groups, and the large charitable foundations did not champion Hispanic causes before the 1970s as seriously as those of black Americans. This low national visibility also helped to allow policymakers to see Hispanic policy issues as simple variations of black problems. The attorney general of the United States in the Carter administration reflected this attitude when he stated at a meeting of the congressional Hispanic Caucus, "I know about Hispanic concerns since I participated in the Civil Rights Movement in the South."

Many factors thus affect the political behavior of American Hispanics. But beyond these factors there is the differing political history of the various Hispanic groups.

MEXICAN-AMERICAN POLITICS

Small numbers, isolation, and Anglo-American hostility greatly limited the impact of Mexican-American political organizations in the early Southwest before 1900. Albert Camarillo characterizes Mexican political relationships in southern California in terms of four major patterns. These were (1) racial partisan politics, (2) political accommodation by the elite Mexican *ranchero* class, (3) political

[7] Evan Anders, *Boss Rule in South Texas* (Austin: University of Texas Press, 1982).

[8] Robert Caro, *The Years of Lyndon Johnson: The Path to Power* (New York: Vintage Books, 1981).

[9] Virginia Sanchez Korrol, *From Colonia to Community* (Westport, Conn.: Greenwood Press, 1983), p. 185.

[10] See Piri Thomas, *Down These Mean Streets* (New York: Alfred A. Knopf, 1967). Thomas uses the term "rainbow people" to describe the color variation present in many Puerto Rican families. See also Jose Villareal, "Mexican Americans in Upheaval," in Matt Meier and Feliciana Rivera, eds., *Readings on LaRaza* (New York: Hill and Wang, 1974), pp. 213-217.

harassment and ostracism by neighboring Anglo communities, and (4) the adoption of policies designed to ensure voter powerlessness. (This last pattern might include gerrymandering and racial exclusion from political parties.)[11] This series of relationships appeared in both Los Angeles and Santa Barbara. Many of the same patterns, if not more intensified, dominated Anglo-Mexican politics in Texas in the late 1800s. Only in New Mexico (largely because of their numbers) were Hispanics able to make their political influence felt. Thus when large numbers of immigrants began to enter the United States during and after the Mexican Revolution, they were trapped by existing patterns. Prejudice toward the Mexican Americans also increased during the Mexican Revolution (roughly 1910 to 1920) and the incursions of Pancho Villa and the subsequent anti-Mexican hysteria (see Chapter 2).

In this atmosphere, such organizations as the *mutualistas* were limited in their political impact. The limits, of course, were set not only by discrimination but by an immigrant membership that could not vote. But other organizations, such as the *Orden de Hijos de America* (which later merged into the now very important League of United Latin American Citizens—LULAC) were not hindered by an immigrant membership because they limited themselves to the emerging Mexican-American middle class. Criticisms of the assimilationist approach of LULAC during this period overlook the pressure of the times. Anglo Americans viewed Chicanos as foreigners, and LULAC was forced to deal with this perception.[12] Discrimination against Mexican Americans during the 1920s and 1930s was strong, and political organizational efforts were kept weak, although a series of groups did make efforts—including the Catholic church, the Communist party, and such community groups as *El Congreso de Pueblos de Habla Espanol.* For Mexican Americans, the prevailing mood did not favor political activity. Notable were the forced repatriations of the depression years, the xenophobic mood of the country (the KKK was active in southwestern states during the 1920s), and the acute suffering and wage competition of the depression itself. World War II changed this atmosphere drastically.

World War II was an event of unparalleled significance in the history of the Mexican-American people. The war profoundly affected Mexicans because (1) Mexican Americans who served in the armed forces were exposed to social climates quite different from those in the Southwest—namely, the novel experience of not being treated as second-class citizens; (2) the war created an expanding economy in the Southwest that drew Mexican Americans much more rapidly into the more politicized urban centers and into industrial employment; and (3) the rhetoric of the national war effort included attempts of the federal government to project a positive image of Latin Americans. (Ironically, during the war years, the zoot suit riots overtly demonstrated the nature of prejudice faced by Mexican Americans.) And (4) the sacrifices and contributions of Mexican Americans increased the legitimacy of their political activism.[13] The LULAC group caught this mood and set new goals

[11] Albert Camarillo, *Chicanos in a Changing Society* (Cambridge, Mass.: Harvard University Press, 1979), p. 110.

[12] Luis Ricardo Fraga, "Organizational Maintenance and Organizational Success: The League of United Latin American Citizens," a paper presented at the annual meeting of the American Political Science Association, Washington, D.C., August 1981.

[13] Mexican Americans and Hispanics served with particular distinction in World War II. Units of the New Mexico National Guard were the men who held out in Corregidor against the Japanese. Twelve Medals of Honor were given to Spanish-surnamed soldiers in World War II, making Hispanics the group with the largest percentage of Medal of Honor winners in the

for itself in 1944. It would seek to eradicate discrimination and seek equal protection under the law. It would seek political unification and take part in local, state, and national political activity. With the end of the war and the return of the Chicano veterans, this stage of political activism developed even further. Newly formed groups emphasized voter registration drives and the articulation of community needs. As just one example, CSO was formed after the defeat of Edward R. Roybal in 1947 for the seat of a Los Angeles city councilman. In 1949, with the help of the CSO in a strong voter registration effort, Roybal became the first Mexican American to be elected to the Los Angeles Council in the twentieth century. With the aid of the Industrial Areas Foundation, the Community Service Organization was also actively involved in civil rights issues during the 1950s—protesting police mistreatment of juveniles, housing restrictions, and related issues.

This new political activism is perhaps best shown by the American G.I. Forum. The Forum appeared as the direct result of an incident in Three Rivers, Texas, in the late 1940s. When private cemeteries and mortuaries refused to handle the body of a Mexican-American soldier, Chicano veterans protested. National attention suddenly focused on the discriminatory conditions of Mexican-American life in Texas. Because of this incident and because he realized the necessity of continued protest activity, Dr. Hector Garcia organized the G.I. Forum in 1948. Composed of Mexican-American war veterans, the Forum is still in existence in over 23 states with a membership of more than 20,000. Officially, the Forum was nonpartisan, but it urged members to participate in politics, and it lobbied for Mexican appointments at the local and state levels. In common with CSO, the G.I. Forum was not as fully committed to assimilationist goals as were the prewar organizations.

In the late 1940s and 1950s, there was continuous effort to develop political power. The G.I. Forum conducted fact-finding investigations of the segregated school system in Texas and lobbied for changes, in some cases bringing law suits. While national attention was centered on black Americans, Mexican Americans also had to contend with segregated public facilities, segregated schools, and discriminatory jury selection procedures. A study conducted in the west Texas city of Ozona showed for example, that the city's drugstores were closed to Mexicans until the 1940s. Restaurants and movie theaters were not desegregated until 1958. As late as 1972, the Chicano residents of Ozona still complained about segregation practices in the city's bowling alleys, cemeteries, and swimming pools.[14] Direct political activity continued in the 1950s but with a low profile. It is probable that this reduction in activity was a consequence not only of the repressive atmosphere of McCarthyism but of the overt hostility shown Mexican Americans during Operation Wetback in 1954. Yet the 1950s were also a time of political efforts by Henry B. Gonzales in Texas, Edward Roybal in California, and Dennis Chávez in New Mexico. With little coverage by the majority press (and almost complete neglect by the political analysts of the time), the incipient Mexican-American efforts went almost

---

United States today. Interestingly, the novels of the war, especially those set in the Pacific, gave the general American public a wide exposure to Hispanic characters. For Hispanics in World War II, see Ralph Guzman, "Politics and Policies of the Mexican American Community," in Eugene Dvorin and Arthur Misner, eds., *California Politics and Policies* (Reading, Mass.: Addison-Wesley, 1966).

[14]"Project Report: De Jure Segregation of Chicanos in Texas Schools," *Harvard Civil Rights—Civil Liberties Law Review,* Vol. 7 (March 1972), pp. 307-390.

unnoticed. In 1954, City Councilman Roybal ran for lieutenant governor of the state of California. Using the Spanish motto of *Solo para Roybal* (only for Roybal), this Mexican-American candidate managed to capture more votes than the Democratic candidate for governor. In Texas Henry B. Gonzales drew national attention when he filibustered against segregationist legislation in the Texas state legislature in 1957. In 1958 Gonzales ran in the Democratic primary for the Texas governorship. (It was an unheard of thing in that state for a Mexican American to seek statewide office. For many voters, especially in west Texas, Gonzales was their first experience with a Mexican-American candidate.)

At the end of the 1950s, a different type of political organization appeared. This was the Mexican American Political Association (MAPA), created in 1960 after the defeat of a Chicano Democratic candidate for state office in California. The Democratic ticket won handily in California, but the single Mexican-American candidate lost. Thus MAPA marks another stage of political activism. Although Mexican Americans had voting bloc strength, the established parties were not recruiting them. Possibly MAPA was the first truly ethnic political organization, as emphasized in an early statement, "MAPA grew out of many sad and difficult experiences of thousands of Mexican Americans throughout California who have tried so hard to elect representatives of our community to state and local government. After defeats in 1954, 1956, and 1958, 150 of the most active Mexican Americans met . . . in 1960 and decided that an organization was needed that would be *proudly* Mexican American, *openly* political, *necessarily* bipartisan."[15] The new MAPA was the beginning of quite a new type of ethnic mobilization. Its pride in its Mexican-American nature, its overt political purposes, and its claim to bipartisanship are the marks of a specialized rather than multifunctional activity. In reality, MAPA was heavily Democratic in its composition, but significantly, it left an opening for bipartisanship. The idea was a success: MAPA in California was followed by the appearance of MAPA in Texas.

Immediately after the birth of MAPA, another event of importance was the 1960 *Viva Kennedy* campaign. The drive expressly worked to bring out the Hispanic vote, drawing leaders from different states with Henry B. Gonzales (Texas), Joseph Montoya (New Mexico), and Edward Roybal (California) as co-chairmen.

The Mexican-American vote was crucial for John Kennedy. Because of *Viva Kennedy,* he carried Texas. The impressive turnouts and the proportions of Mexican Americans who followed Kennedy drew national attention. Some precincts in El Paso and Los Angeles had 100 percent returns from Kennedy and none for Nixon.[16] And, as a consequence, Mexican Americans received patronage positions in the new Kennedy administration.

There were also successes for MAPA. In California, two assemblymen, a congressman, and various judges of Mexican-American descent were elected; all carried MAPA endorsement. Because of these successes, there was a strong effort to develop an organization for national concerns. The consequence was PASSO (Political Association of Spanish Speaking Organizations). While not really national, PASSO

[15] Mexican American Political Association 4th Annual Convention Program, November 1963 (from the files of the author).

[16] "Narrative Report of Spanish Speaking Americans National Political Leadership Conference," Phoenix, Arizona, March 26, 1981 (from the files of the author).

would have its primary influence in Texas, where it replaced MAPA. In combination with the Teamsters' Union, PASSO was able to elect a slate of Mexican Americans to the City Council of Crystal City, Texas, in 1963. Arizona had its counterpart—American Coordinating Council for Political Education (ACCPE)—which also had some success with city council positions.

Complex as these organizations may appear, they were the nucleus of Mexican political power in the Southwest. There were four Mexican-American members of Congress in 1964; state legislators were elected in all the southwestern states and to myriad local offices. By the middle of the 1960s, this power was evident, and Mexicans could expect to be courted by presidential candidates as a matter of course. Yet it was also apparent that the traditional route for ethnic minorities in politics was no longer as rewarding as before. At the local level, where (according to the traditional route for European immigrants) there should be the most impact, local government agencies had been removed from politics by a new set of bureaucracies, usually under the control of civil service. There were fewer patronage positions for the winners of local power, especially in California. This was a serious matter for a community with problems deeply embedded in such institutions as the schools, police, and various forms of social service. Many of these jobs had slipped into state and federal jurisdiction. In short, civil equality was no longer enough reward for a political victory.

Beyond civil equality, a series of events speeded the realization among younger Mexican Americans in the 1960s that the traditional styles of ethnic politics would not accomplish needed changes. Among the most significant of these were the black civil rights movement and the black power movement. The impact was threefold. First, it revealed that civil equality for blacks was not sufficient to achieve meaningful social change. Second, the Black Power movement legitimized an ideology that rejected assimilation and fixed blame on the larger society for the deprivation of black Americans. Mexican Americans occupying similar socioeconomic positions could see the relevance of such terms as "institutional racism." Third (and most important) was the effect of the black riots on the Mexican-American community's view of government. Federal, state, and local governments responded to the black riots with pledges of massive amounts of financial aid. This reaction jolted and politicized all elements of the Chicano community. One question epitomizes Mexican feelings during this time: "Do we have to riot to receive attention?" Many Mexican Americans felt that problems facing them in the Southwest were as severe as (if not worse than) those of the black community. Consequently, when the federal antipoverty programs of the War on Poverty and Model Cities were started, Mexican Americans began demanding a "fair share."

In addition to the black movement, such events as the Vietnam antiwar effort and the whole "counterculture" movement provided alternative ideologies and models of political action to which Mexican Americans and especially young Mexicans could adapt. Inside the community itself, the emergence of ethnic leaders into national prominence gave further legitimacy to unconventional ethnic political efforts.

This new militancy began sometime in the mid-1960s. César Chávez began the strike effort of *La Huelga* in 1965.[17] In the same year, Corky Gonzales resigned

---

[17]Under the charismatic leadership of César Chávez, a new union organization of Mexican (and Filipino) farm workers succeeded in winning a series of labor agreements. Representing as he did the poorest and most exploited group of Mexican workers, the strikes (*La Huelga*)

from the Denver poverty program and founded *La Crusada Para La Justicia,* a movement that later was to support high school strikes, demonstrate against police brutality, and advocate mass action against the Vietnam war. In 1966, the National Farm Workers Association held a highly publicized march in California and Texas to dramatize the conditions of Mexican farm workers. And in 1966 Mexican-American leaders began demanding that Mexicans be included as target populations for federal antipoverty programs. The main target was the Equal Employment Opportunity Commission (EEOC), created in 1964, which was supposed to assure nondiscriminatory hiring practices. Chicano leaders charged that the commission did not show interest in the problems of Mexican Americans or Latinos. This new aggressiveness and militancy was further demonstrated in the walkout by national Mexican-American leaders from an EEOC conference in Albuquerque, New Mexico, that received national media coverage in 1966.[18] An ad hoc group demanded a meeting with President Lyndon Johnson, the appointment of a Mexican American to the EEOC, policy level staff positions in federal civil rights agencies, and participation in the 1968 White House Civil Rights Conference. For the first time the president was forced to respond to press queries on Mexican-American concerns with civil rights issues.[19]

Just as important, the established Mexican political and social organizations began to push an agenda of concerns with the federal government that continues to this day. This agenda holds two basic themes. First, Mexican Americans have unique problems that cannot be remedied by federal programs aimed exclusively at black Americans. Second, there is serious underrepresentation of Mexican Americans in government positions, both civil service and political. The frustration behind these points was particularly acute because the Mexican-American community had given nearly all (more than 90 percent) its votes to President Johnson and his promise of the Great Society.

The actions of mainstream Mexican-American political groups were quickly eclipsed by the more militant factions in the community. Reies Tijerina and his supporters in New Mexico occupied the Kit Carson National Forest to publicize the claims of the *Alianza Federal de Mercedes.* The next year the lieutenant governor of New Mexico called out the National Guard and the State Police (with tanks and helicopters) after a spectacular *Alianza* raid on the courthouse of Tierra Amarilla.[20] This event, along with the drama of César Chávez and the nonviolent and untraditional *Huelga* (strike) of the farm workers captured the sympathy of most Mexican Americans. In particular it grasped the imagination of a new generation of younger Hispanics.

It was now possible to point to something called the *Movimiento* (movement). At a La Raza Conference in October 1967, young Chicanos (the word Chicano was

and a national boycott of grapes and lettuce won great support among Hispanics. For an accurate and interesting account of Chávez and his movement, see John Gregory Dunne, *Delano* (New York: Farrar, Straus and Giroux, 1967).

[18] Rowland Evans and Robert Novak, "Inside Report . . . the Mexican Revolt," *Washington Post,* March 31, 1966; also Paul Beck, "Mexican American Walkout Mars U.S. Job Conference," *Los Angeles Times,* March 29, 1966.

[19] "Text of President's News Conference," *Washington Post,* May 21, 1966; also, Robert Thompson, "President Pledges Aid to Mexican Americans," *Los Angeles Times,* April 1, 1966.

[20] The national media viewed this event in a manner indicative of the times. The *Washington Post* headlines read; "15 Land Claiming Desperados Hunted," *Washington Post,* June 7, 1967.

now being used by many Mexicans for the first time) displayed frustrations and anger at the traditional style of politics. Armando Rendon captures this anger when he quotes one participant, "The young Chicanos see this conference as the last chance you older Chicanos have to come through. If nothing happens from this you'll have to step aside—or we'll walk over you."[21] The United Mexican American Students (UMAS), the Mexican American Youth Organization (MAYO), and the Brown Berets were all organized the same year (1967). Common to all three organizations was an active rejection of traditional styles of political action.

These events and their conjunction with the Black Power movement (and the antiwar effort) provided the genesis of ethnic militancy. While today the word "Chicano" is synonymous for some with Mexican American, in the mid-1960s the term was something new. In the 1960s, it began to represent an ethnic viewpoint. Chicano ideology or *Chicanismo* was most actively (but not exclusively) promulgated by Mexican-American student and youth organizations. These included UMAS, the Mexican American Student Association (MASA), the Mexican American Student Confederation (MASC), the *Movimiento Estudiantil Chicano de Aztlán* (MECHA), and MAYO.

In its essence, Chicanismo was an eclectic ideology that at times drew inspiration from the black experience, the Latin American revolutionary experience, and the Mexican revolutionary tradition. Many Chicanos felt that the traditional forms of political participation were the least effective, especially within the two-party system. Others favored confrontation-type tactics—mass demonstrations and "walkouts." A small minority endorsed the active self-defense tactics of the Brown Berets, and an even smaller number sympathized with the revolutionary activities of the Chicano Liberation Front.

Chicanismo saw Chicanos as basically a conquered people—a people who were stripped of their land, their history, and their culture as the result of Anglo exploitation. The Chicanos in the American economy were victims of an exploitative relationship. Chicanos were used as a source of cheap labor for the economy of the Southwest for which they received little economic reward. Deculturation meant that Chicanos were ashamed of their Mexican Indian heritage. Chicanos should have pride in their cultural heritage and in their unique adaptation to Anglo-American society. The process of deculturation was carried out in schools that failed to teach the children their bilingual-bicultural heritage. *Chicanismo* emphasized the concept of *la raza* and rejected materialistic standards of individualistic self-achievement, favoring collective goals based on *la raza*. It was an ideology that profoundly affected Mexican-American communities in the late 1960s and early 1970s and, most particularly, the youth and the college students. The impact may have been greatest in the politics of education. Here there were increased demands for ethnic studies programs, ethnic heritage classes, and ethnic personnel, all reflecting the ideological approach of *Chicanismo*. The wave of high school "blow-outs" (walkouts) that swept throughout the southwest show the strong appeal of *Chicanismo* for students.

But the general course of ethnic militancy after 1968 followed old issues that long had been important to everyone in the community. Many of the issues that

---

[21] Armando Rendon, "La Raza—Today, Not Mañana," in John Burma, ed., *Mexican Americans in the United States,* (Cambridge, Mass.: Schenkman, 1970), pp. 307–326.

were important rallying points—protests against police brutality, protests against miseducation, demands for more political voice—always were active grievances. But young Chicanos spoke for these issues in a way that was unconventional and grasped the attention of all American society. Activism in school reform is an example. Efforts by Mexican Americans to reform Southwestern school systems reach back into the 1930s (see Chapter 9). The new Chicano approaches were marked by walkouts and protest demonstrations in California (1968), Texas (1969), and Colorado (1969). The general community watched them with interest, knowing that they would bring the inevitable police reprisals and revive old tensions.[22] Colleges and universities felt Chicano protests for the first time, reflecting the greater number of young Mexican Americans entering these institutions.

The height of ethnic militancy was reached in the early 1970s. A Chicano protest against the Vietnam war in August 1970 in East Los Angeles resulted in large-scale violence between the police and the demonstrators. In a terrifying manner, it brought to national consciousness the anger and the frustration always latent in the *barrios.* (A noted Mexican-American journalist, Ruben Salazar, was shot to death by the police, and a great deal of property was damaged.) Urban violence by Mexican Americans also occurred in Denver and Albuquerque.

In addition to this outburst of long-standing grievances and new issues, the most highly publicized aspect of ethnic militancy in the Mexican community was the formation and growth of a separatist third party—*La Raza Unida* Party (LRU). Just as MAPA was an ethnic response in the 1960s, the new party was a militant ethnic separatist reaction in the late 1960s and early 1970s. The concept was developed by José Angel Guitiérrez, a cofounder of MAYO and the leading spirit of the LRU in Texas. There were numerous rationales for such a third party: third-party organizations can reach the media during elections, and third-party campaigns need not compromise with either of the established parties and thus allow clear expression of goals. Tactically, a Chicano third party in areas where Chicanos are a majority presents opportunities for Mexicans to gain control of their own communities. An additional advantage is that, by running candidates in general elections (even where there is little, if any, chance to win), the potential for a Chicano bloc vote is further developed.

La Raza Unida had some noteworthy successes, particularly in Crystal City, Texas.[23] Here LRU candidates gained control of the city council and board of education in the 1970 elections. It was successful in such other Texas towns as Cotulla and Carrizo Springs. Even in defeat, *La Raza Unida* made its presence felt. Thus in the Texas state elections of 1972, the LRU candidate for governor, Ramsey Muñiz, captured close to 6 percent of the vote.

At first glance the impact and actual gains of the Chicano political militancy may appear to be minimal. Chicano militant organizations came and went. By the 1980s *La·Raza Unida* in Texas was no longer a viable force. In retrospect, however, Chicano militancy had a tremendous impact on the Mexican-American community

---

[22] Dial B. Torgerson, " 'Brown Power' Unity Seen Behind School Disorders," in Burma, ed., *Mexican Americans,* pp. 279–288; and Carlos Muñoz, "The Politics of Educational Change in East Los Angeles," in *Mexican Americans and Educational Change,* (collected papers from a symposium at the University of California, Riverside, May 21–22, 1971).

[23] John Shockley, *Chicano Revolt in a Texas Town* (Notre Dame, Ind.: University of Notre Dame Press, 1974).

and on the larger political system. In the American system, protest activity always has the potential of a political resource.[24] The protest activities of young Chicanos built a new awareness of ethnic political activity. The third-party efforts of young Chicanos allowed mainstream politicians to extract greater concessions from the established political parties. Skilled Mexican-American politicians could enhance their political power by invoking images of ethnic militancy in the community.

Mexican American politics: 1970s and 1980s. Although Chicano political militancy captured most of the media attention and the imagination of college-age young people, the American political system was changing. These changes would have important consequences for Mexican-American mainstream electoral politics.

The first of these changes was the passage of the Voting Rights Act in 1965. It was designed to protect the civil rights of black Americans, but it also helped Chicano communities in the Southwest and the Puerto Ricans. In fact, the literacy test was often used as a means of disenfranchising minority voters by making the test so difficult that even minority college graduates could not pass. Moreover, because many Mexican Americans are poorly educated, the literacy examination further discourages registration to vote. Eliminating this test enfranchised new voters. In California, the legal case of *Castro* v. *California* removed literacy tests based solely on the English language. Finally, the 24th Amendment to the U.S. Constitution eliminated poll taxes. (Poll taxes were widely used to discriminate by selectively enforcing deadlines for payment or not announcing locations for payment.) Court cases replacing "at large" elections with single-member district elections have also had significant impact.[25] These legal changes tended to enfranchise a much larger Mexican voting population.

Second, two new organizations appeared. In 1968 both the Mexican American Legal Defense and Education Fund (MALDEF) and the Southwest Voter Registration Project were created (with the assistance of Ford Foundation grants). These organizations began a variety of activities: voter registration, litigation to support voter registration, get-out-the-vote activities, and legal advocacy, all on behalf of Mexican Americans.

Third, both Democrats and Republicans began to see the *barrios* as a "swing vote" that could affect elections. As an example, the Mexican American vote in 1966 probably defeated the Democratic candidate for governor of Texas. In 1968, Hubert Humphrey carried Texas by 39,000 votes, an edge made possible by his 90 percent vote in Mexican-American districts. Third-party efforts by *La Raza Unida* also demonstrated the possible impact of a bloc vote in a close election in Texas or California. Both political parties showed increasing support for Mexican candidates after the mid-1960s. As shown in Table 10.4, the number of southwestern Hispanic state legislators jumps abruptly after 1965—and continues to grow into the 1980s.

---

[24] See Harry Pachon, "Politics and the Mexican American Experience" in *Mexican Americans* (Englewood Cliffs, N.J.: Prentice-Hall, 1976), p. 157. Also see Carlos Muñoz and Mario Barrera, "La Raza Unida Party and the Chicano Student Movement in California," *The Social Science Journal,* Vol. 19 (April 1982), pp. 101–120.

[25] Rodolfo de la Garza, "Social Change and the Chicano Community: Patterns of the 1970s and Issues for the 1980s," a paper presented at the International Conference of Condiciones Sociales, Economicas y Culturales en Mexico Contemporano," El Paso, September, 1978.

TABLE 10.4   Mexican American State Legislators in Five Southwestern States 1950–1983

	1950	1960	1965	1974	1983
Arizona	0	4	6	11	12
California	0	0	0	8	7
Colorado	0	1	1	6	7
New Mexico	20	20	22	33	30
Texas	0	7	6	15	19
	20	32	35	73	85

Sources: Numbers were determined by consulting the *Book of the States,* Supplement I, State Elected Officials and the Legislatures (Chicago: Council of State Governments, 1950, 1960, 1965). Figures for these years are approximate and involve the author's determination of Spanish surnamed legislators by name. Data for 1974 taken from *Southwest Voter Registration Project,* San Antonio, Texas. Data for 1983, NALEO, *A Preliminary Listing of Hispanic State Legislators* (Washington, D.C.: NALEO, 1983).

Even a relatively small number of state legislators (as in Colorado and California) can have significant effect. Mexican legislators in Colorado are firm advocates of bilingual education. In California, the Chicano caucus is deeply involved in issues of increased representation in the government bureaucracy, farm worker problems, and bilingual education.

Political parties concerned with victory in the presidential election increasingly court the Mexican vote in Texas and California because of the peculiarities of the Electoral College.[26] California and Texas share approximately 25 percent of the electoral votes needed for a presidential victory and thus become critical states. Table 10.5 shows that critical vote differences often rest with the Hispanic vote. In a close election, the victory edge might be only one or two percentage points. For every 8 percent of the Mexican-American vote drawn by a presidential candidate in Texas in 1980, a 1 percent difference appeared in the general election. While the majority of the Chicano population traditionally votes Democratic (because of the New Deal, Kennedy, the Great Society, and the social liberalism associated with Democrats), there is also a segment of the community that responds to Republican conservatism and an emphasis on family moral values and self-reliance. This variability makes the Mexican community one of the true "swing" votes in America today. It is not enough for Democratic candidates to capture a majority of the Mexican-American voters. It is only necessary to split the vote for benefits to accrue to Republican candidates. Further, the Democrats cannot be satisfied with a simple majority. Every couple of percentage points that the Democratic candidate gains over 50 percent may make a crucial difference in the election.

This crucial edge of victory leads to what some observers call "fiesta politics." Every four years presidential candidates start making overtures to the community.

[26] For recent elections, see Neal Peirce and Jerry Hagstrom, "Democratic Primaries in California and Texas May Hinge on Chicano Vote," *National Journal,* April 26, 1980, pp. 681–684; Phil Gailey, "Courting Hispanic Voters Now a Reagan Priority," *The New York Times,* May 19, 1983; and Dick Kirschten, "The Hispanic Vote–Parties Can't Gamble That the Sleeping Giant Won't Waken," *National Journal,* November 19, 1983, pp. 2410–2416.

TABLE 10.5   Presidential Elections and Hispanic Votes, 1980

STATE	PRESIDENTIAL VOTE IN 1980[a]	HISPANIC VOTE[b]	PERCENTAGE OF HISPANIC VOTE NEEDED FOR A 1% SHIFT IN ELECTION		NUMBER OF ELECTORAL VOTES
Arizona	853,483	77,704	11%	8,535	7
California	8,348,319	586,978	14	83,483	47
Colorado	1,150,906	65,043	18	11,509	8
Illinois	4,686,261	120,483	39	46,862	24
New Mexico	448,064	165,687	3	4,480	5
Texas	4,503,465	557,291	8	45,034	29

[a]"Official 1980 Presidential Election Results," *Congressional Quarterly Almanac* (Washington, D.C.: Government Printing Office, 1981).

[b]U.S. Bureau of the Census, "Voting and Registration in the Election of November 1980," *Current Population Reports,* April 1982.

It is no coincidence that the first national commission on Mexican-American affairs was set up in 1967, one year before a presidential election. Watergate hearings substantiated the efforts of the Nixon administration in 1971 in its "Responsiveness" and "Incumbency" programs to court the Mexican-American vote in 1972.[27] Later, Jimmy Carter began a series of "Town Hall meetings" that publicized the efforts of his administration to help Mexican Americans. In 1983, President Ronald Reagan appointed a Mexican American from Texas to the White House and made a series of highly publicized visits to Hispanic groups in Texas. All these activities demonstrate the value placed on the "swing" vote and its power. By the 1980s Mexican Americans had won governorships in Arizona and New Mexico, congressional represen-'ation had nearly doubled, and there were a host of elected officials at all levels of government. The result, of course, is much more political power. Yet there is still much dissatisfaction with the responsiveness of governmental agencies to Mexican concerns—and the slowness of the federal government to consider critical Mexican-American (and Hispanic) issues.

PUERTO RICAN POLITICS

The Puerto Rican political experience is quite different from that of the Mexicans and highlights the differences inside the Hispanic community. There are similarities, of course, such as the early development of *mutualistas* both in the Southwest and

[27]These hearings also raised a host of questions about the role of the Republican party and ethnic militant politics. Charges were made that the *Raza Unida* party in Texas received federal grants because of its important role in splitting the Mexican-American vote in 1972. See Tony Castro, *Chicano Power* (New York: Saturday Review Press/E. P. Hutton, 1974). Also U.S. Congress, Senate, 93rd Congress, 1st Session, *Hearings before the Select Committee on Presidential Campaign Activities, Watergate and Related Activities,* Vol. 13 (Washington, D.C.: U.S. Government Printing Office, 1973).

in New York City, and through this century both discrimination and gerrymandering were prevelant. But Puerto Ricans are much more recent arrivals in the mainland United States. Furthermore, they entered not the southwestern political environment but New York City, a city rich in the history of ethnic politics. Finally, many Puerto Ricans were deeply involved with the politics of their homeland, Puerto Rico. In this respect, from a political perspective, segments of the Puerto Rican community may have had more in common with the Cuban community in at least one regard: their attachment and identification with the politics of the original homeland (emigré politics).

Politics before 1960.   It is possible to trace the presence of Puerto Ricans in New York City as far back as the 1820s because apparently there were Puerto Rican exiles during the late 1700s.[28] But Puerto Ricans did not appear in any numbers until after 1900. Yet, in spite of these small numbers, there was political activity. As an example, one year after the passage of the Jones Act, several thousand Puerto Rican voters participated in the election of Governor Alfred E. Smith.

But Puerto Ricans were not confined to voting in elections. Political clubs appeared as early as 1918. They were multifunctional, offering health referrals, social services, legal aid, and other counseling. Yet other groups formed during the 1920s and 1930s tended to mix social and political objectives. Furthermore, most of these organizations were concerned with the homeland, Puerto Rico itself. As an early community activist told Virginia Korrol:

> Many Puerto Ricans did not exercise their right to vote . . . Puerto Ricans also believed they had nothing to look for in American politics.

In 1922 the Puerto Rican Democratic Club petitioned Congress on behalf of Puerto Rico. "The only way for our island to get political recognition is through the Puerto Ricans here in New York and in many other states of the union . . . congressmen who in exchange for our help to elect them will help our beloved Puerto Rico."[29]

There were yet other signs of this concern. In 1936, more than 10,000 Puerto Ricans marched in New York to protest the arrest of an independence leader in Puerto Rico and living conditions on the island. In fact, Puerto Ricans are more faithful to the Democratic party than are any other Hispanic group, in part at least because of the perceived more favorable treatment of Puerto Rico. During Democratic administrations, the Jones Act was passed. The Democratic platform of 1928 called for Puerto Rican statehood, and the New Deal program included Puerto Rico in rural rehabilitation, electrification, reforestation, and housing programs.[30] Dur-

---

[28] James Jennings, *Puerto Rican Politics in New York City* (Washington, D.C.: University Press, 1977), p. 22.

[29] Virginia Sanchez Korrol, *From Colonia to Community* (Westport, Conn.: Greenwood Press, 1983), gives an excellent account of Puerto Ricans in New York before 1940. Much of this material is based on this work.

[30] Lawrence Chenault, *The Puerto Rican Migrant in New York City* (New York: Russell and Russell, 1938), p. 22; and American Council on Public Affairs, *Puerto Rican Problems* (Washington, D.C.: Women's International League for Peace and Freedom, 1940), p. 3.

ing the administration of Franklin D. Roosevelt, recommendations were made for Puerto Rico to elect its own governor instead of receiving appointees.[31]

The strength of nationalist feeling in Puerto Rico and among its sympathizers on the mainland cannot be overestimated. Even after Puerto Rico adopted its commonwealth form of government in 1952, nationalist sentiment remained strong. Nationalists engaged in political violence on the island during 1950, mounted an assassination attempt on President Harry Truman, and even opened fire on the floor of the U.S. House of Representatives in 1954. In 1950 the pro-independence party gained 19 percent of the vote. There is now less support for independence, but the issue is still important, even as late as the 1980s. The future political status of Puerto Rico (a choice of statehood, continuing status as a commonwealth, or independence) continues to be an open issue. It is still of critical importance to all Puerto Ricans. Even to this date, some Puerto Ricans in the northeast U.S. return to Puerto Rico to vote.

The importance of Puerto Rico island politics is reflected in the Puerto Rican Commonwealth Office in New York and other cities. Throughout the 1950s, this office was a significant social service agency for Puerto Ricans, maintaining branch offices in several northeast cities. Job placements, referrals, and housing were all performed by this office, and it continues to play a key role. Its significance was demonstrated during the street riots in the Puerto Rican community in the 1960s when the city of New York called on the Commonwealth Office (as well as community representatives) for counsel.[32]

According to Glazer and Moynihan, the Commonwealth Office may have served to perpetuate dependency between Puerto Ricans and government agencies.[33] Yet it is very probable that the Commonwealth Office was a much less hostile bureaucratic environment than were other social service agencies in New York. One obvious difference is the presence of Spanish-speaking personnel in the Commonwealth Office but not in the municipal and state agencies. In the 1970s Puerto Rican groups would bring suit against New York social service agencies for failing to provide equitable services to the Spanish speaking.

Another factor affects the development of Puerto Rican politics on the mainland. Puerto Rican political efforts took place, by and large, within the political environment of New York—a milieu characterized by strong partisan and ethnic politics. This is unlike the Mexican-American experience in California where traditional political party organizations were weakened by the progressive reforms. Political "clubs" in the Manhattan and Brooklyn Puerto Rican communities emerged quite early as did certain politicians catering to Puerto Rican voters.

The presence of politically strong partisan organizations also helps to explain why the first Puerto Rican to be elected to the New York legislature (Oscar García Rivera) was a Republican from the East Harlem area in 1937. The Republi-

[31] Kal Wagenheim, *Puerto Rico: A Profile* (New York: Praeger, 1975). Wagenheim states that these appointees left much to be desired: "With rare exception they were an undistinguished lot. None mastered Spanish; few were familiar with the island's culture; few could have run their own home state" p. 78.

[32] Jennings, *Puerto Rican Politics*, p. 40.

[33] Nathan Glazer and Daniel Patrick Moynihan, *Beyond the Melting Pot: The Negroes, Puerto Ricans, Jews, Italians, and Irish of New York City* (Cambridge, Mass.: M.I.T. Press, 1963), p. 110.

cans ran García Rivera to counter the strong presence of the Democratic party. Yet the Puerto Rican community mobilized for García Rivera in spite of the fact that East Harlem was a Democratic stronghold. Rivera's beliefs, however, were too liberal for the Republicans of the era, and he did not receive nomination at the next election. Under the label of the American Labor Party, Rivera recaptured his seat for one more term.[34]

Strong partisan organizations also help to explain the high popularity of Congressman Vito Marcantonio in the Puerto Rican community during the 1930s and 1940s.[35] Marcantonio (of Italian descent) recognized and fought for issues that affected the Puerto Rican community. On one occasion, for example, he flew down to Puerto Rico to defend Albizu Campos in a 1936 sedition trial. Marcantonio also addressed the issue of Puerto Rico's status before the Congress on numerous occasions.[36] The Marcantonio district office staff was fluent in Spanish long before other New York governmental agencies hired Spanish-speaking personnel. His strength was aided by an organization.

The presence of political institutions that recognized ethnic group issues and the strong partisan atmosphere in New York (where both parties at times courted the Puerto Rican voter) should not, however, obscure the fact that Puerto Rican political development, much like its Mexican-American counterpart in the Southwest, took place in an environment of struggle and discrimination. The available studies show that mainstream political clubs in New York (dominated by the Irish, Italians, and Jews) did not welcome Puerto Ricans. One author states, "Only the American Labor Party tried to recruit Puerto Ricans." It appears that the main reason for excluding the Hispanics were fears that their presence in the political machine would alienate working-class whites.[37] Puerto Rican political efforts in New York were hampered by two other factors. Gerrymandering was obvious in the Manhattan community.[38] Also, urban renewal meant that old housing was demolished and thus displaced Puerto Ricans from Manhattan were relocated into the South Bronx and other areas. In 1960, 37 percent of the Puerto Ricans in the city lived in Manhattan; by 1980, only 19 percent did, and 70 percent were living in Brooklyn and the Bronx. No specific studies have been done on the effects of these movements, but one can speculate that political representation both at the local and the state level was certain to be affected by the displacement of entire communities. In spite of these obstacles, by the 1950s Puerto Ricans were beginning to win elected offices. Three assemblymen were elected to the state legislature. Herman Badillo became the first Puerto Rican to hold a citywide post (and, ironically, it was that of commissioner of Urban Renewal Relocation).[39]

Puerto Rican politics: beyond the 1960s.   Just as in the Mexican community, the Puerto Ricans were profoundly affected by the changes of the 1960s. The *Viva*

[34] Rene Torres Delgado, *El Primer Legislador Puertorriqueñno en Nueva York: Oscar García Rivera* (Santurce, P.R.: Departamento de Instrucción Pública, 1979).

[35] Warren Moscow, *Politics in the Empire State* (New York: Alfred A. Knopf, 1981).

[36] Peter Jackson, "Vito Marcantonio and Ethnic Politics in New York," *Ethnic and Racial Studies,* Vol. 6 (January 1983), pp. 50–71.

[37] Jennings, *Puerto Rican Politics,* pp. 86, 115.

[38] Personal Communication, Congressman Robert Garcia.

[39] Clarence Senior, *Our Citizens from the Caribbean* (New York: McGraw-Hill, 1965).

Kennedy campaign also had its impact—and its rewards. Herman Badillo became the president of the John F. Kennedy Democratic Club (for Puerto Ricans) in the East Harlem area; this kind of support brought some appointments. Most notably, Teodoro Moscoso became ambassador to Organization of American States.

The changes of the 1960s continued. The forces that mobilized American young people, blacks, and Mexican Americans were also present in New York and in other cities with large Puerto Rican populations. Young Puerto Ricans began questioning the progress being made in mainstream politics. They were bolstered by the deplorable socioeconomic conditions of their community. Ethnic militancy appeared in the form of the Young Lords—and, later, the Puerto Rican Revolutionary Workers Organization and other militant ethnic organizations captured the attention of the media and the sympathy and support of the young.[40] There were also gains in mainstream politics, particularly at the Democratic party level. City councilmen and state legislators were elected in the late 1960s in both the city and state. And of great significance, the Black and Puerto Rican Caucus was established at the state level—the first formal coalition between Hispanic and black elected officials.[41] These gains were gradual and hardly noticed by the larger society. There were defeats both at the city level and for higher offices. But by the 1970s the Puerto Rican community had elected its first Puerto Rican congressman, Herman Badillo; its first state senator, Robert Garcia; and yet other state and municipal officials. The federal War on Poverty was helpful also in furthering developing Puerto Rican community organizations. As just one example, the Hunts Point Multi-Service Center was headed by Ramon Velez, who was later elected to municipal office. And other community organizations grew out of the Office of Economic Opportunity (OEO) to express Puerto Rican needs.

In general, political accomplishments of the Puerto Ricans match those of Mexican Americans at the state level. But congressional representation lags considerably. Robert Garcia won Herman Badillo's seat in 1977—and is still the only mainland Puerto Rican federal elected official. There are six members of the state legislature, equaling that of California's Mexican population. Moreover, their seniority is such that they occupy the chairs of key committees.

What is the political future of the Puerto Rican community? There is no question but that Puerto Ricans have established an important presence as a voting bloc. In New York State, the 1982 elections for governor show that Puerto Ricans and Hispanics were significant in the victory of Governor Mario Cuomo. And, given the highly politicized nature of their base in New York, one can expect Puerto Ricans to continue running for city offices. In Congress, several districts (notably the 11th in Brooklyn) have substantial numbers of Puerto Ricans and a sufficient number of Puerto Rican locals elected and appointed to make viable candidates. There should, therefore, be further gains in Congress. The rapid expansion to other northeast states, particularly New Jersey and Connecticut, suggests substantial political gains. Some such accomplishments are already appearing in Chicago, Philadelphia, and Bridgeport, Connecticut.

[40] For a thorough review of the limited literature on Puerto Rican politics, see Angelo Falcón, "Puerto Rican Politics in Urban America: An Introduction to the Literature," *La Red* (July 1983), pp. 2–9.

[41] The Black and Puerto Rican Caucus was established after recognition that in New York City both blacks and Puerto Ricans are intermingled in electoral districts, such as Harlem.

Yet Puerto Ricans, much like their Chicano counterparts, face difficult political issues. At a time of fiscal retrenchment, how does the community achieve representation in the state and municipal bureaucracies? Studies show that Puerto Ricans lag seriously in their share of these jobs.[42] Then also the continued migration from the home island will affect ethnic mobilization. And decisions in Puerto Rico about its political status in future years will significantly affect the mainland politics of Puerto Ricans.

One unique factor affecting Puerto Ricans is the presence of other Hispanics in their communities. East Harlem (as a single example) has substantial numbers of Dominicans and Panamanians. In New York State, 40 percent of the population of Hispanic origin is non-Puerto Rican. The Puerto Rican political movement will be affected by these other Hispanics. Some Puerto Rican officials such as Congressman Robert Garcia have begun to address issues of particular importance to them. For example, Congressman Garcia has led in recognizing democratic institutional developments in the Dominican Republic as a result of the interests of the large number of Dominicans in his district.

Yet the political issues facing Puerto Ricans (who are U.S. citizens by birth) are far different from those of other Latin Americans. The presence of nonnaturalized Latin Americans in Puerto Rican *barrios* will also reinforce the stereotype that Puerto Ricans do not vote. At the present time, these other Latin and Central American immigrant groups are politically active in the issues of their home countries. Dominican presidential candidates make fund-raising tours and political campaign stops in New York City. Colombian absentee ballots are cast in significant numbers from the Borough of Queens. Just how Puerto Rican communities interact with these other Central and Latin American Hispanic groups (especially as they become naturalized citizens) will be a significant factor in the future development of Puerto Rican politics.

CUBAN-AMERICAN POLITICS

Although a vast number of Cuban Americans arrived in the United States after 1960, their political development in the south Florida area is very impressive in recent years.[43] Thus it is unfortunate that (like other Hispanic groups) Cubans have become associated with certain political stereotypes, even among other Hispanic groups. This is the simple stereotype of the "Golden Cuban." He is a right-wing political refugee who unquestionably supports all ultraconservative causes and has little in common with other Hispanic groups in this country. But while Cuban Americans are the only group among the Hispanics who in the 1970s and 1980s were identified with the Republican party, the reality of Cuban-American political development is more complex. When Cuban refugees started to arrive in Miami, their unquestionable preoccupation was politics in the homeland, or more specifically, the overthrow of Fidel Castro. The history of this period suggests that this was not an unrealistic goal. As soon as Castro's socialist and communist orientations

[42] William Blair, "Study Says Hispanic Workers Don't Get Enough State Jobs," *The New York Times,* October 31, 1982.
[43] Sonia L. Nazario, "After a Long Holdout, Cubans in Miami Take a Role in U.S. Politics," *The Wall Street Journal,* June 7, 1983.

were known by the American government, and Castro was seen as a threat to hemispheric security, planning began to overthrow this government. Just six years previously, the United States had successfully overthrown the left-wing government in Guatemala (1954), and there was no reason to doubt it could not be successful in Cuba.[44] During this time Cuban refugee politics can best be described as "emigré" politics.[45]

In 1960, for example, the Anti-Castro Liberation Alliance was formed in Miami Beach. Other groups organized during this time were the Revolutionary Movement of the People, headed by Manuel Ray, and the Democratic Revolutionary Front, led by Antonio de Varona.[46] In 1961 at the time of the pending invasion, the last two groups merged.

The invasion of the island ended in the disaster of the Bay of Pigs. The Cuban community felt that the invasion effort had failed because President Kennedy reneged on his promise of air and naval support for Brigade 2500 and blamed Kennedy—and the Democrats. The failed invasion was quickly followed by the U.S.-Soviet Cuban missile crisis of 1962. Again the outcome was seen as negative by Cubans. As part of the agreement to withdraw Russian missiles from Cuba, the United States agreed not to invade or overthrow the Cuban government. The Cuban community felt it had been misled and deceived.

One cannot understand contemporary Cuban-American politics without recognizing the importance of foreign policy events and the significance of the Cuban experience. In the 1970s and 1980s, a large segment of the Cuban-American population experienced life under Fidel Castro. Communism and anticommunism are experienced realities and, until very recently, were constantly reinforced by relatives and friends entering from Cuba. (See Chapter 2 for a short history of Cuban emigration.)

Dissatisfaction with the foreign policies of the Democrats had quick repercussions in the Cuban-American community of south Florida. Once it was no longer possible to hope for a quick return, Cuban refugees took a more serious interest in American politics. Politically, the anticommunist posture appeared in the "Cubans for Goldwater" in the 1964 election. Richard Nixon's perceived anticommunism also captured Cuban support in 1968. The George McGovern campaign promise to "normalize" relations with Cuba acted to drive yet more Cubans into the Republican party. But the growth of support for conservative anticommunist candidates is but one component of political developments in the Cuban community.

In the mid-1960s Cubans realized they were more or less permanent residents of the United States. The result was one of the highest rates of naturalization among any Hispanic group. In 1966, five years after the Bay of Pigs, the legal waiting

[44] U.S. and Cuban relationships during this period are subject to a wide variety of interpretations—and there is an extensive literature. For American plans to overthrow Fidel Castro, see Peter Wyden, *Bay of Pigs: The Untold Story* (New York: Simon & Schuster, 1979).

[45] There is an interesting similarity to the Mexican immigrant communities in Arizona and Texas border towns in the early 1900s. These easily reached refuges contained Mexican exiles and fugitives from virtually every defeated Mexican cause. See Mario T. Garcia, *Desert Immigrants: The Mexicans of El Paso, 1880-1920* (New Haven, Conn.: Yale University Press, 1981), Ch. 9.

[46] Patrick Gallagher, *The Cuban Exile: A SocioPolitical Analysis* (New York: Arno Press, 1980).

period, Cuban naturalization jumped abruptly. There was another great increase in 1970 as a result of Public Law 89-732, which allowed Cubans to become permanent resident aliens without having to leave the country.[47] The lower rates after 1979 reflect in part the backlog of cases built up in the Immigration and Naturalization offices in the southern Florida area (11,000 cases in 1982).

The high rate of citizenship among Cubans is underscored in a comparison with other Hispanic groups. Approximately 80 percent of Cubans become naturalized as against only 12 percent of the Mexicans during a comparable time. In such south Florida communities as Hialeah, Allapatah, and Little Havana, these rates quickly made Cubans a significant electoral force in local and state elections. In 1980, for example, 4 of Florida's 19 congressional districts contained close to 40 percent of the entire U.S. Cuban population. Cuban Americans won state legislative office as well as mayoral and council seats. But electoral power is only one dimension of Cuban influence. The strong Cuban business community in the state contributes to its influence in local and national politics.[48] A Cuban-American political action committee, The National Coalition for a Free Cuba, composed of Cuban businessmen, gave nearly $50,000 to political candidates in the 1982 elections.[49]

Ethnic political mobilization has followed a different path among Cubans. The ethnic militancy, so obvious in the Mexican-American and Puerto Rican communities, has not occurred. The amalgam of socialist and revolutionary symbols of the 1960s did not influence Cuban Americans as it did other young Hispanics. Cubans fled a regime that utilized many of the same symbols so attractive to young militants. Nor did the first wave of Cuban refugees identify with the *barrios* of the Southwest and the Northeast. And perhaps most important, Cuban refugees were quite different from Mexican Americans or Puerto Ricans: they were older (the average age was 41 years), better educated, earned more, and were received more generously by American society. The Cuban Refugee Program provided funding for social and educational services for several years even before the War on Poverty.[50] Between 1969 and 1979, the federal government appropriated more than $1 billion to the Cuban refugee program, most of these funds going into South Florida.[51]

Yet it would be a mistake to see Cuban Americans as completely different from other Hispanics. Although there was no ethnic militancy, there has been ethnic political mobilization. Much like Puerto Ricans who identify with Democrats because of the party's stance toward Puerto Rico, Cubans supported Republicans be-

[47] Rafael Prohias and Lourdes Casal, *The Cuban Minority in the U.S.* (New York: Arno Press, 1980), p. 55.

[48] Kenneth Wilson and W. Allen Martin, "Ethnic Enclaves: A Comparison of the Cuban and Black Economies in Miami," *American Journal of Sociology,* Vol. 88 (July 1982), pp. 135-160.

[49] Lucette Lagnado, "Anti Castro PAC in Washington," *The Nation,* Vol. 237 (October 1983), pp. 332-333.

[50] Richard Fagen, Richard Brody, and Thomas O'Leary, *Cubans in Exile* (Stanford, Calif.: Stanford University Press, 1968). See also Hearings Before a Subcommittee on Appropriations, Department of Health, Education and Welfare, U.S. House of Representatives, 95th Cong., 2d sess., 1978, p. 422.

[51] A movie of this period captures the disparity in treatment between Cubans and Puerto Ricans. Alan Arkin in *Popi* portrays a Puerto Rican father who puts children into a boat off the Florida coast so they can enjoy the benefits of being Cuban refugees.

cause of a more conservative foreign policy and strong anticommunism. Emigré politics is still important among large segments. At one time, there were more than 100 Cuban exile political organizations. Some of these groups, such as Alpha 66, Omega 7, and Abdala received widespread American news coverage of their bombings and acts of political violence.[52] But the political strength was growing. The first sign of this strength came when Maurice Ferre, a Puerto Rican with support from the Cuban community, became mayor of Miami in the 1970s. In following years, however, Ferre had to contend with Cuban-American candidates who mounted stiff campaigns in 1981 and 1983.[53] Surveys of the Cuban-American community show the strong support for Cuban candidates.

But Cuban Americans have not automatically supported conservative causes. An example is Cuban support of Representative Claude Pepper, a liberal congressman with more than a 50 percent Cuban constituency in 1980. But Pepper's social liberalism is offset by his conservative approach to Cuban-American relations. Pepper's popularity is also made more secure by his identification with issues of aging, another area of concern to the Cuban-American community.[54] Cubans also share with other Hispanic groups a strong support for bilingual education. South Florida has had such programs since the early 1960s; language obstacles are still seen as a significant problem.[55]

In common with the Puerto Ricans, the Cuban Americans show a high degree of racial tolerance. This is of some importance politically. Not only is it at odds with the ultraconservative image of Cubans, but it facilitated in Chicago the support of the majority of the Cuban community for a black mayoral candidate in 1983.[56] But how this racial liberalism will be affected by the black riots in Miami of the 1980s remains to be seen.

In the 1980s, Cuban-American politics were in a stage of change. A young generation was coming into positions of power. While anticommunism was still present, the memories of Cuba among the young were not as vivid as for the older refugees. Domestic political issues were of increasing importance.

NATIONAL HISPANIC POLITICS

Just as activist political movements have developed in the Mexican-American and Puerto Rican communities, a national focus began to coalesce the larger Hispanic world. This national movement is primarily the work of Hispanic organizations and

[52] Bruce McCohen and Francis Maier, "Fighting Castro from Exile," *The New York Times Magazine,* January 4, 1981, p. 28.

[53] Fred Stasser, "Ferre Rides in on Black Vote," *Miami Herald,* November 16, 1983, p. 1. See also "Election Highlights Ethnic Splits," in *The Hispanic Monitor,* Vol. 1 (January 1984), p. 4.

[54] For an overview of Cuban concern with the elderly, see Catherine McHugh and Susanne Landerghini, "Elderly Cuban Refugees in the United States and Programs for the Elderly in Dade County, Florida," report of the Congressional Research Service, March 23, 1978.

[55] Orlando Alvarez, *Estudio Demografico, Social y Economico de la Comunidad del Condado Dade* (Miami: Editorial AIP, 1976).

[56] Antonio Mejias-Rentas, "Hispanic Vote in Chicago—A Message Missed," *Hispanic Link,* no. 534, April 24, 1983.

Hispanic elected officials. It has also been greatly helped by the response of the federal government.

One of the earliest Washington organizations to articulate national concerns was the National Organization of Mexican American Services (NOMAS). This group was established in 1964 to coordinate the efforts of Mexican-American organizations such as the G.I. Forum, LULAC, MAPA, and others at the national level. It also worked to disseminate federal policy information down to the community level. NOMAS was nonpartisan, primarily serving Mexican-American interests. When Mexican-American leaders walked out of the EEOC conference in Albuquerque, President Johnson chose to deal directly with the leaders, thereby bypassing and splintering the unity efforts of NOMAS.

But NOMAS did have its usefulness, lasting two or three years, as a precursor of the National Council of La Raza, a service and advocacy group that is active to this date. People in NOMAS also were successful in reaching the Ford Foundation and gathering some important support for a variety of organizations.[57]

This organizational effort was being supplemented by the middle of the 1960s by a group of newly elected Mexican-American congressmen. These include Henry B. Gonzales (Democrat, Texas), elected in 1961; Edward R. Roybal (Democrat, California), elected in 1962; Kika de la Garza (Democrat, Texas), elected in 1964; and Manuel Lujan (Republican, New Mexico). Later there would be a Puerto Rican, Herman Badillo (Democrat, New York), elected in 1970. They joined Senator Joseph Montoya, elected to the U.S. Senate in 1964.[58] (It is interesting to note that most Hispanic congressmen were elected in the 1960s and that no new congressmen appeared in the 1970s, except when Robert Garcia replaced Herman Badillo in New York. Not until the 1982 elections did four new Hispanic congressmen join the original five.)

Hispanic congressmen are thrust into two roles. Not only are they expected to represent their districts, but the larger Hispanic world expects them to be sympathetic and to understand Hispanic concerns far outside their constituencies. If one examines federal legislation focused on the Hispanic community (such as bilingual education or the Cabinet Committee on Spanish Speaking Opportunities), it is the small group of Hispanic legislators elected in the 1960s who shepherded the legislation. Senator Montoya worked tirelessly to bring pressure on federal agencies and to recruit Hispanics and as a member of the U.S. Senate Appropriations Committee to ensure that federal education programs reaching the Hispanic community were adequately funded.[59]

[57]Interview with Raul Yzaguirre, executive director, National Council of La Raza, January 8, 1983.

[58]New Mexico was the first state to elect Hispanics to Congress. Senator Dennis Chavez, for many years senator from New Mexico, is recognized by older Hispanic politicians as an early leader.

[59]The same distance between Washington, D.C., and the Southwest that made Hispanics invisible at the national level for so many years also works to make national efforts by these legislators almost invisible at the local level in the Southwest. Many people working in bilingual education, for example, still believe that the growth of funding for bilingual education was an automatic process. Instead, the continuous efforts of Senator Montoya and, later, Congressman Roybal were responsible for the increased funding. (Interview with Manny Fiero, former executive director, El Congreso.)

The federal government responded to Hispanic national pressure by setting up mechanisms that would voice Hispanic community concerns within the bureaucracy. The first of these was the Inter-Agency Committee on Mexican-American Affairs, established by President Johnson in 1967. It evolved into the Cabinet Committee on Opportunities for Spanish Speaking People, designed to "advise and counsel federal agencies on the needs of Spanish speaking peoples."

At first, this committee offered hopes to Hispanics who saw it as a mechanism to affect federal program managers. In retrospect, one questions how a small agency outside the standing executive departments could influence federal policy throughout the government.[60] But it did serve as a symbol that Hispanic concerns were being recognized at the national level. Unfortunately, President Nixon politicized the committee and used the personnel so heavily during the reelection campaign of 1972 that it was vulnerable to charges of tokenism.[61] Its partisan identification with the Republican presidential effort meant that it was abolished by Congress in 1974.

There were yet other sporadic efforts to establish national Hispanic organizations. And there were some reverses. In 1971 an attempt was made to draw together major Hispanic groups for a national coalition. The "Unidos" conference brought Mexican Americans, Puerto Ricans, Cubans, and other Hispanics from across the country to Washington. Originally, only 200 were expected to attend; the conference brought nearly 1,000. But there were conflicts between the more militant representatives (such as Reies Tijerina of New Mexico) and the mainstream politicians. An effort was made to exclude Cubans. And, finally, Puerto Rican nationalists quarreled with the organizers of the conference over the priority given the status of Puerto Rico.

But these efforts continued. The most successful was *El Congreso* in 1975, formed by a coalition of Hispanic organizations to create a Washington presence. Its director, Manny Fiero, became the first lobbyist associated with Hispanic issues. *El Congreso* reached the height of its power in 1976 when it attempted to serve as a clearinghouse for Hispanic appointments in the Carter administration. Lack of funding and some internecine rivalries between the founding organizations contributed to its death in the late 1970s. Yet during its existence it lobbied effectively for such Hispanic concerns as bilingual education and the Roybal Act (Public Law 94-311), which mandated improved statistics on the Hispanic population. In general, it was able to increase the visibility of Hispanic concerns in the federal bureaucracy.[62] Politicization of the community meant increased response from federal agencies when Hispanic organizations asked directly for funding. SER, for example, is an organization created by LULAC and the G.I. Forum to promote employment training. It was almost entirely dependent on federal money. Also, in 1973, the LULAC group received a grant from the Ford administration to run its LULAC Educational Service programs, a scholarship plan for Hispanic youth.

[60] Harry Pachon, "Hispanic Underrepresentation in the Federal Bureaucracy: The Missing Link in the Policy Process," in *The State of Chicano Research in Family, Labor and Migration Studies* (Stanford, Calif.: Stanford Center for Chicano Research, 1983), pp. 209–219.

[61] Hearings Before the Committee on Government Operations on the Activities of the Cabinet Committee on Opportunities for Spanish Speaking People, 93rd Cong., 1st sess., July 23 and September 12, 1973, p. 42.

[62] Interview with Manny Fiero, December 2, 1983.

But accepting such grants presents certain problems: First, do the grant awards imply approval of the administration by the organization? And, second, what happens when a new administration takes power? Are those organizations linked to the previous administration? Unfortunately, the second problem often appears. In 1976, one of the first acts of the Carter administration (through the office of the Community Service Administration, headed by Grace Olivares, a long-term community activist) was to cut funding to the LULAC centers. LULAC then became involved in a long series of battles to restore the funding, an effort that ultimately succeeded.[63] Much the same thing happened in 1980 when the new Reagan administration cut funding to the National Hispanic Housing Urban Coalition at a critical time in its development, thereby destroying it. These examples illustrate a weakness of the growing national Hispanic organizations.

Throughout the 1970s, most Hispanic organizations tried to place branches in Washington, D.C. These included the Puerto Rican Forum, Aspira (a Puerto Rican group), LULAC, MALDEF, and the Cuban National Planning Council. And, after the demise of *El Congreso,* there were attempts to get the organizations to work together. One such effort was the Forum of National Hispanic Organizations. Two other efforts marked this growth of a national Hispanic presence: the first was the formation of the National Association of Latino Elected and Appointed Officials (NALEO) at the midterm Democratic conference in Kansas City in 1975. NALEO embodies some of the principles of older Hispanic organizations and also encompasses new ideas. Like its antecedents, NALEO is bipartisan. Its political leadership is aware of the necessity of working through the two-party system. By using the term "Latino" and by having both Mexican-American and Puerto Rican leadership, it is, in effect, the first coalition of Mexican Americans, Puerto Ricans, Cubans, and other Hispanics represented by political leaders. It also—significantly—rejects government funding. The other effort, a year later, was the congressional Hispanic Caucus formed by Hispanic congressmen. Like NALEO, it institutionalized coalition leadership. The president, Representative Edward Roybal, is of Mexican descent and Herman Badillo, secretary treasurer, is Puerto Rican.

The new Congressional Hispanic Caucus was very visible at the national level. It was small in membership (in the 1970s it operated with only six members). Nonetheless, it made its presence felt.[64] Seniority was very helpful; by 1983 three of its members chaired important House committees. Beginning in 1978, the Hispanic Caucus began to meet with President Jimmy Carter to discuss issues of concern, such as Hispanic underrepresentation in the federal bureaucracy, education issues, and employment opportunities. Furthermore, the Caucus became a convenient avenue of approach by other Hispanic organizations with policy concerns. In the 1980s, the Caucus helped to place new Hispanic congressmen on committees of their choice and prevent the inclusion of bilingual education into a block grant (an effort of the Reagan administration). Four new members of Congress brought the Caucus up to 11 members by 1984. It was able to maintain paid management staff since 1977 and a common approach in spite of the great difference between conservative Texas rural districts and urban New York *barrios.*

[63] Luis Fraga, "Organizational Maintenance and Organizational Success: The League of United Latin American Citizens," unpublished, 1980.

[64] Dick Kirschten, "The Congressional Hispanic Caucus," *National Journal,* November 19, 1983, p. 2412.

Yet another measure of the Hispanic coalescence is NALEO's success in attracting Hispanic elected officials. In the early 1980s, in fact, it held more than 2,500 members from all regions of the country, ranging from conservative Cuban businessmen to Puerto Rican community activists. Even the older and established ethnic organizations are beginning to reach out to other sectors of the Hispanic community. LULAC has chapters in Puerto Rican communities in the northeast. The National Council of La Raza has held meetings in Puerto Rico to widen its constituency.

In spite of these gains, in the early 1980s the Hispanic community still lacks the political representation to match its numbers. While Hispanic lobbying is felt in bilingual education and immigration, many national issues are developed in the White House and considered by Congress with little or no Hispanic comment. An example is the collapse of the National Hispanic Housing Coalition, an event important to Hispanics because one of the largest components of inner-city residents is almost completely left out of federal urban policymaking. After the Department of Labor employment programs were decentralized, SER (one of the few Hispanic organizations with a focus on labor policy) closed its Washington offices. But the permanent significance of the growth in a Hispanic political presence is that in less than 20 years, such a presence is firmly established.

THE FUTURE OF HISPANIC POLITICS

Mobilization of the Hispanic community is now a fact of American politics. Elections of Hispanics to the mayoralities of such large cities as San Antonio and Denver symbolize this change. The growing number of state legislators has not received as much publicity, particularly in states with smaller numbers of Hispanics—notably New Jersey, Indiana, Connecticut, and Minnesota. These are people who are forming a political leadership base for statewide offices and congressional seats. The 1982 elections showed a dramatic change in the number of Hispanic congressmen. The same effects can be expected from the 1990 reapportionments. Moreover, the aging of the Hispanic population means more voters in key states.

Certain basic issues are almost sure to be the fuel of future political activity. Representation is still a problem, both politically and in bureaucratic positions. Thus a civil rights report of November 1983 noted that although Los Angeles has the largest Mexican-American population in the United States, it has not elected an Hispanic city councilman since the 1960s. In classic fashion, the Hispanics may well duplicate the experience of other ethnic groups in time, but bureaucratic representation is another story. It still lags far behind other groups.[65] This is especially true as public policy issues become more complex and technical. A growing body of literature argues that national and state bureaucracies are growing factors in the development and implementation of policy. A common result is that Hispanic organi-

[65] See "Federal Employment Problems of the Spanish Speaking," Hearings Before the Civil Rights Oversight Committee, Committee on the Judiciary, U.S. House of Representatives, 92nd Cong., 2d sess., March 8, 9, 10, 1972. Also "Equal Employment Opportunity for Hispanics Within the Federal Government," Hearings Before the Subcommittee on Appropriations, U.S. House of Representatives, 92nd Cong., 2d sess., November 3, 1972.

zations and elected officials are forced to "react" to complex public policy options without being involved in the development of these options. Despite pressure and activism, the rate of increase of Hispanics in the federal bureaucracy is so slow that Hispanics will not be able to achieve parity until the year 2025. Future Hispanic political activity will continue to press on this issue.

A second major factor that will mobilize the community is the continued perception of discrimination against Hispanics. The following incidents (at high governmental levels) illustrate this perception:

A U.S. congressman stated that the chair of the congressional Hispanic Caucus "didn't look like a Mexican. He wasn't short and didn't wear a mustache."

A top industrialist, Peter Grace, states the U.S. Food Stamp program is "mostly a Puerto Rican program and should be discontinued."

Passage of "English-only" ordinances by two major cities (Miami and San Francisco), have been aimed at the Spanish-speaking residents.

Finally, education of the youth is an important concern of all the Hispanic groups and always a potent force for instant coalition. At the present time, bilingual education is the focus of effort. But the continued disparities in education will generate trouble in the future.

In general, the political future of the Hispanics is bright. Yet the shape and direction of this future depends largely on the reaction of the larger American society.

EPILOGUE

No glimpse into the future of America's Hispanics can possibly anticipate all the changes to come, many of them now in process. Yet there are some obvious trends, and these will support some interesting guesses.

The first trend is the unquestioned major shift in the ethnic composition of this country. In large part, this shift is a result of the immigration legislation of 1965, which for the first time allowed non-Europeans to enter this nation in large numbers. Most of the new immigrants now come from Latin America and from Asia. It is a shift that already has changed the social and cultural life of many American cities, particularly in the West. There is no sign of any decline in this immigration pressure. Thus the continuous immigration, legal and undocumented, flows into an urban context that is increasingly non-European. No longer are Mexicans the *only* non-Europeans entering our cities. Now they are joined by Central Americans, South Americans, Chinese, Asiatic Indians, Filipinos, and yet others with an appearance and culture and goals that share very little with the traditional American "mainstream." This is the context of the Hispanic future, and the concept of "mainstream" is becoming increasingly hackneyed.

But immigration is only part of the story. The average Hispanic growth rate of 8 percent per year since 1970 is a result not only of immigration but of high fertility. Eight percent is the measurable growth rate; the true rate is probably higher.

The second trend is that Hispanics continue to be poor and their poverty is guaranteed by a steady influx of poor and badly educated workers and by the high birth rate. There are real gains in both education and income as older arrivals gradually make their way more deeply into the American economy and society and as some of the affluent newcomers find their special niche. But these gains tend to be obscured by the prevailing poverty.

The third point is that the relative youth and poverty of America's Hispanics will continue to put pressure on the educational, health, welfare, and criminal justice systems. Thus, the Hispanic population will continue to be labeled as a "problem," and this label will place a special meaning on their growing political weight.

Fourth, the steady appearance of Hispanics far from the regions with which they were traditionally associated (especially the isolated and exotic Southwest) is making them much more obvious to all Americans—Midwestern, Eastern, and Southeastern. Hispanic groups are becoming noticeable in dozens of cities whose populations had no awareness of the Hispanic minority as recently as a generation ago.

Most of these trends can be seen easily and provoke educated guesses about public policy and forthcoming changes in American opinion. For Hispanics themselves, as an example, it is likely that the forced cohabitation of Mexicans, Puerto Ricans, and an increasingly differentiated residual category of "other Hispanics" seems to be increasing the acceptability of Hispanic coalitions—cultural, social, and especially political. Meanwhile, immigration will probably reinforce ethnic identities based on the national origins of Mexico, Puerto Rico, Cuba, and other nations.

These trends also imply that the national biracial preoccupation with blacks and European ethnics must disappear. The conceptualizations of social science tend to follow societal preoccupations, and accordingly, American scientists have quite generally failed to deal realistically with the rather obvious misfitting of Hispanics. They have never been easy to fit into either the black relationship to American society or to the European ethnic pattern. Thus, changing circumstances will eventually force a change in American social science. In the process, a great deal of simple information is still lacking. We are even yet largely ignorant of the settlement patterns and stresses of all but the largest of the Hispanic groups.

Even with them (as we discovered in the writing of this book), there is comparatively little descriptive or historical material. This places a most special burden on those young social scientists now working and those scientists yet to be found.

INDEX

Compensatory education, 156–57
Conflict between cultures, 129–30
Congressional Hispanic Caucus, 197
Congressional representation, 170–72, 190,
  191, 195
Contraception, use of, 105
Contracting of workers, 30, 33, 137–38
Cooney, R.S., 104
COPS (Community Organized for Public
  Service), 115, 153
Cordasco, F., 96*n*
Cornelius, W., 91*n*, 135*n*, 137*n*, 138*n*, 141–42,
  163*n*
Corrada, B., 155
Cortez, G., 14*n*
Costilla, A.T. de, 102*n*, 113*n*
Cotera, M., 106*n*
Cottrell, C., 134*n*
Counterculture movement, 30, 180
Court decisions on education, 150
Crime, poverty and, 82–85
Criminal justice system, 164–68
Criollos, 32
Crusada Para La Justicia, La., 181
Crystal City, Texas, 150–51, 183
Cuban Americans
  acculturation, 131
  demographics, 53, 56–58, 62, 66, 70, 72,
    75–76
  drug trafficking by, 84
  family size, 100
  field dependence of, 126
  housing, 80–81
  immigration of, 35–37, 54, 55
  in Miami, 44–46
  "parole" provision for, 139
  politics of, 36–37, 191–94
  recent images of, 8, 9
Cuban missile crisis, 192
Cuban Refugee Program, 193
Culture
  acculturation and change, 118, 130–31
  defining, 122–25
  health and, 158–60
  importance of, 125–30
  persistence of, 87–88
  of poverty, 98–99, 124
  Spanish language and, 118–22
Cuomo, M., 190
Curanderas, 158–59

D

Dale, C.V., 73*n*
Dayan, E., 162*n*
Deignan, P., 150*n*
De Leon, A., 4*n*
Delgado, R.T., 189*n*
Delinquency, juvenile, 82–84

Democratic party, 179, 184–88, 192
Demographics, 51–66
  age patterns and family structure, 62–65,
    87
  income and occupation, 69–78, 85, 94–95,
    128–29
  nativity and generation patterns, 61–62
  political significance of, 172–73
  population, 50–61, 172
"Dependency ratio," 64–65
Deprivation, relative, 174
Desegregation of schools, 30
"Diagnostic stereotypes," 161
Díaz, P., 25–26, 29
Diaz-Guerrero, R., 96*n*, 124, 125–26, 127
Dirschten, D., 185*n*
Discrimination
  employment, 73, 74
  language, 73, 154
  political organization and, 177
  in schools, 30, 145–47
Distribution, geographic, 38–49, 56–61
Diversity, regional, 38–49
  Cubans in Miami, 36, 37, 44–46
  in declining snowbelt, 46–48
  in Southwest, 39–44
Dobie, J.F., 6
Down These Mean Streets (Thomas), 14–15
Dropout rates, 68. *See also* Education
Drug trafficking, 84, 85
Dunne, J.G., 181*n*

E

Economics
  Hispanic-Anglo relationship in, 17–18
  of snowbelt, 46–48
  in Southwest, 19–20, 27–28, 39–41,
    48–49
  Sunbelt boom, 42–44
Edgerton, R., 159*n*
Edgewood experiment (ESP), 152–53
Education. *See under* Institution(s)
El Congreso, 196, 197
Elderly, care of, 107
Elementary and Secondary Education Act,
  153
Elites, 94, 134
Emigre politics, 187, 192
Employment. *See* Occupation
"Enclave economy," 45
Enforcement, law, 164–68
Enforcement, immigration policy, 140–43
Enriquez, E., 98*n*, 106*n*
Equal Employment Opportunity Commission,
  181
Eribes, R., 76, 80*n*
Erie, S., 162*n*
Ethnicity, confusion of race and, 3–4

World War II, effect of, 28, 177–78
Wyden, P., 192*n*